Frances Eales
Steve Oakes

speakout

Elementary
Students' Book

with ActiveBook and MyEnglishLab

CONTENTS

LESSON		GRAMMAR/FUNCTION	VOCABULARY	PRONUNCIATION	READING
UNIT 1 WELCOME page 7		Video podcast | What's your name?			
1.1	Nice to meet you page 8	present simple: *be*	greetings; countries and nationalities	stressed syllables	read a general knowledge quiz about world facts
1.2	Travel light page 10	*this/that, these/those*; possessives	objects	stressed syllables /ðɪs/, /ðæt/, /ðiːz/ and /ðəʊz/	read an article about travelling light
1.3	Can I have a coffee? page 12	making requests	tourist places	sentence stress and polite intonation	
1.4	Fawlty Towers page 14		hotel services; phrases for booking in at a hotel		
UNIT 2 LIFESTYLE page 17		Video podcast | What's your daily routine?			
2.1	Join us! page 18	present simple: *I/you/we/they*	activities	strong and weak forms of *do you*	read an article about social online groups
2.2	High flyers page 20	present simple: *he/she/it*	daily routines; jobs	Present simple verb endings: /s/, /z/ and /ɪz/	
2.3	What time does it start? page 22	asking for information	the time	polite intonation	read tourist leaflets
2.4	Chalet Girl page 24		household routines; phrases to describe life at home		read a web posting about pen pals
UNIT 3 PEOPLE page 27		Video podcast | What do you like doing with friends/family?			
3.1	Just good friends page 28	frequency adverbs: *sometimes, usually, always, often, hardly ever* and *never*; modifiers *quite, not very, really* and *very*	personality	stressed syllables	read a quiz about what type of friend you are
3.2	Big happy families page 30	*have/has got*	family	contracted forms of *have/has got*	read an article about unusual families
3.3	Are you free tonight? page 32	making arrangements	time expressions	positive and negative intonation	
3.4	A Celebration In Crete page 34		special occasion activities; phrases to describe special occasions		read an invitation
UNIT 4 PLACES page 37		Video podcast | Where do you live?			
4.1	Small place, big style page 38	*there is/are*	rooms/furniture; prepositions (1)	/ðeəzə/ and /ðeərə/	
4.2	An English village? page 40	*can* for possibility	places in towns; prepositions (2)	strong and weak forms of *can* and *can't*	read an article about a special kind of village
4.3	Can I help you? page 42	shopping	things to buy; shops	polite intonation	
4.4	Favourite Places page 44		phrases to describe places		read a web posting about a favourite place
UNIT 5 FOOD page 47		Video podcast | What's your favourite dish?			
5.1	MyFridge.com page 48	countable and uncountable nouns; nouns with *a/an, some, any*	food/drink		
5.2	A lifetime in numbers page 50	*how much/many*; quantifiers	containers		read an article about how much an average person gets through in a lifetime
5.3	Are you ready to order? page 52	ordering in a restaurant	restaurant words	fast speech: linking	
5.4	A Chef In Goa page 54		ingredients; phrases for writing a recipe		read a recipe
UNIT 6 THE PAST page 57		Video podcast | Did you go out last night?			
6.1	Favourite things page 58	*was/were*	dates and time phrases	strong and weak forms of *was* and *were*	
6.2	Time twins page 60	past simple	common verbs (1)	past simple regular verbs with /t/, /d/ and /ɪd/	read an article about 'time twins'
6.3	How was your weekend? page 62	making conversation	weekend activities	learn to show interest	
6.4	Carlos Acosta page 64		phrases for interviewing		read an essay about a special person

IRREGULAR VERBS page 127   LANGUAGE BANK page 128   PHOTO BANK page 152

CONTENTS

LISTENING/DVD	SPEAKING	WRITING
listen to short conversations showing different ways to introduce people	introduce people; do a quiz	improve your use of capital letters
	identify objects	
listen to conversations in various tourist places; learn to listen for key words; listen to prices and numbers	give information for numbers, prices, etc; make simple requests	
BBC Fawlty Towers: watch an extract from a sitcom about a hotel	arrival and check in at a hotel	complete a hotel registration form; write an email to book a hotel room
listen to a conversation between two friends choosing the right online group for them	talk about activities; talk about a group/team	
listen to people describing their jobs; listen and identify a variety of jobs	talk about routines; describe other people's routines	learn how to use linkers: *and*, *but* and *or*
learn to get a speaker to slow down and grade their language	learn to show you don't understand; ask questions at a tourist information centre	
BBC Holiday: Fasten Your Seatbelt: watch an extract from a reality programme about a difficult job	talk about life at home: likes and dislikes	write an internet posting to a penpal describing yourself
listen to people describing their friends	describe personality; do a quiz and find out what kind of friend you are	
	talk about your family	improve your use of apostrophe 's; write about your family
learn to show interest when you listen	make arrangements to meet friends	
BBC Francesco's Mediterranean Voyage: watch an extract from a documentary about a special occasion	talk about a special occasion	write an invitation
listen to a conversation between two people talking about a special flat	describe your home	improve your use of commas; write an email about your home
	talk about things you can do in towns; describe a favourite place in your town/city	
learn to say *no* politely in a shop; listen to various shopping conversations	have a conversation in a shop	
BBC 50 Places To See Before You Die: watch an extract from a documentary about some amazing places	describe your favourite place of all	write a blog about your favourite place
listen to people talk about food	talk about your eating and drinking habits	
	talk about diets and lifestyle	learn to use paragraphs and write a short report
understand fast speech; listen to a man ordering in a fast food restaurant	order a meal in a restaurant	
BBC Rick Stein's Seafood Odyssey: watch an extract from a cookery programme about a famous chef	describe a special dish	write a recipe
listen to people describing famous people's favourite things	talk about people's favourite things; describe your favourite childhood things	
	talk about your life/past events	link sentences with *because* and *so* and write your life story
learn to keep a conversation going; listen to someone describing their weekend	describe a perfect/terrible weekend	
BBC The Culture Show: watch an extract from a documentary about a famous dancer	interview a special person	write a profile essay about a special person

COMMUNICATION BANK page 160 AUDIO SCRIPTS page 167

CONTENTS

LESSON	GRAMMAR/FUNCTION	VOCABULARY	PRONUNCIATION	READING
UNIT 7 HOLIDAYS page 67 — Video podcast | How was your last holiday?					
7.1 Travel partners page 68	comparatives	travel	stressed syllables	
7.2 The longest bus ride page 70	superlatives	places (1)	strong and weak forms of *the*	read an article about a long journey
7.3 Can you tell me the way? page 72	giving directions	places (2)	sentence stress for correcting	
7.4 Buenos Aires page 74		phrases to describe a town/city		read a travel article
UNIT 8 NOW page 77 — Video podcast | What was the last film you saw?					
8.1 In the picture page 78	present continuous	verbs + prepositions	weak forms of prepositions and articles	read blogs about what people are doing now
8.2 Looking good page 80	present simple and present continuous	appearance		
8.3 What do you recommend? page 82	recommending	types of film	word linking	
8.4 Festival Highlights page 84		festival activities; phrases to describe an event		read a festival review
UNIT 9 TRANSPORT page 87 — Video podcast | How do you get to work?					
9.1 Travel in style page 88	articles: *a/an*, *the*, no article	transport collocations	strong and weak forms of *a* and *the*	
9.2 Citybikes page 90	*can/can't*, *have to/don't have to*	adjectives (1)	strong and weak forms of *can*, *can't*, *have to* and *don't have to*	read an article about Paris Citybikes
9.3 Sorry I'm late page 92	apologising	excuses	intonation to show being happy or unhappy	
9.4 Airport page 94		phrases to describe and complain about problems		read an email
UNIT 10 THE FUTURE page 97 — Video podcast | What are your plans for the future?					
10.1 Life's a lottery page 98	*be going to*; *would like to*	plans	*going to* and *would*	read a news story about a lottery win
10.2 Survive! page 100	*will*, *might*, *won't*	phrases with *get*	contracted form of *will*	read an extract from a survival instruction book
10.3 Let's do something page 102	making suggestions	adjectives (2)	stressed syllables	read an article about things to do with friends
10.4 Wild Weather page 104		phrases to describe weather		
UNIT 11 HEALTH page 107 — Video podcast | Do you have a healthy lifestyle?					
11.1 My head hurts page 108	*should/shouldn't*	the body; health	consonant clusters	read an article about cold cures around the world
11.2 Never felt better page 110	adverbs of manner	common verbs (2)		read a quiz about how fit you are
11.3 Help! page 112	offering to help	problems		read an article about a social experiment
11.4 The Optician page 114		phrases to describe a problem and to give advice		
UNIT 12 EXPERIENCES page 117 — Video podcast | What's the most exciting thing you've done?					
12.1 Unforgettable page 118	present perfect	outdoor activities		
12.2 Afraid of nothing page 120	present perfect and past simple	prepositions (3)		read an article about a dangerous job
12.3 I've got a problem page 122	telephoning	telephoning expressions	sentence stress	
12.4 Shark Therapy page 124		phrases to describe an experience		

IRREGULAR VERBS page 127   LANGUAGE BANK page 128   PHOTO BANK page 152

CONTENTS

LISTENING/DVD	SPEAKING	WRITING
listen to people discuss how they like to travel	talk about how you like to travel; compare places and holidays	
	plan and talk about a long journey	learn to check and correct information; write about a holiday
understand directions; learn to check and correct directions	give directions in the street	
BBC **Holiday 10 Best:** watch an extract from a travel show about Buenos Aires	describe a town/city you know	write a short article about a town/city
	talk about taking photos; talk about what people are doing	write a blog entry about what you are doing
listen to a radio programme about ideas of beauty	discuss what you know about various film stars; describe people's appearance	
learn to link words to speak faster	ask and answer a questionnaire about films; ask for and give recommendations	
BBC **Inside Out:** watch an extract from a documentary about an English music festival	describe an event	write a review of an event
listen to a guide giving a tour around a transport museum	talk about types of transport	
	talk about ways to travel around towns/cities	
listen to a man talk about his problems getting to work	apologise for being late; tell a long story	learn to use linkers and write a story
BBC **Airport:** watch an extract from a documentary about a day at Heathrow airport	deal with problems when flying	write an email about an experience at an airport/on a plane
listen to a radio interview with lottery winners	talk about your future plans/wishes	
	make predictions about situations	improve your use of linkers: *too*, *also* and *as well* and write a short story
learn to respond to suggestions; listen to people discussing which activities they want to do	make some suggestions and invite your friends to join you	
BBC **Wild Weather:** watch an extract from a documentary about the wettest place in Europe	talk about weather and how it makes you feel	write a message board notice about your country
listen to a radio programme about colds and flu	talk about what to do when you don't feel well and give advice; discuss cures for the common cold	
	do a quiz about your fitness; talk about healthy weekends	learn to use adverbs in stories and how to make stories more interesting
listen to different scenarios of people needing help and thanking someone	give advice and offer help; thank someone	
BBC **The Two Ronnies:** watch an extract from a sitcom about an unusual shopping experience	ask for help in a pharmacy	write some advice for a health message board
listen to people talking about their experiences	talk about unusual experiences	learn to use postcard phrases and write a postcard
	describe movement from one place to another; talk about past experiences	
listen to different scenarios on the phone	describe difficult situations/problems; say telephone numbers; phone someone about a problem	
BBC **Shark Therapy:** watch an extract from a documentary about sharks	describe an exciting/frightening experience	write a story about an exciting/frightening experience

COMMUNICATION BANK page 160   AUDIO SCRIPTS page 167

LEAD-IN

OBJECTS AND COLOURS

1A Look at the words in the box. Which objects are in your classroom?

| chair   bag   notebook   table   whiteboard   pen   book |
| CD player   pencil   noticeboard   projector   picture |

B Work in pairs and take turns. Student A: point to objects in the classroom. Ask your partner. Student B: name the objects.

A: *What is it?*
B: *It's a book.*

C Write the colours.

1 _____   4 _____   7 _____
2 _____   5 _____   8 _____
3 _____   6 _____   9 _____

D Work in pairs. Ask and answer *What's your favourite colour?*

THE ALPHABET

2A ▶ L.1 Listen and write the letters in the correct column. Each column has the same vowel sound.

A̶ B̶ C̶ D E F G H I̶ J K L M N O̶ P Q̶ R S T U V W X Y Z

A	B	F	I	O	Q	R
	C					

B Listen and repeat.

C Work in pairs and take turns. Student A: spell an object or colour. Student B: say it.

A: *b-l-u-e*
B: *Blue!*

QUESTION WORDS

3A Underline the correct question word.
1 How / *What* 's your name?
2 Who / Where are you from?
3 How / When are you today?
4 What / Who 's your favourite actor?
5 When / Where 's your birthday?
6 What / Why are you here?
7 Which / What spelling is correct: c-h-i-a-r or c-h-a-i-r?

B Work in pairs. Ask and answer the questions above.

CLASSROOM LANGUAGE

4A Complete the questions with a word from the box.

| ~~mean~~   repeat   don't   that   could   page |

1 A: What does 'capital' __mean__ ?
   B: It means capital city, for example, London or Tokyo.
2 A: 'Work in pairs'? I _____ understand.
   B: It means 'Work together'. So, you two …
3 A: Could you _____ that?
   B: Yes. Page ninety-five.
4 A: Could you spell _____ ?
   B: Yes, m-e-e-t.
5 A: _____ you write it?
   B: Yes, of course.
6 A: Which _____ is it?
   B: Thirty-five.

B ▶ L.2 Listen and check. Then listen and repeat.

NUMBERS

5A Write the numbers.

_1_ one	___ twelve	___ fifteen
___ three	___ eight	___ thirteen
___ nine	___ two	___ fifty
___ four	___ seven	___ thirty
___ ten	___ eleven	___ a hundred
___ six	___ five	___ twenty

B ▶ L.3 Listen and write the numbers.

C Work in pairs. Student A: say five numbers. Student B: write the numbers.

6

UNIT 1

SPEAKING
- Introduce yourself and others
- Make requests
- Check into a hotel

LISTENING
- Understand people in tourist situations
- Listen for key information
- Listen to prices and numbers
- Watch an extract from a sitcom about a hotel

READING
- Read about travelling light

WRITING
- Improve your use of capital letters
- Complete a registration form at a hotel
- Write an email to book a hotel room

BBC CONTENT
- Video podcast: What's your name?
- DVD: Fawlty Towers

welcome

▶ Nice to meet you   p8

▶ Travel light   p10

▶ Can I have a coffee?   p12

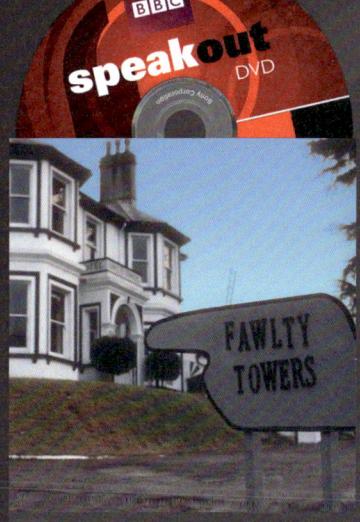

▶ Fawlty Towers   p14

1.1 NICE TO MEET YOU

▶ GRAMMAR | present simple: be   ▶ VOCABULARY | greetings; countries and nationalities   ▶ HOW TO | introduce people

VOCABULARY | greetings

1A Match photos A–E to the places in the box below.

| TV studio A   airport |
| street   office   classroom |

B ▶1.1 Listen and match conversations 1–5 with the photos.

1 Hello. Are you Mr and Mrs Burns?
   Yes, we are.
   Hello. I'm Elena Garcia from YouTourist.
   Hello. _____ to meet _____.
   And you.

2 Hi, Lily. _____ are _____?
   Great, thanks. And _____?
   Not so bad.

3 Juan, this is Ana.
   _____, Juan.
   Hi. _____ to _____ you.
   Are you in the same class?
   No, I'm not a student. We're friends.

4 Good _____ and welcome to the BBC News at One.

5 _____ _____. Can I help you?
   Yes, I'm here to see Mr. Miller.
   Is your name Simpson?
   No, it isn't. My name's Jackson.
   Oh, sorry. Please take a seat, Mr Jackson.

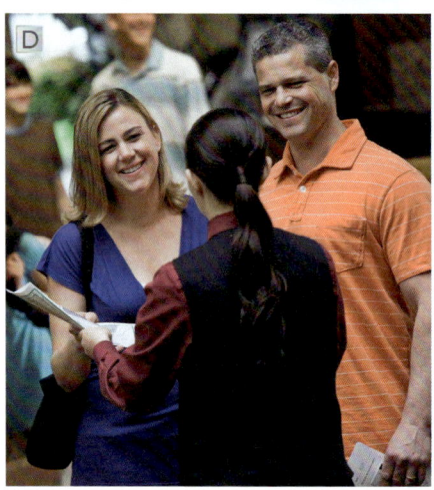

C Listen again and complete the conversations.

GRAMMAR | present simple: be

2 Look at the conversations in Exercise 1B and complete the tables.

Positive and negative statements		
I	_'m_	Elena Garcia.
My name	_____	Jackson.
I	_____ not	a student.

Questions and short answers			
_____	you	Mr and Mrs Burns?	Yes, we _____.
_____	your name	Simpson?	No, it _____.

▶ page 128 **LANGUAGEBANK**

speakout TIP

It's a good idea to write a personal example with all new grammar. In your notebook, write two sentences beginning: *I'm … . My name … .*

PRACTICE

3A Complete the conversation. Then practise it in groups.

A: Hi, Muhammed. This ¹ _is_ Cristina. She ² _____ a student in my class.
B: Hi, Cristina. Nice ³ _____ meet ⁴ _____.
C: Hi. ⁵ _____ you a student?
B: Yes, I ⁶ _____.

B Work in groups. Take turns to introduce each other.

VOCABULARY countries and nationalities

4A Which nationalities do you know? Complete the table.

Country	Nationality
Spain, Britain	Spanish
Italy, Brazil	
China, Japan	
France, the USA	

B Circle your country and nationality above or add them to the table.

C ▶ 1.2 Listen to the countries and nationalities. Underline the stressed syllable.

<u>Spain</u>, <u>Span</u>ish

D Work in pairs and take turns. Student A: say a country. Student B: say the nationality. Remember to stress the correct syllable.

A: <u>I</u>taly

B: <u>I</u>talian

➡ page 152 **PHOTOBANK**

PRACTICE

5A ▶ 1.3 Work in pairs and do the quiz below.

B Check your answers on page 161.

WRITING capital letters

6A Tick the correct information below to complete the rule.

> Rule:
> Use capital letters for the first letter of:
> countries ✓   all nouns   famous places   jobs   cities
> names of people   nationalities   food   languages
> the first word in a sentence

B Correct the sentences.
1 the eiffel tower is in france.
2 'buenos días!' is spanish for 'hello'.
3 sake is japanese.
4 spaghetti is food from italy.

SPEAKING

7A Write the names of four countries. For each one, add one or two piece(s) of information. E.g. a famous place, a word or a phrase or a type of food or drink.

India – Taj Mahal, curry

B Work in pairs and take turns. Student A: read out your information. Student B: guess the country.

A: *The Taj Mahal, a curry.*
B: *Is it India?*
A: *Yes, it is.*

Hear it, see it, taste it!

1 Listen and match the countries with the music (A–D) you hear.

1 Russia _____   2 Ireland _____   3 Greece _____   4 Brazil _____

2 Look at the maps and match the countries with the shapes.

1 France _____   2 Egypt _____   3 the USA _____   4 Australia _____

3 Look at the pictures and match the countries with the food.

1 Italy _____   2 Japan _____   3 India _____   4 Spain _____

1.2 TRAVEL LIGHT

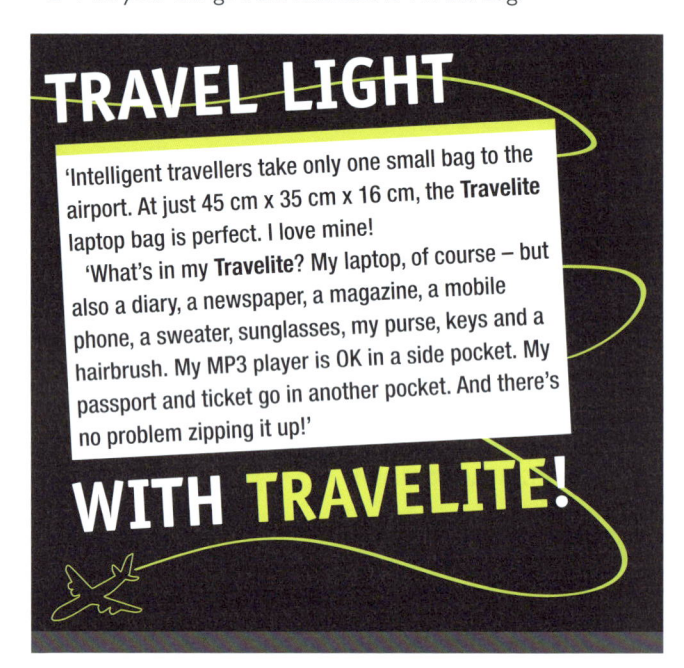

▶ **GRAMMAR** | *this/that, these/those; possessives* ▶ **VOCABULARY** | objects ▶ **HOW TO** | identify objects

VOCABULARY | objects

1A Look at the picture below. Match the words in the box with objects A–O. Which object isn't there?

| camera A   mobile phone   laptop   purse   keys |
| diary   passport   MP3 player   magazine |
| hairbrush   watch   newspaper   toothbrush |
| sweater   sunglasses   ticket |

B ▶ 1.4 Listen and underline the stressed syllable in the words.
<u>ca</u>mera

C Work in pairs and take turns. Student A: point to an object in the picture. Student B: name the object.
A: *What's this?*
B: *It's a camera.*

D What do you remember? Close your book and make a list of the objects in the picture.

speakout TIP

Always write new vocabulary in your notebook. Underline the stressed syllable of the words to help you with the pronunciation.

READING

2A Work in pairs and discuss. What five things are <u>always</u> in your bag/pocket?

B Read the article and discuss.
1 Why is Travelite a good bag?
2 Are your things from Exercise 2A in the bag?

TRAVEL LIGHT

'Intelligent travellers take only one small bag to the airport. At just 45 cm x 35 cm x 16 cm, the **Travelite** laptop bag is perfect. I love mine!

'What's in my **Travelite**? My laptop, of course – but also a diary, a newspaper, a magazine, a mobile phone, a sweater, sunglasses, my purse, keys and a hairbrush. My MP3 player is OK in a side pocket. My passport and ticket go in another pocket. And there's no problem zipping it up!'

WITH TRAVELITE!

10

1.2

GRAMMAR this/that, these/those

3A Work in pairs. Look at the picture above. Where are the people? What objects are in the picture?

B ▶ 1.5 Listen and check. Is Rob's bag A, B or C?

C Listen again and underline the correct answer.
1 The DVDs are *Rob's/Kate's/Marco's*.
2 The book is *Rob's/Kate's/Marco's*.
3 The sunglasses are *Rob's/Kate's/Marco's*.

D ▶ 1.6 Listen and write *this, that, these* or *those* in the extract below.
Kate: Wait a minute. Is ¹_____ my bag?
Rob: No, ²_____'s mine. ³_____ is your bag.
Kate: Wait, look. What are ⁴_____?
Rob: ⁵_____? They're DVDs. But they aren't mine.

E Write *this, that, these* or *those* under the pictures below.

1 _____   2 _____   3 _____   4 _____

F ▶ 1.7 Listen to the pronunciation. Then listen and repeat.
1 This /ðɪs/ key.   3 That /ðæt/ key.
2 These /ðiːz/ keys.   4 Those /ðəʊz/ keys.

▶ page 128 **LANGUAGEBANK**

PRACTICE

4 Work in pairs and take turns. Student A: point to an object in the classroom and ask your partner what it is. Student B: name the object.
A: What's *this* in English?
B: It's a dictionary.
A: What are *those* in English?
B: They're windows.

GRAMMAR possessives

5 Underline the correct alternatives.
Kate: It's a book about Rome, but it isn't *my/mine*. Is it *you/yours*?
Rob: Oh, no. That's *Marco/Marco's*.

▶ page 128 **LANGUAGEBANK**

PRACTICE

6 Complete the conversation. Use the words in brackets to help.
A: Is that ¹ *my* book? (I)
B: No, it isn't. It's ²_____. (Ana)
A: Where's ³_____? (I)
B: Is this ⁴_____? (you)
A: Yes, thanks. Is this ⁵_____ bag? (you)
B: No, it isn't ⁶_____. (I)
A: Maybe it's ⁷_____. (Ali)

SPEAKING

7A Work in groups. Put two objects from your bag/pocket on a table. Identify the objects.
Silvia's bag, Cheng's keys, my watch …

B Work with a partner from another group. Look at their objects. Ask and answer questions.
A: Is that your pen?
B: No, it isn't. It's Bruno's.
A: Are these Jack's glasses?
B: No, they aren't. They're Veronika's.

▶ page 152 **PHOTOBANK**

1.3 CAN I HAVE A COFFEE?

▶ FUNCTION | making requests   ▶ VOCABULARY | tourist places   ▶ LEARN TO | listen for key words

VOCABULARY | tourist places

1A Match photos A–D to the places below.

1 a souvenir shop _____
2 a sandwich bar _____
3 a money exchange _____
4 a train station _____

B Write the words from the box in the word webs below. Add one more word to each place.

~~postcard~~   cola   euros   battery
single ticket   money   return ticket
coffee   sandwich   platform
exchange rate   souvenir

postcard

(souvenir shop)

(sandwich bar)

(money exchange)

(train station)

C ▶ 1.8 Listen and check. Then listen and repeat.

D Work in pairs and take turns.
Student A: say a place from Exercise 1B.
Student B: say three things you can buy/find there.

FUNCTION | making requests

2A ▶ 1.9 Listen to four conversations. Where are the people?
1 _____
2 _____
3 _____
4 _____

B Listen again. What does each tourist buy?
1 _____
2 _____
3 _____
4 _____

3A ▶ 1.10 Listen and complete the requests.
1 _Can_ _I_ _have_ a sandwich, please?
2 ___ ___ ___ one of those batteries, please?
3 ___ ___ ___ a single to Sydney, please?
4 ___ ___ ___ this money, please?

B Look at the question. Listen to the polite pronunciation. Then listen and repeat.

Can I have a sandwich, please?

▶ page 128 **LANGUAGEBANK**

12

1.3

6 ▶ **1.13** Listen to three conversation extracts and circle the correct prices.

Extract 1
1 an orange juice   a) 2.00   b) 2.10   c) 2.20

Extract 2
2 a single ticket   a) 4.20   b) 4.50   c) 4.80
3 a taxi   a) 13   b) 23   c) 30

Extract 3
4 a coffee   a) 2.15   b) 2.50   c) 3.50
5 a sandwich   a) 2.25   b) 2.75   c) 3.75
6 a bottle of water a) 1.30   b) 1.40   c) 1.60

7 Work in pairs and take turns. Student A: look at page 160. Student B: look at page 162.

SPEAKING

8A Work in pairs. Complete the menu with prices.

B Take turns to role-play the conversation in a sandwich bar. Student A: look at the menu. Choose and order your food and drink. Student B: take your partner's order. Say how much it costs.

A: *Could I have a coffee and a cheese sandwich?*
B: *A coffee and a sandwich? That's four euros fifty.*

4A ▶ **1.11** Listen to the speakers. Are they polite (P) or impolite (I)?

B Work in pairs and take turns. Student A: you are in one of the places in the photos. Make requests. Student B: only answer if Student A is polite.
A: *Could I have one of those postcards, please?*
B: *Yes. Here you are.*

LEARN TO listen for key words

5A Read the conversation. Underline the key words in each sentence.

A: Can I have a <u>sandwich</u> and a <u>cola</u>, please? (2 words)
B: That's six euros. (2 words)
A: Ah, I only have five euros. How much is the sandwich? (4 words)
B: Four euros fifty, and the cola is one fifty. (6 words)
A: OK. Could I have the sandwich, but no cola? (3 words)
B: That's four fifty. (2 words)

speakout TIP

Key words are the important information words in a sentence. These words are stressed and are l o n g e r, LOUDER and ʰⁱᵍʰᵉʳ.

B ▶ **1.12** Listen to the conversation and check your answers. Then listen and repeat.

MENU — Little DORRIT

DRINKS
Coffee €1.50
Tea .... ____
Hot chocolate .... ____
Mineral water .... ____
Cola .... ____

SANDWICHES
Cheese €3.00
Egg .... ____
Chicken .... ____

CAKES
Chocolate cake .... ____
Coffee cake .... ____

13

1.4 FAWLTY TOWERS

DVD PREVIEW

1 Look at the photo and read the programme information. Who are the people in the photo?

BBC Fawlty Towers

Fawlty Towers is a hotel in a BBC TV comedy. The manager's name is Basil Fawlty and he's married to Sybil. Polly and Manuel work at the hotel. Polly is British and Manuel is Spanish. Manuel speaks a little English but he sometimes has problems with his translations! The hotel is terrible and Basil often gets angry with his staff and guests!

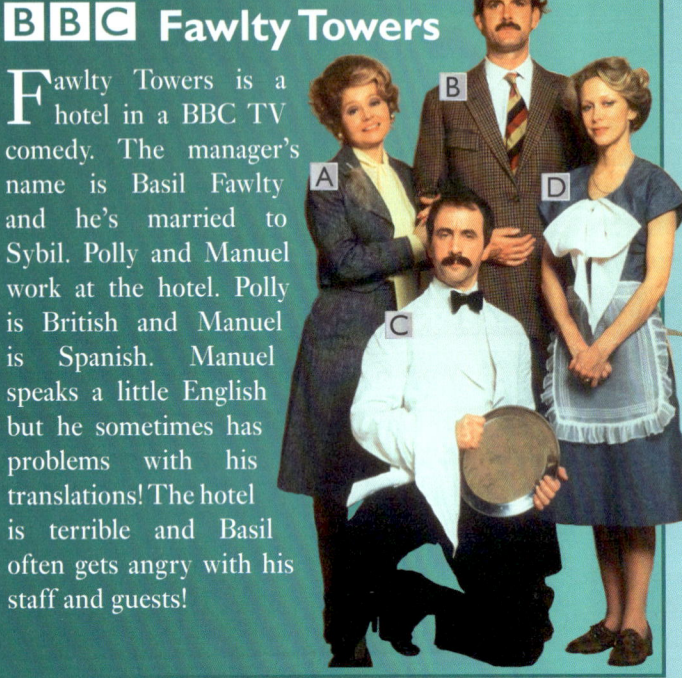

2A Match the words in the box with pictures A–H.

lift A   restaurant   stairs   keycard   reception
internet connection   room service   parking

B Work in pairs and take turns. Student A: point to a picture above. Student B: say the word.

C Discuss. What do you look for in a hotel?

DVD VIEW

3A Watch the DVD. Are the sentences true (T) or false (F)?
1. Manuel speaks English.
2. The moose speaks English.
3. The Major is surprised.
4. Basil Fawlty is angry.

B Watch again and underline the word you hear in the sentences.
1. *How*/*Who* are you, sir?
2. I speak English *good*/*well*.
3. I learn it from a *book*/*cook*.
4. Hello, Major. How are you *OK*/*today*?
5. I'm *tired*/*fine*, thank you.
6. That's a remarkable *animal*/*antique* you have there, Fawlty.
7. Er … *£20*/*£12*, I think.
8. *Canadian*/*American*, I think, Major.

speakout at a hotel

4A Look at the key phrases below. Who says them? Write guest (G) or receptionist (R) next to each phrase.

keyphrases
Good evening. Can I help you?   R
Yes, I have a reservation.
For two nights?
What's your family name?
Could you spell that?
You're in room 407.
This is your keycard.
What time's breakfast?

B ▶ 1.14 Listen and check.

C Listen again and write the guest's name and telephone number.
Guest: _____
Phone: _____

5 Work in pairs and take turns to role-play the situation. Student A: you are the receptionist. Welcome the guest and complete the hotel registration form. Student B: you are the guest. Answer the receptionist's questions.

HOTEL REGISTRATION
Family name: _____
First name: _____
Address: _____
_____
Phone: _____
Email: _____
Number of nights: _____

A: *Good evening, can I help you?*
B: *Yes, I have a reservation. My name's Pirez.*
A: *Ah, yes. Could you spell that?*
B: *Yes. It's p-i-r-e-z.*

writeback an email to a hotel

6A Number the phrases in the correct order in the email below.

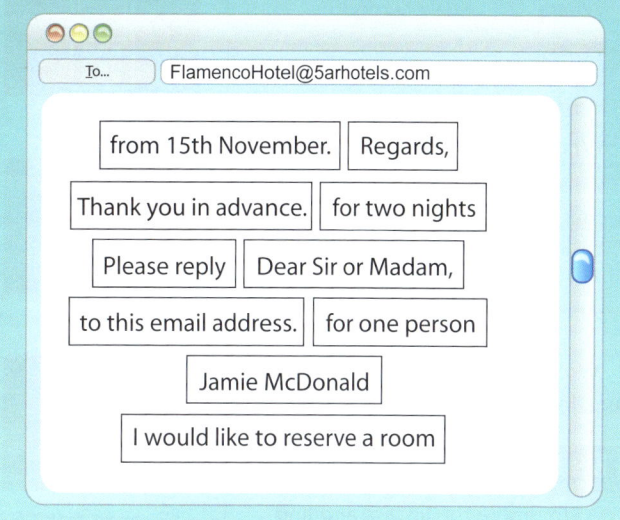

To... FlamencoHotel@5arhotels.com

- from 15th November.
- Regards,
- Thank you in advance.
- for two nights
- Please reply
- Dear Sir or Madam,
- to this email address.
- for one person
- Jamie McDonald
- I would like to reserve a room

B Write an email to book a room. Decide where and how many nights you want to stay. Choose one of the cities and hotels below.
- New York / The Hilton
- Edinburgh / Castle Bed & Breakfast
- Sydney / The Ritz

1.5 « LOOKBACK

PRESENT SIMPLE: BE

1A Complete sentences 1–5 with the correct form of *be*.
1 Where'___ Kuala Lumpur?
2 Where ___ these people from: Oprah Winfrey, Daniel Radcliffe, Kazuo Ishiguro, Cristiano Ronaldo?
3 Where'___ the Blue Mosque?
4 What ___ the names of four countries in South America beginning with A, B or C?
5 I'___ the President of the USA. What ___ my name?

B Work in pairs and answer the questions.

SPELLING AND COUNTRIES

2A Unjumble the letters and find six countries below.
aanpj = Japan
1 isusar
2 typeg
3 isnap
4 hutso cifara
5 omicxe
6 diain

B Write five new words from Unit 1.
___
___
___
___
___

C Work in pairs and take turns. Student A: say one of your words. Student B: spell it.
A: *sandwich*
B: *s-a-n-d-w-i-c-h*

QUESTIONS WITH BE

3 Work in pairs. Student A: choose a famous person. Student B: ask questions to identify him/her.
B: *Is it a man?*
A: *Yes, it is.*
B: *Is he French?*
A: *No, he isn't.*
B: *Is he on TV?*
A: *Yes, he is.*

OBJECTS

4A Write the name of each object.

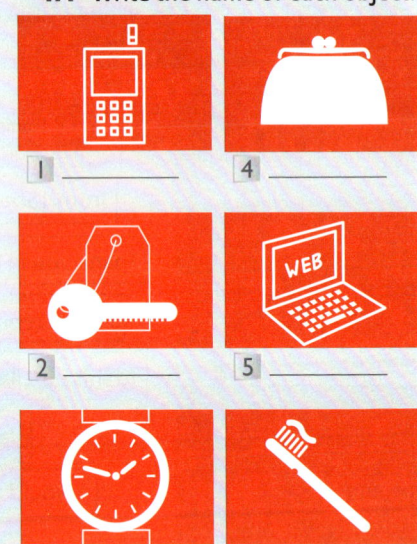

1 _____   4 _____

2 _____   5 _____

3 _____   6 _____

B Underline the correct alternatives.
1 A: Which newspaper is *that/those*?
  B: It's The Times.
2 A: What are *this/these*?
  B: They're my new sunglasses.
3 A: What are *that/those*?
  B: They're English magazines.

C Work in pairs and take turns. Student A: give your partner an object from your bag/pocket. Student B: close your eyes and take an object from your partner. Guess what it is.
A: *What's this? / What are these?*
B: *It's a … / They're …*

WORD GROUPS

5A Write five words from Unit 1 for the three groups below:
1 electrical objects
  mobile phone, …
2 two-syllable words
  passport, …
3 places
  money exchange, …

B Work in pairs and take turns. Student A: read out the words but don't say which group. Student B: guess the group.

POSSESSIVES

6A Work in pairs. Complete the poems with words from the box.

| ~~my~~ your my mine yours |
| hands fine Ann's |

A: This is ¹___*my*___ book.
B: No, it's ²_____.
A: Here's ³_____ name. Look!
B: Oh! That's ⁴_____.
B: Are these ⁵_____ pens?
A: No, they're ⁶_____.
B: Where are ⁷_____ then?
A: In my ⁸_____!

B Read the poems to each other.

AT THE STATION

7A Complete the conversation with the words in the box.

| ~~could~~ is return there you it |

  Could
A: Hello,∧I have a ticket to Rome, please?
B: A single or ?
A: A return, please. How much is ?
B: Twenty-five euros.
A: And which platform it ?
B: Platform three. Over .
A: Thank .

B Make a list of twelve key words from the conversation.

C Work in pairs. Compare your list of the key words and practise the conversation.

BBC VIDEO PODCAST
Watch people talking about where they are from on ActiveBook or on the website.

Authentic BBC interviews

www.pearsonELT.com/speakout

UNIT 2

SPEAKING
> Talk about activities you do
> Talk about your daily routine
> Talk about people's jobs
> Ask questions at a tourist information centre

LISTENING
> Listen to people discussing online groups
> Listen to people talk about their daily routines
> Check when you don't understand
> Watch an extract from a reality programme about a difficult job

READING
> Read about online groups

WRITING
> Link sentences with *and*, *but* and *or*
> Write an internet posting to a penpal

BBC CONTENT
Video podcast: What's your daily routine?
DVD: Holiday: Fasten Your Seatbelt

UNIT 2

lifestyle

▶ Join us! p18
▶ High flyers p20 
▶ What time does it start? p22 
▶ Chalet Girl p24

2.1 JOIN US!

▶ **GRAMMAR** | present simple: I/you/we/they   ▶ **VOCABULARY** | activities   ▶ **HOW TO** | talk about activities

READING

1A Read the website extracts. Answer the questions.
1 How many online groups are there?
2 Which is the right group for these people?

'I eat a lot of fruit and no fast food.'

'I watch everything with Johnny Depp in it.'

'Sleep? I love it.'

'I send a postcard to my mum from every city.'

B Work in pairs and compare your ideas.

VOCABULARY activities

2A Complete phrases 1–8 below with words from the box. Use the website extracts to help you.

~~drink~~   read   listen to   do   eat play   go   watch

1 _drink_ coffee / water
2 _____ films / TV
3 _____ tennis / football
4 _____ junk food / popcorn
5 _____ books / magazines
6 _____ music / an MP3 player
7 _____ running / to the cinema
8 _____ sport / exercise

B Add these words to phrases 1–8.

tea   a sandwich   DVDs   swimming golf   newspapers   nothing the teacher

C Work in pairs. Student A: say a noun from Exercise 2A. Student B: say the verb that goes with it.

A: *football*
B: *play* football

speakout TIP

Look for words that go together (collocations). When you write new words in your notebook, write the words that go with them, e.g. *drink coffee/tea/water*. Look at the website extract about the Travel group. In your notebook, write the words that go with *meet* and *take*.

GROUPTALK.net

Profile   edit   Friends ▼   Inbox ▼

Search

🎥 Film group

We love films – old black and white films, new films – all kinds of films. We write about films on our group forum. We watch DVDs and films on TV, and sometimes we go to the cinema together. And yes, we like popcorn, too!

▶ Join us

🧳 Travel group

We love travel! We go everywhere. We meet people from different countries and we chat with them about their lives. We take photos of our travels, and post them on our website. We read travel books and we like maps.

▶ Join us

🏀 Sport group

We love sport! We do lots of sport. We play tennis and go running or swimming every day. At the weekend, we do exercise in the gym or we play football. We also watch sport on TV. We don't eat junk food, only good food. We don't drink coffee, only water; 2–3 litres a day.

▶ Join us

🎧 Laid-back group

We do nothing … just relax … all the time! We don't like work and we hate sport, but we listen to our MP3 players a lot. We watch TV every evening … for 4–5 hours! We don't read books or newspapers, but sometimes we read magazines. Easy magazines, of course!

▶ Join us

LISTENING

3A ▶ 2.1 Listen to two friends talk about the online groups. Complete the table for the man. Tick the boxes.

	like	don't like
sport		✓
films		
travel		
relaxing		

B Discuss. Which is the right group for the man?

GRAMMAR present simple: I/you/we/they

4A ▶ 2.2 Listen and complete the table.

Questions and short answers					
____	you	like	films?	Yes,	I ____
		travel	a lot?	No,	____

B Listen again. Underline the stressed words.

C Look at the pronunciation of *do you*. Then listen and repeat.

do‿you /dʊjʊ/
/dʊjʊ/ like films?

▶ page 130 **LANGUAGEBANK**

PRACTICE

5A Work in pairs. Write three questions for each online group. Use the website extracts to help.

Film group – Do you like films? Do you watch films on TV? Do you go to the cinema a lot?

B Work in groups. Ask other students your questions. Which is the right group for them?

GRAMMAR present simple: I/you/we/they

6A Read the website extract about the Laid-back group again. Complete the table.

Positive and negative statements	
We	_____	magazines.
	_____	books.

B Look at the sentences in the table. How do you make the negative?

C Underline the correct word(s) to complete the rule.

Rule: We use the present simple for activities we do *regularly* / *at the moment of speaking*.

▶ page 130 **LANGUAGEBANK**

PRACTICE

7 Cover the website extracts on page 18. Complete the information below. Use a verb in the positive or negative form.

In the Laid-back group they ¹ *don't like* work and they ² _____ all the time. They ³ _____ nothing all day.

In the Sport group they ⁴ _____ tennis and ⁵ _____ running or swimming every day. At the weekend, they ⁶ _____ exercise at the gym. They ⁷ _____ junk food and they ⁸ _____ coffee.

8A Work in pairs. Start a new online group. Choose one of the groups below or think of another. Then write answers to the questions.

Party group   *Good food group*

Car group   *English group*

1 What do people in your group do? (four activities)
2 What don't you do? (two activities)

B Work with another pair. Tell them about your group. Find out about their group.

Our group is the Party group. We love parties. We …

SPEAKING

9 Work in pairs and take turns. Talk about a group or team you are in.

A: *Are you in a group or team?*
B: *Yes, I'm in a football team.*
A: *Where do you play?*

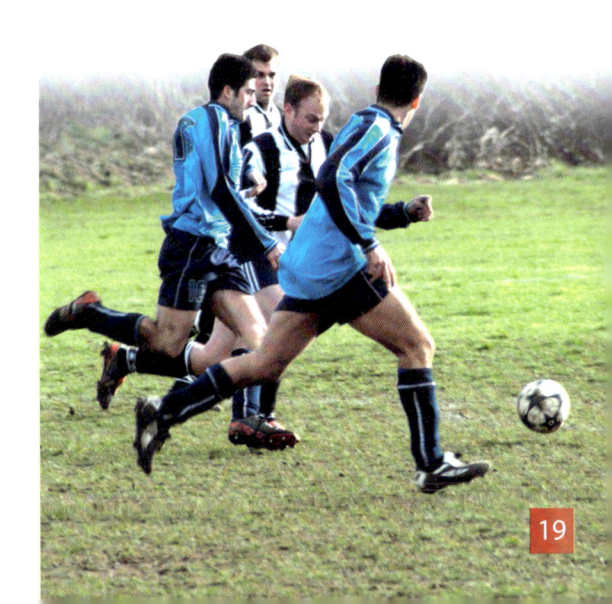

2.2 HIGH FLYERS

▶ **GRAMMAR** | present simple: *he/she/it*   ▶ **VOCABULARY** | daily routines; jobs   ▶ **HOW TO** | talk about routines

VOCABULARY daily routines

1A Match the phrases in the box with photos A–I below.

| get up A   go to bed   have breakfast   get home |
| have lunch   start work/school   leave home |
| finish work/school   have dinner |

B Complete the questions.
1 Do you ___get___ up early?
2 Do you _____ breakfast at home?
3 What time do you _____ home?
4 When do you _____ work/school?
5 Where do you _____ lunch?
6 When do you _____ home?
7 Do you _____ to bed late?

C Work in pairs. Ask and answer the questions above.

WRITING *and*, *but* and *or*

2A Complete the sentences with *and*, *but* and *or*.
1 Every morning, I have coffee, _____ I don't like it very much.
2 Every morning, I have coffee at home _____ I drink another coffee on the train.
3 Every morning, I have coffee _____ tea at home.

B Complete each sentence in three different ways. Use *and*, *but* and *or*.
1 In the week, I get up early …
2 At the weekend, I play tennis …

C Work in pairs and compare your answers.

LISTENING

3 Look at the person in the photo on page 21. What is his job? Do you think it is a good job?

4A ▶ 2.3 Listen and answer the questions.
1 Do the people like their jobs?
2 Do their families think they are good jobs?

B Listen again and complete the table.

	Daniel	Ted
¹where/breakfast?	London	
²where/lunch?		
³where/dinner?		Singapore
⁴when/leave home?		
⁵when/get home?		

GRAMMAR present simple: *he/she/it*

5A Look at audio script 2.3 on page 168 and complete the table.

Present simple positive statements		
He	_____	home on Monday.
He	_____	home on Thursday.
My father	_____	windows.

B Look at the sentences in the table above and complete the rule.

Rule: To make the present simple with *he/she/it* add _____ or _____ to the verb.

C ▶ 2.4 Listen to the verbs. Write them in the correct group below according to the sound of the ending.

/s/	/z/	/ɪz/
get*s*		

D ▶ 2.5 Listen to other verbs. Write them in the correct group. Then listen and repeat.

E Look at the sentences in the table and complete the rule.

Present simple negative statements		
He	doesn't want	to fly.
My wife	doesn't like	it.

Rule: Make the negative with *he/she/it* + _____ + verb.

▶ page 130 **LANGUAGEBANK**

20

PRACTICE

6A Complete the text. Use a verb in the positive or negative form.

A day in the life …

Sian Williams ¹*gets up* at 3.45 in the morning but she ² _____ (not) breakfast at home because there's no time. She ³ _____ home at 4.15 and ⁴ _____ to the BBC1 studio by taxi. She ⁵ _____ work at 5.30 and is live on air from 6 to 9.15 in the morning. In the afternoon she prepares for the next day's show. She ⁶ _____ work at about 4 and ⁷ _____ home at 5. She ⁸ _____ (not) TV in the evening because she ⁹ _____ music and ¹⁰ _____ dinner for her family!

B Read the information again. What's the woman's job?

7A Work in pairs. What do you know about your partner? Write four true and two false sentences about him/her.

Pilar gets up early.
She doesn't watch TV in the evening.

B Work with another partner. Take it in turns to read your sentences. Guess which are true and which are false.

GRAMMAR present simple: *he/she/it*

8A Look at the sentences in the table and complete the rule.

Present simple questions			
Does		he	want	to be a pilot?
What	**does**	your family		**think**?

Rule: Make the question with _____ + *he/she/it* + verb.

B ▶ 2.6 Listen and underline the stressed words.
1 Does he want to be a pilot?
2 What does your family think?

C Listen again and repeat the sentences.

▶ page 130 **LANGUAGEBANK**

PRACTICE

9 Work in pairs. Student A: look at page 160. Student B: look at page 164.

VOCABULARY jobs

10A ▶ 2.7 Listen to the sounds A–F and write the names of the jobs.

1 _____   3 _____   5 _____
2 _____   4 _____   6 _____

B Work in pairs. How many other jobs do you know in English? Make a list.
▶ page 153 **PHOTOBANK**

SPEAKING

11 Work in groups. One student: choose a person from the photo bank on page 153. The other students: ask ten questions to find the job.

B: Is it a woman?
A: Yes, it is.
C: Does she work with animals?
A: No, she doesn't …

21

2.3 WHAT TIME DOES IT START?

▶ **FUNCTION** | asking for information ▶ **VOCABULARY** | the time ▶ **LEARN TO** | show you don't understand

VOCABULARY the time

1A Match the times 1–6 to the photos A–F.

1 four o' _clock_   C
2 _____ past five
3 two fifteen OR quarter past _____
4 one thirty OR _____ past one
5 nine forty-five OR _____ to ten
6 five _____ six

B Look at the photos again and complete the times above.

C Work in pairs and take turns. Student A: point to a photo. Ask the time. Student B: say the time.
A: *What's the time?*
B: *It's …*

2A ▶ 2.8 Look at the times below. Listen and circle the correct times.

1	10.30	12.30	2.30
2	3.15	3.45	4.15
3	6.40	7.20	7.40
4	4.25	4.35	5.25

B Work in pairs. Student A: look at page 166. Student B: look at page 164.

3 Work in pairs and take turns. Ask and answer the questions below.
At the weekend, what time do you …
- get up?
- have breakfast?
- have lunch?
- go to bed?

On Saturday I get up at 8 but on Sunday I …

FUNCTION asking for information

4A Work in pairs. Look at the photos and leaflets. Answer the questions.
1 What city are the tourists in?
2 What tours can they take?
3 What can they do on the tours?

B ▶ 2.9 Listen and answer the questions.
1 Which tour do the tourists want?
2 Do they book the tour?
3 What's the problem?

5A Put the questions about the bus tour in the correct order.
1 it / does / what / time / start?
2 leave / where / from? / does / it
3 when / the tour / finish? / does
4 much / cost? / it / how / does
5 take / do / credit cards? / you

B ▶ 2.10 Listen and check. Then listen again and underline the stressed words in the questions above.

C Look at the pronunciation of *does it*. Listen again and repeat the questions.
does it /dəzɪt/
What time /dəzɪt/ start?

D ▶ 2.11 Listen and answer the questions in Exercise 5A.
▶ page 130 LANGUAGEBANK

2.3

HONG KONG ISLAND TOUR

Start with a tram ride to Victoria Peak to see the fantastic views from the top. Visit the fishing village of Aberdeen, and go shopping in the 'Shopper's Paradise' at Stanley market. Finish with a visit to the beach at beautiful Repulse Bay.

HONG KONG HARBOUR TOUR

Go round the harbour on a Chinese-style tour boat. Relax with a coffee in the air-conditioned café or stand outside and enjoy the sun. See the city buildings, the mountains of Kowloon Island behind and the busy shipping port.

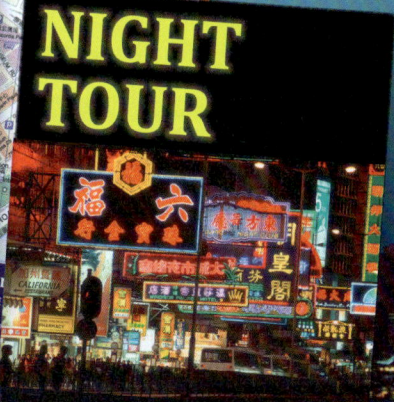

NIGHT TOUR

Start with dinner at the famous revolving '66' restaurant with amazing views over all Hong Kong. Then walk with a guide in the streets of the night market in Kowloon. Go on a Chinese junk in the harbour and enjoy the city lights on the buildings and in the water.

LEARN TO show you don't understand

6A ▶ 2.12 Read and listen to part of the conversation again. Underline three phrases the woman (A) uses when she doesn't understand.

A: Hello. We're back.
C: Hello again! So, do you want the Hong Kong Island tour?
A: Yes. Er. Could you speak more slowly, please?
C: Of course. Would you like to take the tour tomorrow morning or afternoon?
A: Tomorrow morning. What time does it start?
C: At eight o'clock exactly.
A: Excuse me, eight o'clock … ?
C: Yes, at eight.
A: And where does it leave from?
C: The bus leaves from the front gate here.
A: Sorry, could you repeat that?
C: The bus leaves from the front gate.

B ▶ 2.13 Listen again to the three phrases. Then repeat and practise the polite intonation.

speakout TIP

When you don't understand, stop the other person and ask them to slow down or to repeat.

C Work in groups. Ask each student for their address and telephone number. Use the phrases from Exercise 6A to check the information.

SPEAKING

7A Work in pairs. Student A: you work at the Tourist Information centre. Look at page 161.

Student B: You are a tourist in Hong Kong. Ask Student A questions and complete the notes below.

Excuse me. Can you give me some information about the … ? What time does it … ?

	Start time	Finish time	Leaves from	Price
Harbour tour				
Island tour				

B Change roles. Student B: now you work at the Tourist Information centre. Look at the information below. Answer Student A's questions.

	Start time	Finish time	Leaves from	Price
Night tour	7.15p.m.	10.15p.m.	Temple Street	HK$410
Rock concert	8.00p.m.	11.30p.m.	Asia-World Expo	HK$980

23

2.4 CHALET GIRL

DVD PREVIEW

1 Read the programme information and answer the questions.
1 What is Toyah's usual job?
2 What job does she try?

BBC Holiday: Fasten Your Seatbelt

Toyah Willcox is a TV presenter, a singer and actress. In this BBC programme she takes a new holiday job as a chalet girl in Verbier, Switzerland. Her job is to clean the chalet and cook for six guests. The problem is that Toyah isn't a good cook and it's her first time in this kind of job!

2 Work in pairs. Read Toyah's list of jobs. Which are about food, cleaning or people?

Today's jobs
- Cook breakfast
- Go shopping for food 1
- Clean the rooms
- Wash the floors
- Make a cake
- Meet the guests
- Go out with the guests
- Buy bread
- Make soup

DVD VIEW

3A Watch the DVD. Number Toyah's jobs in the correct order.

B What five problems does Toyah have? Use the prompts below to help.
1 shopping / 174 / 100 francs
2 salt / soup
3 guest / professional cook
4 not have / key
5 guest / not want / egg

C Work in pairs and discuss. What are two good things and two bad things about this job?

speakout life at home

4A Think about your life at home. Make a list of:
- three things you like doing
- three things you don't like doing

B ▶ 2.14 Listen to two people talking about their life at home. Write man (M) or woman (W) next to phrases 1–3.
1 likes cleaning
2 doesn't like cleaning
3 likes relaxing

C Listen again and tick the key phrases you hear.

keyphrases

Do you like [cleaning/cooking/washing]?
Yes, I love it! It's OK. / No, not really. / No, I don't. I hate it.
I don't [clean/cook/relax]!
What do you like doing? Why?
I like [playing video games/watching TV].
Me, too.

D Work in groups. Ask and answer questions about life at home. Use the key phrases to help.

E Discuss. Which student has a similar life at home to you?

writeback an internet posting

5A Read the internet posting. Is Leona a good penpal for you?

penpalfinder.com

About me: I'm Leona. I live in the Czech Republic. I'm a student of law at Prague University and I also study English in the evenings. I'm twenty-two and I love meeting people, but I don't know many people from other countries.

Interests/Hobbies: I like rock music. and my favourite band is Radiohead. I'm very active. I go running or swimming every morning and I like sports – tennis is my favourite, but I don't play it well.

Requests: Please email me. I want to practise English and to have friends from other countries, especially from South America or Asia. I want to know about different lifestyles.

B Write a posting about you. Remember to use *and*, *but* and *or*.

About me: Give your name, your country/city, your occupation (work/study)
Interests/Hobbies: What do you like doing?
Requests: What do you want?

C Read other students' postings. Match two students with each other.

2.5 « LOOKBACK

JOBS

1A What are the jobs? Find and circle twelve jobs.

nurse teacher waiter hairdresser receptionist engineer lawyer actress accountant doctor politician chef

B Work in pairs. Which jobs are right for these people? Write two jobs for each person.

1. I like people.
2. I talk a lot.
3. I work well alone.
4. I love numbers.
5. I'm very active.
6. I like food.

ACTIVITIES

2A Complete the questions with a suitable verb.

1 Do you _read_ magazines? Which ones?
2 Do you _____ sport on TV? Which sport?
3 Do you _____ a lot of photos? When?
4 Do you _____ music when you work or study? What kind?
5 Do you _____ exercise every week? What do you do?
6 Do you _____ a lot of junk food? What and when?
7 Do you _____ books in English? Which ones?
8 Do you _____ to the cinema a lot? When?

B Work in pairs. Ask and answer the questions.

PRESENT SIMPLE QUESTIONS

3A What do you know about your partner? Complete the sentences with the positive or negative form of the verb in brackets.

1 He/She _doesn't like_ (like) shopping.
2 He/She _____ (play) computer games.
3 He/She _____ (go) out a lot in the evenings.
4 He/She _____ (do) his/her homework every night.
5 He/She _____ (study) a lot at the weekend.
6 He/She _____ (watch) breakfast television.
7 He/She _____ (go) to bed very late.
8 He/She _____ (cook) every night.

B Work in pairs and check your answers.
A: *Do you like shopping?*
B: *No, I don't.*

DAILY ROUTINES

4A On a piece of paper write:
- a place you like
- your job or study subject
- the time you get up
- two things you do in the evening

B Work in pairs. Exchange papers. Ask and answer questions.
A: *Moonbucks. What's that?*
B: *A coffee bar.*
A: *Why do you like it?*
B: *Well, …*

C Take your partner's paper. Work with a new partner and exchange papers. Ask and answer questions about your first partner.
Why does he get up at six?
What does he study?

ASKING FOR INFORMATION

5A Look at the leaflet below. Write questions to ask for the information in the leaflet.

Malta full day tour	
Start time:	9.45a.m.
Finish time:	4.30p.m.
Leaves from:	Hotel lobby
Adult:	15 euros
Payment:	All major credit cards accepted.

B Work in pairs. Student A: you are a tourist. Ask questions about the Malta tour. Student B: you work at the Tourist Information centre. Answer your partner's questions. Use full sentences.
A: *What time does the tour start?*
B: *It starts at nine forty-five in the morning.*

BBC VIDEO PODCAST
Watch people talking about their daily lives on ActiveBook or on the website.

Authentic BBC interviews

www.pearsonFLT.com/speakout

26

UNIT 3

SPEAKING
- Describe a friend and why you like them
- Make arrangements to meet friends
- Talk about a special occasion

LISTENING
- Learn to show interest when you listen
- Watch an extract from a documentary about a special occasion

READING
- Read and understand a quiz about friends
- Read about an unusual family

WRITING
- Improve your use of apostrophe 's
- Write about your family
- Write an invitation

BBC CONTENT
- Video podcast: What do you like doing with friends/family?
- DVD: Francesco's Mediterranean Voyage

people

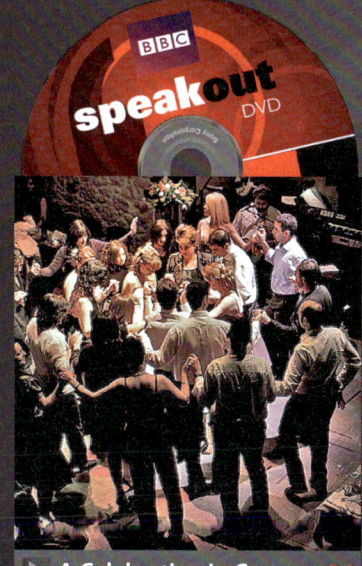

▶ Just good friends   p28
▶ Big happy families   p30
▶ Are you free tonight?   p32
▶ A Celebration In Crete   p34

3.1 JUST GOOD FRIENDS

▶ GRAMMAR | frequency adverbs; modifiers   ▶ VOCABULARY | personality   ▶ HOW TO | describe personality

VOCABULARY | personality

1A Match adjectives 1–5 with pictures A–E.
1 intelligent B
2 kind
3 talkative
4 friendly
5 funny

B Look at the adjectives in the box below. Match each adjective with its opposite from Exercise 1A.

| stupid 1 serious unfriendly quiet unkind |

C Look at audio script 3.1 on page 168. Underline the stressed syllables in the adjectives.

D ▶ 3.1 Listen and check. Then listen again and repeat.

E Work in pairs. Think of a friend and describe him/her. Use adjectives from Exercise 1A.
My friend's name is David. I like him because he's kind and funny.

speakout TIP

We often make words negative with *un-*. In your notebook, write the negative of these words: *happy, usual, well, real, safe, common*, e.g. *unhappy*.

LISTENING

2A ▶ 3.2 Listen and answer the questions.
1 Are the two men very close friends?
2 Are the two women very close friends?

B Listen again. Tick the adjectives that describe José and Rosa.

adjective	José	Rosa
friendly		
funny		
intelligent		
kind		
quiet		
serious		
stupid		
talkative		

GRAMMAR | frequency adverbs

3A Read the sentences and put the adverbs in bold in the correct place on the line below.
1 He's **sometimes** very funny – not all the time, but sometimes.
2 We **usually** understand each other well.
3 We **often** go out to clubs – two or three times a week.
4 We **hardly ever** do things together, maybe two or three times a year.

never   always
0%   100%

B Read the sentences again and complete the rule below.

Rule: The adverb goes *before/after* the verb *be*.
The adverb goes *before/after* other verbs.

▶ page 132 LANGUAGEBANK

PRACTICE

4A Put the words in the correct order.
1 My / quiet / usually / very / friend / is *My friend is usually very quiet.*
2 always / 're / together / We
3 around / feel / I / him/her / stupid / sometimes
4 funny / My / very / usually / is / friend
5 always / him/her / to / I / listen
6 other / understand / don't / each / We / always

B Work in pairs. Discuss which sentences are true for you and your friend from Exercise 1E.

READING

5A Think of another friend. Read the quiz on page 29 and answer the questions.

B Work in pairs and compare your answers.

28

3.1

Are you TRUE friends, just GOOD friends or FAIR-WEATHER friends?

Do the quiz and find out how close you really are!

1 **Do you like doing things together?**
a) Yes, we do. We like the same things and we often do them together.
b) Yes, we do. We sometimes do things together.
c) No, we don't. We don't like the same things and we hardly ever do things together.

2 **How often do you phone, text or talk to your friend?**
a) every day
b) once or twice a week
c) not very often

3 **What do you do when your friend has a problem?**
a) I usually make time to listen to him/her.
b) I sometimes listen, but not always.
c) I go away and leave him/her alone.

4 **What does your friend know about your life?**
a) everything
b) some things but not everything
c) almost nothing

5 **Do you think you're a good friend to him/her?**
a) Yes – we're lucky to have each other!
b) Yes, usually.
c) Not all the time.

Key

3 or more a's: True friends! You're very close, you like a lot of the same things and you understand each other well. You're really good friends and you are always ready to help each other.

3 or more b's: Just good friends. You're quite close to your friend, but sometimes you don't understand each other very well.

3 or more c's: Fair-weather friends. You like each other but you aren't very close. You have fun together, but you don't help each other when one of you has a problem.

GRAMMAR   modifiers

6A Read the key again and underline these words: *quite*, *not very*, *really* and *very*.

B Complete phrases 1–4 with the correct modifiers and adjectives in the box below.

| ~~very good~~   not very good   good |
| really good   quite good |

1 ✓✓✓ = We're _very good_ friends, we're _____ friends.
2 ✓✓ = We're _____ friends.
3 ✓ = We're _____ friends.
4 ✗ = We're _____ friends.

C ▶ 3.3 Listen and repeat.

▶ page 132 LANGUAGEBANK

PRACTICE

7A Correct the modifiers in four of the sentences below. Two sentences are correct.

1 I'm ~~not very~~ friendly. I love people.
    very/really
2 I'm very quiet. I speak all the time.
3 I'm quite intelligent. I usually get about 65% in tests.
4 I'm not very funny. People often laugh at my jokes.
5 I'm really kind. I always help my friends.
6 I'm not very serious. I like studying and I don't like relaxing.

B Change the sentences above so that they are true for you. Then compare your answers with a partner.

I'm very funny. People always laugh at my jokes.

SPEAKING

8A Complete the table with the names of three people you know.

How close?	Who?
not very close	Felipe
quite close	
very/really close	

B Work in pairs. Ask and answer questions about the people.

A: *Who's Felipe?*
B: *We work together. He's very intelligent and quite serious. We're not very close.*

3.2 BIG HAPPY FAMILIES

▶ **GRAMMAR** | have/has got   ▶ **VOCABULARY** | family   ▶ **HOW TO** | talk about your family

VOCABULARY | family

1A Work in pairs. Look at the photo of the Chernenko family. Can you find:
- the parents?
- the number of children?
- a son and a daughter?
- a brother and a sister?
- a husband and a wife?

B Look at the family words above. Do you know any other 'family' words? Make a list.

➡ page 154 **PHOTOBANK**

READING

2A Discuss. What do you think are the good/bad things about life in a big/small family?

B Work in pairs. Student A: look at page 165. Student B: read the text on this page. Circle the numbers in the box which are in your text. What do they refer to?

| 12 (17) 11 8 1 7 |
| 9 6 15 |

17 children in the Chernenko family

C Work in pairs. Tell your partner about your text. Use your numbers as prompts.

D Work in pairs. Draw lines to complete the information. Use the texts to help.

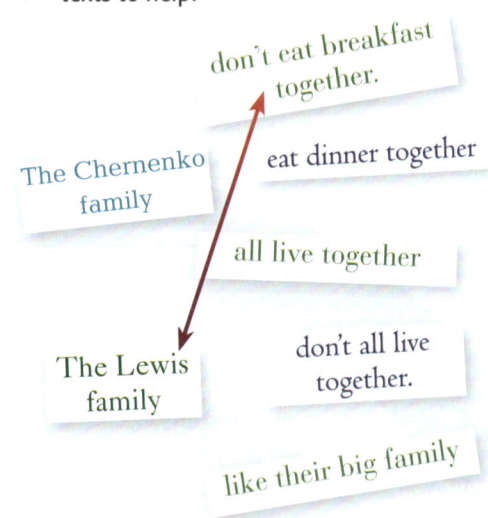

- don't eat breakfast together.
- eat dinner together
- all live together
- don't all live together.
- like their big family

The Chernenko family
The Lewis family

RealLIVES

Family welcomes baby seventeen

BABY DAVID is the latest child of Vladimir and Zynaida Chernenko. The Chernenkos come from Ukraine and now live in the USA. They have got 17 children, 8 girls and 9 boys. (Sergey, 22, isn't in the photo.)

Life in the Chernenko house is noisy! The house has got 7 rooms but each child sleeps in his or her own bed. They don't always eat at the same time, but in the evenings they have dinner together. They travel everywhere in their 15-seat car.
Vladimir Chernenko doesn't think his family is unusual. Large families are quite normal in the Ukraine. Vladimir says, 'We love singing and now we've got lots of voices for our family *choir!'

One daughter, 20-year-old Liliya, is married and doesn't live with her brothers and sisters. The other children live at home. 'It's good,' says 18-year-old Dmitry. 'I like it. My best friend says he's bored because he hasn't got a brother or a sister. I come home from school and I'm never bored. I've always got something to do.'
And how about another child? 'We haven't got any plans,' says Zynaida, 'but who knows?'

*****choir** – a group of people who sing together

GRAMMAR have/has got

3A Look at the article on page 30 again and complete the sentences.
1 They _____ seventeen children.
2 The house _____ seven rooms.
3 They _____ any plans for another child.

B Complete the table.

I/You/We/They	_____	got	eight sisters.
He/She	_____		
I	_____n't		a brother.
He/She	_____n't		

C ▶ 3.4 Listen and underline the alternative you hear.
1 David *'s/has* got eight brothers.
2 I *'ve/have* got a sister and two brothers.
3 They *'ve/haven't* got a big car.
4 She *'s/hasn't* got a small family.

D Listen again and repeat. Notice the contracted forms. Which word is stressed in the sentence?

➔ page 132 LANGUAGEBANK

PRACTICE

4A Complete the text. Use the correct form of *have got* or *be*.

I ¹ __'ve got__ a brother and a sister. My sister, Lisa, ² _____ thirty-five, my brother, Mark, ³ _____ thirty and I ⁴ _____ twenty-seven. My sister ⁵ _____ married to Andreas and they ⁶ _____ a daughter, Eva. Eva ⁷ _____ (not) any brothers or sisters. My brother ⁸ _____ (not) married, but he ⁹ _____ a girlfriend. I ¹⁰ _____ married to Marek. We ¹¹ _____ two sons, Vlad and Henryk. They ¹² _____ three and one.

B Use the information above to complete the family tree.

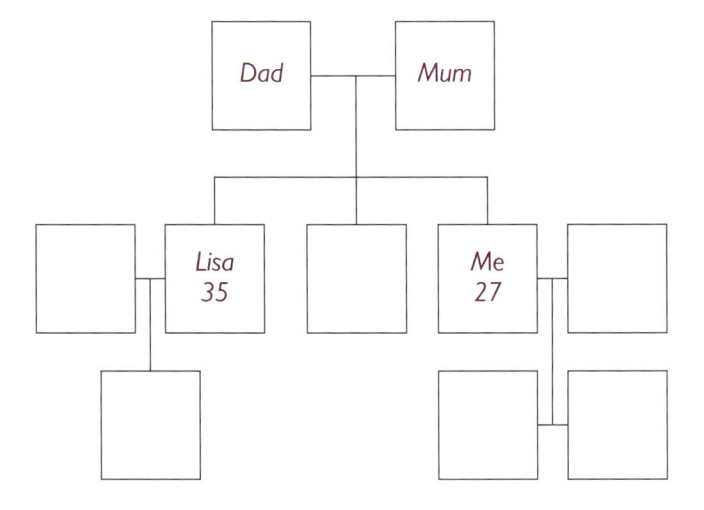

```
    Dad —— Mum
         |
   ——————————————
   |      |      |
         Lisa   Me
         35     27
```

SPEAKING

5A Complete the questions.
1 _____ you _____ any brothers or sisters?
2 How many brothers _____ you _____ ?
3 _____ your brother _____ any children?
4 How many children _____ he _____ ?

B Draw your family tree in your notebook. Write your name and two family members in your tree.

C Work in pairs. Exchange family trees with your partner. Ask and answer questions. Add names, ages and jobs to your partner's family tree.
A: *How many brothers and sisters have you got?*
B: *I've got two brothers and one sister.*
A: *What are their names?*
B: *Joel, Santiago and Cecilia.*
A: *And how old are they?*

D Look at your own family tree again. Check the information and correct any mistakes.

WRITING apostrophe *'s*

6A Read the sentences. Underline six examples of *'s*.

Stuart's got one sister and two brothers. His sister's name's Jane and she's a doctor. Jane's husband is also a doctor and he's got four children from his first marriage.

B Work in pairs. Which *'s* means *has*, *is* or possessive *'s*?

C Read the text. Put in six missing apostrophes (').

Ive got two brothers, Aleksis, and Pavel. Aleksis is forty. Hes an engineer and hes married to Katia. They live in an apartment in Moscow. Theyve got one daughter, Lara. Shes at school and she lives at home with them. Aleksis is quite serious, but my other brother, Pavel, is very energetic and lively. He likes sport and he writes for a magazine. Hes single.

D Write about two people in your family. Write 50–70 words.

3.3 ARE YOU FREE TONIGHT?

▶ FUNCTION | making arrangements ▶ VOCABULARY | time expressions ▶ LEARN TO | show interest

VOCABULARY time expressions

1A Match the time expressions 1–5 with the examples a)–e).

1 every day
2 once a week
3 once a month
4 twice a year
5 three times a day

a) on Fridays
b) in June and December
c) Sunday, Monday, Tuesday, etc.
d) at 8a.m., 1p.m. and 6p.m.
e) on the first Saturday of every month

B How often do you do these activities with friends?
- go to a club, restaurant or a café
- go to the cinema or a concert
- chat about work/school

C Work in pairs and compare your answers.
I go to a café with my friends twice a week.
Alicia and I chat about work every day.

LISTENING

2A ▶ 3.5 Listen to a phone call between Ron and Jack. Which two things in Exercise 1B do they talk about?

B Listen again. Are the sentences true (T) or false (F)? Correct the false sentences.
1 Ron doesn't like his new job.
  F *Ron likes his new job.*
2 Ron likes all the people in his office.
3 Ron wants to meet Jack tonight.
4 They agree to meet.

C Is Jack a good listener? Why/Why not?

3A ▶ 3.6 Listen to a phone call between Ron and Denise. Complete the note with the information you hear.

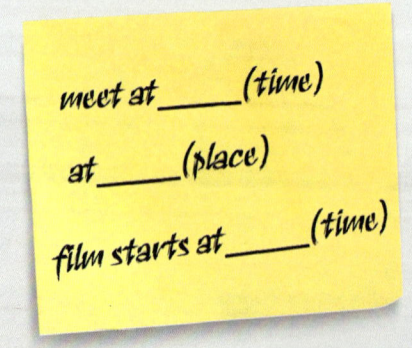

meet at _____ (time)
at _____ (place)
film starts at _____ (time)

B Is Denise a good listener? Why/Why not?

LEARN TO show interest

4A Look at the extract. How does Denise show interest? Underline three of her phrases.

Denise: How's your new job?
Ron: Good. The work's quite interesting and the people are quite friendly…
Denise: Uh-huh.
Ron: … and the work isn't too difficult.
Denise: That's great!
Ron: It's not perfect. I haven't got my own office, and one of the people in my room is really unfriendly …
Denise: Oh, that's a shame!

B Which of the three phrases is positive (+), negative (−) or neutral (N)?

C Complete the phrases with the words in the box.

| ~~interesting~~ ~~a shame~~ terrible great |
| awful fantastic wonderful |

Positive   Negative
That's *interesting* !   That's *a shame* !
_____ !   _____ !
_____ !   _____ !
_____ !

D ▶ 3.7 Look at the intonation. Then listen and repeat.

That's interesting!   That's a shame!

E ▶ 3.8 Listen to the sentences. Reply with a positive or negative phrase.
I've got a new job!
You: That's fantastic!

3.3

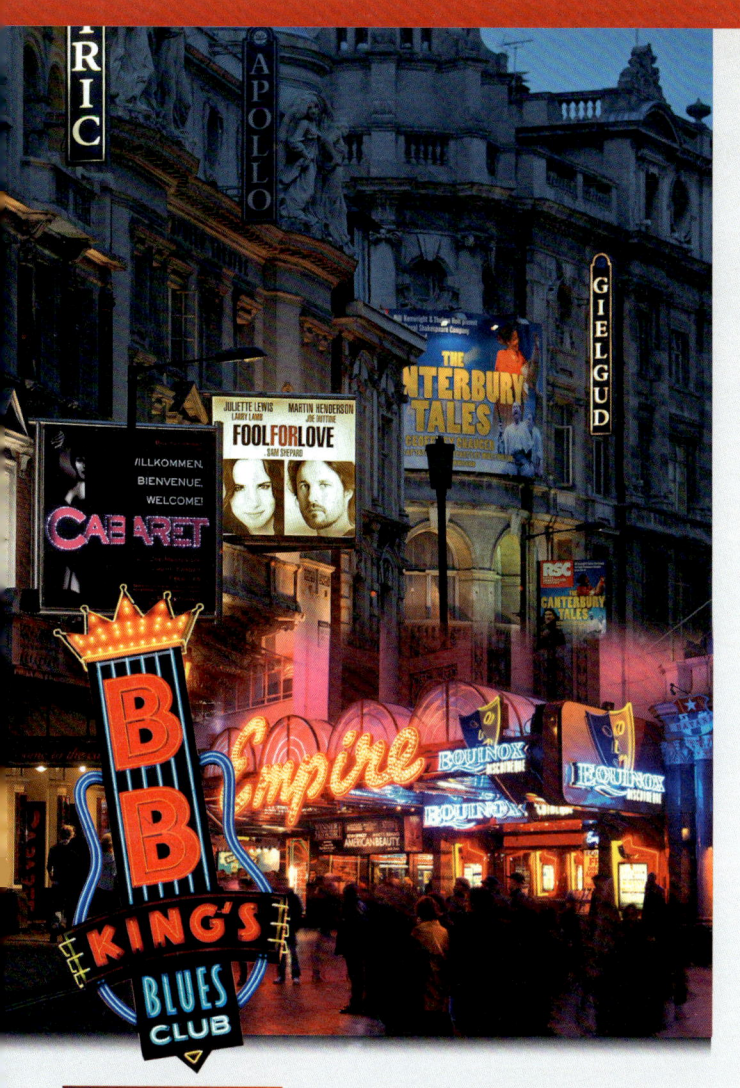

FUNCTION making arrangements

5A Underline the correct alternative.
1 *Do/Are* you free tonight?
2 What *you want/do you want* to do?
3 *How/Who* about going to the cinema?
4 Where's *it on/the town*?
5 What time do you *want/when* to go?
6 *It's/This is* on at six o'clock.
7 *What's/Was* good for you?
8 How about *meeting/to meet* at half past five?

B ▶ 3.9 Listen and check. Then listen and repeat.
➤ page 132 LANGUAGE BANK

6 Work in pairs and take turns. Student A: say a number below. Student B: say the complete sentence/question.
1 free / tonight?
2 What / want / do?
3 How about / cinema?
4 Where / on?
5 What time / go?
6 It's on / seven
7 good / you?
8 How about / at half past five?

A: Six
B: It's on at seven.

SPEAKING

7A You want to go to the cinema. Write down:
- the name of a film
- the name of the cinema
- two start times

B Work in pairs and role-play the situation. Student A: invite your partner to see a film. Student B: ask about the film and accept the invitation. Use the flowchart to help.

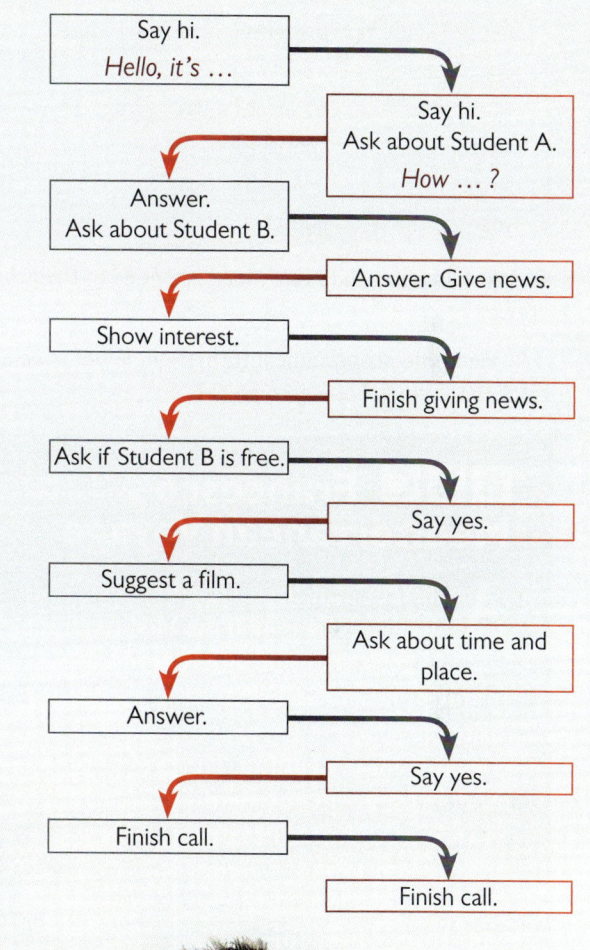

```
Say hi.
Hello, it's ...
        ↓
              Say hi.
              Ask about Student A.
              How ... ?
        ↓
Answer.
Ask about Student B.
        ↓
              Answer. Give news.
        ↓
Show interest.
        ↓
              Finish giving news.
        ↓
Ask if Student B is free.
        ↓
              Say yes.
        ↓
Suggest a film.
        ↓
              Ask about time and place.
        ↓
Answer.
        ↓
              Say yes.
        ↓
Finish call.
        ↓
              Finish call.
```

33

3.4 A CELEBRATION IN CRETE

DVD PREVIEW

1 Discuss. What special occasions do people usually celebrate in your country? What do people usually do on these occasions?

2A Match the verbs and the phrases they go with.

1 have	a restaurant
2 eat	football on TV
3 go to	special clothes
4 sing	presents/gifts to each other
5 give	a party
6 watch	to special music
7 invite	special food
8 dance	'Happy Birthday'
9 wear	guests

B Work in pairs. Add two more activities to the list above.

3A Read the programme information. What special celebration does Francesco go to?

BBC Francesco's Mediterranean Voyage

Architect and historian Francesco da Mosto travels around the Mediterranean Sea and goes to lots of different places. In this programme, Francesco visits the island of Crete and goes to a local wedding. He meets the gorgeous bride Maria and her nervous bridegroom Jorgos, watches the preparations and the wedding, then joins the guests for the reception – a big party to celebrate the occasion!

B Read the information again and check any new words in your dictionary.

▶ DVD VIEW

4A Watch the DVD. Which of the activities in Exercise 2A do you see?

B Watch the DVD again. Are sentences 1–5 true (T) or false (F)?
1 Men make the special wedding bread. *F*
2 There are 1,000 guests for the wedding.
3 Maria arrives at the wedding with her father.
4 The wedding party starts with a dance.
5 Maria and Jorgos dance with their whole family.

C Complete sentences 1–6 with words from the box below.

| ~~married~~ | dance | food | money |
| wedding | family | wife | man |

1 The whole of Maria's village has turned out to see her get ___married___.
2 This is the nervous bridegroom, Jorgos. In a few minutes he and Maria will be _____ and _____.
3 It's certainly the largest _____ reception I've ever been to.
4 At Cretan weddings, guests give _____ as gifts.
5 And now the _____ is served. The meat of 150 sheep … and a whole lot more.
6 Maria and Jorgos's first _____ as man and wife includes all their close _____.

D Watch the DVD again and check your answers.

34

speakout a special occasion

5A Work in pairs. Think of a special occasion, e.g. a birthday, a national holiday or a wedding. Use the questions below to make notes about it.
- What's the name of the occasion?
- When and where does it happen?
- What do you usually do? Describe three/four activities.
- What's your favourite thing on that day?

B ▶ 3.10 Listen to someone talking about Hogmanay. Number the pictures in order.

A   B   C   D

C Look at the key phrases below. Listen again and tick the key phrases you hear.

key phrases

[I want to talk/Let me tell you] about …
[This/It] happens in (place) on (date) …
On [this day/the day before], we [always/usually/often] …
We (also) have a special custom …
I like it because …

D Work in groups and take turns. One student: talk about your special occasion. Use the key phrases to help. Other students: listen and make notes. Then ask two questions about the occasion.

writeback an invitation

6A Read the invitation and answer the questions.
1 What's the special occasion?
2 Where is it?
3 When is it?

Come and join us at our New Year Party!

Place
16A Abbey Street Dublin
(map attached)

Date
Saturday 31st December (of course!)

Time
8.00 till late
Celebrate the New Year with some friends instead of watching TV!

R.S.V.P.
Tel: Sean on 94938 284
or email sean@webmailer.com

B Write an invitation to a special occasion. Use the invitation above to help. Choose from the list:
- a birthday party
- a housewarming
- a wedding
- a school leaving party
- a graduation party

C Work in groups and exchange invitations. Read them and reply to two.

35

3.5 ◀◀ LOOKBACK

PERSONALITY

1A Rearrange the letters to make adjectives. Then write the opposites.
1 itspud   *stupid – intelligent*
2 alavetkit
3 relyfind
4 eurosis
5 dink

B Complete the sentences below. It is important/not important that:
- a doctor is …
- a parent is …
- a TV presenter is …

C Work in pairs and discuss your answers.
A: *I think it's important that a doctor is intelligent and kind.*
B: *Yes, I agree./I don't agree.*

FREQUENCY ADVERBS

2A Add the vowels to the frequency adverbs.
1 _lw_ys
2 _s__lly
3 _ft_n
4 s_m_t_m_s
5 h_rdly _v_r
6 n_v_r

B Choose six events and write six sentences that are true about you. Use each adverb of frequency only once.

make breakfast
watch TV in the morning
eat lunch at work/school
drink coffee in the evening
do the food shopping
clean up after dinner
go to bed early
get home late

I always get home late.

C Work in pairs. Read out your six sentences. What things are the same/different?

FAMILY

3A Complete the sentences with the correct family word.
1 My mother's father is my _____.
2 My brother's son is my _____.
3 My sister's daughter is my _____.
4 My father's sister is my _____.
5 My grandmother's son is my _____ or my _____.
6 My sister's mother and father are my _____.

B Write four more sentences to test your partner.
My mother's daughter is my …

C Work in pairs and take turns. Student A: read out your sentences. Student B: say the family word.

HAVE/HAS GOT

4A Work in pairs. Write questions to ask other students.
Find someone who …
1 _____ has got a cat.
   Have you got a cat?
2 _____ has got a laptop.
3 _____ hasn't got children.
4 _____ has got brothers and sisters.
5 _____ has got a job.
6 _____ hasn't got a car.

B Ask other students the questions. Write a different student's name in each gap above.
1 *Naomi* has got a cat.

MAKING ARRANGEMENTS

5A Complete the phrases with a suitable verb.
1 *go* shopping / running
2 _____ a club / a concert / the cinema
3 _____ lunch at a restaurant / breakfast at a café
4 _____ a film on TV / a DVD
5 _____ football / tennis / golf

B Write three activities from above in the diary below. Leave three spaces empty.

SATURDAY
morning:
afternoon:
evening:

SUNDAY
morning:
afternoon:
evening:

C Work in groups. Take turns to invite other students to do the activities with you. When they accept, write their names and the activity in your diary.
A: *How about going shopping on Saturday morning?*
B: *Sorry, I'm busy./Great! I'm free.*

PUNCTUATION

6A Rewrite the text message with spaces and punctuation.

1/1
Hiareyoufree
tonighthowa
boutgoingto
TXclubmeet
at8oclockout
side
OK

B Write a reply.

BBC VIDEO PODCAST
Watch people talking about family and friends on ActiveBook or on the website
Authentic BBC interviews
www.pearsonELT.com/speakout

UNIT 4

SPEAKING
- Describe your home
- Talk about things you can do in town
- Have a conversation in a shop

LISTENING
- Listen to a man describing his flat
- Understand conversations in shops
- Watch an extract from a documentary about some amazing places

READING
- Read about an English village not in England

WRITING
- Improve your use of commas
- Write an email about your home
- Write a blog about your favourite place

BBC CONTENT
- Video podcast: Where do you live?
- DVD: 50 Places To See Before You Die

UNIT 4

places

▶ Small place, big style p38 　　▶ An English village? p40 　　▶ Can I help you? p42　　▶ Favourite Places p44

4.1 SMALL PLACE, BIG STYLE

▶ **GRAMMAR** | there is/are   ▶ **VOCABULARY** | rooms/furniture; prepositions   ▶ **HOW TO** | talk about homes

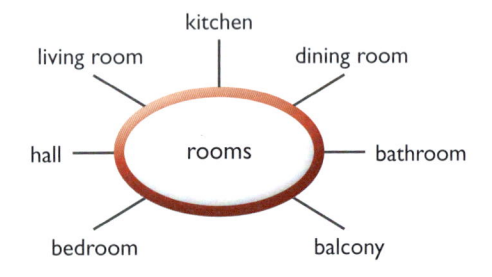

VOCABULARY rooms/furniture

1A What do you need in a flat? Tick the necessary things in the word webs below.

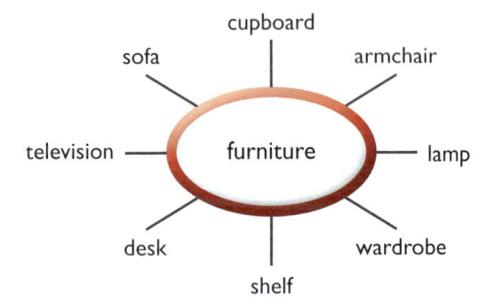

rooms: kitchen, living room, dining room, hall, bathroom, bedroom, balcony

furniture: cupboard, sofa, armchair, television, lamp, desk, wardrobe, shelf

B Work in pairs and compare your ideas.

C ▶ 4.1 Listen and underline the stress in each word. Then listen and repeat.

D Work in pairs and take turns. Student A: say a room. Student B: say the furniture which is usually in that room.
A: *Living room*
B: *a sofa, an armchair, …*

▶ page 155 **PHOTOBANK**

speakout TIP
Write words on Post-its and put them around your home. Choose eight words for furniture from the photo bank. Label them in your home. When you look at the Post-its, say the words aloud.

LISTENING

2A Read the advert and answer the questions.
1 Who are 'microflats' for?
2 Where are they?
3 Are they expensive to buy?
4 Which rooms and furniture can you see in the pictures?

Micro**flats** for you
Do you work in the city centre?
Are you a student or teacher?
Or maybe a police officer, doctor or nurse?
Then we've got the flat for you!
Twenty-four microflats for sale in the city centre.
Low price, high quality, available now!
Contact us on **0118 324168**
to see one today!

B ▶ 4.2 Listen to two people talk about a microflat. Number the rooms in the order they talk about them.
dining room *1*
balcony
bathroom
bedroom
kitchen
living room

C Listen again. What's one thing the woman likes about the flat? What's one thing she doesn't like?

38

GRAMMAR there is/are

3A Look at audio script 4.2 on page 169 and complete the table.

There	___'s___	a bathroom.
	_____	two chairs.
	_____	a separate living room.
	_____	any shelves.
Is	_____	a bedroom?

B ▶ 4.3 Listen and repeat. Notice the pronunciation of /ðəzə/ and /ðeərə/.

➤ page 134 **LANGUAGEBANK**

PRACTICE

4 Complete the email. Use *there's, there isn't, there are* or *there aren't*.

To: |

Hi Jaime and Laura,

I'm so happy that you want to stay in my flat. Here's some information about it.
¹ _There are_ four rooms – a bedroom, a living room, a bathroom and a kitchen. ² _____ a double bed in the bedroom and ³ _____ a desk where you can study and work. ⁴ _____ a DVD player in the living room and ⁵ _____ lots of films (in English!). Have you got a laptop? ⁶ _____ wireless broadband everywhere in the flat. ⁷ _____ a dining room but ⁸ _____ two chairs and a table in the kitchen. My flat is on the top floor and ⁹ _____ any neighbours, so it's OK to play loud music! Tell me about your flat. Where is it and how big is it?

Paul

---

5 Work in pairs and take turns. Ask your partner about his/her home.
How many rooms? Garage? Garden? Washing machine? Shower? Balcony? Wireless broadband? TV / kitchen?

A: *How many rooms are there?*
B: *There are six. There's a …*

WRITING commas

6A Look at the sentences below. How are they different? Which one is correct?
1 There are four rooms – a bedroom and a living room and a bathroom and a kitchen.
2 There are four rooms – a bedroom, a living room, a bathroom and a kitchen.

B Put commas in the sentences if necessary.
1 There are three bedrooms two bathrooms and a balcony upstairs.
2 We've got a bathroom and two bedrooms.
3 I get up at 7 have a shower have breakfast in the kitchen and go to work.

C Write an email to a friend about your home. Use the email in Exercise 4 to help. Remember to use commas.

VOCABULARY prepositions

7A Match the prepositions in the box with the pictures below.

in A	under	above	in front of
on	behind	between	next to

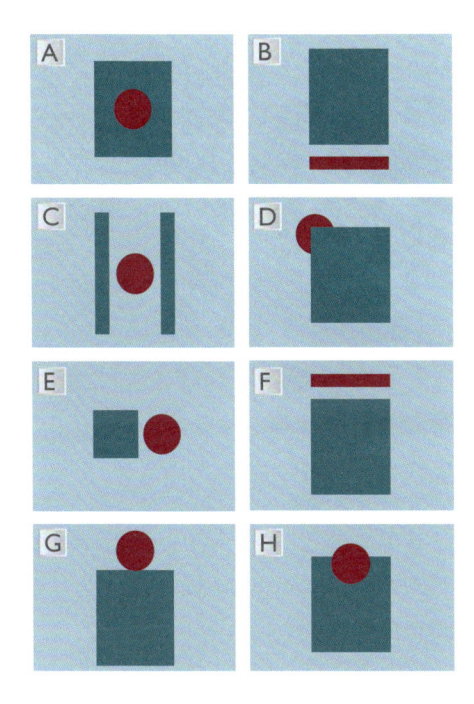

B Work in pairs. Look at the picture on page 163 for fifteen seconds. Then correct sentences 1–6 below.
1 There are four books on the shelves.
2 There's a sofa near the television.
3 There's a table in front of the door.
4 There are two chairs next to the table.
5 There's a lamp above the armchair.
6 There's a chair between the door and the shelves.

C Look at the flat on page 163 again. Write three false sentences about where things are.

D Work in pairs. Look at the flat and correct your partner's sentences.

SPEAKING

8A In your notebook, draw the outline of your favourite room at home. Draw only the windows and door.

B Work in pairs and take turns. Exchange notebooks. Student A: describe the furniture in your room. Student B: draw the furniture in the room.

This is my living room. There's a table under the window.

4.1

39

4.2 AN ENGLISH VILLAGE?

▶ **GRAMMAR** | can for possibility ▶ **VOCABULARY** | places in towns; prepositions ▶ **HOW TO** | talk about towns

Studying English is very important for young people in South Korea. The problem is that many South Korean students learn grammar but don't learn how to speak.

They say that English-speaking countries are far away and they can't visit and practise. So what's the answer? Bring England to South Korea and build an English village!

These villages have got all the buildings of a typical village in England so it's easy to do English activities all day. There are also English teachers from Britain, the USA and Australia working there and they help the guests speak English all the time!

READING

1A Look at the picture. Where do you think it is? Read the article and check.

B Read the article again and answer the questions.
1 Who studies there?
2 Who works there?
3 What buildings does it have?
4 How does the village help people?

C Work in pairs and discuss. Do you think the English village is a good idea? Why/Why not?

VOCABULARY   places in towns

2A Look at sentences 1–10 below. Where do you think you can do the things in the village? Complete the sentences with the words in the box below.

| post office   bank   cinema   theatre   supermarket   museum |
| town hall   school   pharmacy   sports centre |

1 You can post a letter with British stamps on it in a _post office_.
2 You can buy English food like baked beans in a _____.
3 You can watch films from English-speaking countries in a _____.
4 You can buy medicine in a _____.
5 You can see Shakespeare plays in a _____.
6 You can play tennis and football in a _____.
7 You can find out about British history in a _____.
8 You can go to an English class in a _____.
9 You can change money into British pounds in a _____.
10 You can meet the mayor in a _____.

B ▶ 4.4 Listen and check your answers.

C ▶ 4.5 Look at the place words in Exercise 2A and underline the stressed syllables. Then listen and repeat.

3 Look at the sentences in Exercise 2A again. Say which things you can do in your town/city.

speakout TIP

When you see places in town, think to yourself in English: *That's a cinema. That's a sports centre*, etc. Do this to practise and revise vocabulary.

4.2

GRAMMAR can for possibility

4A Look at the sentence and underline the correct alternative.

You can go to an English class. = It's *possible/ impossible* to go to an English class.

B Complete the sentences about the village. Use *can* or *can't*.

You	_____ watch films from Australia.
	_____ change money into dollars.

C ▶ 4.6 Listen and check. Then underline the correct alternatives to complete the rules below.

Rules:
1 In sentences, *can* is usually *stressed/ unstressed* and pronounced /kən/.

2 In sentences, *can't* is usually *stressed/ unstressed* and pronounced /kɑːnt/.

D ▶ 4.7 Listen and write positive (+), negative (−) or question (?) for each sentence.
1 _____
2 _____
3 _____
4 _____
5 _____
6 _____

E Listen again and repeat the sentences.
▶ page 134 **LANGUAGEBANK**

PRACTICE

5A Choose a place from the box in Exercise 2A. Write two sentences about what you can/can't do there.

Post office: You can buy postcards there. You can't play tennis there.

B Work in pairs and take turns. Student A: read your sentences. Student B: guess the place.

C Choose another place. Work with a new partner and take turns. Student A: ask questions with *Can you … ?* and guess the place. Student B: answer.
A: *Can you change money there?*
B: *No, you can't.*

VOCABULARY prepositions

6A Match the prepositions in the box with pictures A–F.

| opposite   in front of   on the left of   on the right of |
| next to   near |

A _____ B _____ C _____

D _____ E _____ F _____

B Look at the map of one of the villages. Can you find the bank?

shopping centre   pharmacy
bank

YOU ARE HERE

C ▶ 4.8 Listen and write the places on the map.

D Work in pairs. Student A: look at page 160. Student B: look at page 162.

SPEAKING

7A Think of a favourite place in your town/city. Make notes about where it is and what you can do there.

B Work in groups. Tell each other about the places. Which places would you like to visit?

There's a good cinema called the Rialto. It's in the main square opposite the metro, next to a big pizza restaurant. It's got six screens and you can also have a coffee there.

41

4.3 CAN I HELP YOU?

▶ FUNCTION | shopping   ▶ VOCABULARY | things to buy   ▶ LEARN TO | say *no* politely in a shop

VOCABULARY   things to buy

1A Work in pairs and discuss.
1 Do you enjoy shopping? Why/Why not?
2 Is there a big shopping centre in your town/city? Do you like it? Why/Why not?
3 Where do you usually buy these things in your town/city?
- clothes
- food
- books
- electronic equipment
- music or DVDs
- things for the home
- magazines/newspapers

B Work in pairs. What different kinds of shops do you know? Make a list.

⟹ page 156 **PHOTOBANK**

2A Where can you buy the things in the box? Complete the table below.

| jacket C   swimming costume |
| jeans   blank DVD   paperback book |
| T-shirt   magazine   headphones |
| memory stick   trainers   dictionary |
| football shirt   battery   sweater |

Shop	Item
clothes shop	jacket
sports shop	_____
electronics shop	_____
bookshop	_____

B ▶ 4.9 Listen and check. Then listen and repeat.

C Work in pairs. Write one other thing you can buy in each shop.
1 _____
2 _____
3 _____
4 _____

D Work in pairs and take turns. Student A: say one of the shops. Student B: say four things you can buy there.
A: *A newsagent.*
B: *Newspapers, magazines, urm ... , sweets and drinks.*

FUNCTION   shopping

3A ▶ 4.10 Listen to the customers. What do they want? Write the correct item in the table.

Customer	Item	Price
1	nothing	_____
2	sweater	_____
3	_____	_____
4	_____	_____
5	_____	_____

B Listen again and write the correct prices next to each item.

C Look at audio script 4.10 on page 170 and complete the sentences below.
1 Have you got it in large ?
2 It's too _____.
3 It's not _____ enough.
4 That's fine. I'll _____ it.

D Use the words/phrases in the box below to complete sentences 1–4.

| expensive   have   long enough   medium |

1 It's too _____.
2 That's fine. I'll _____ this one.
3 Have you got it in _____?
4 Sorry, but it isn't _____.

⟹ page 134 **LANGUAGEBANK**

42

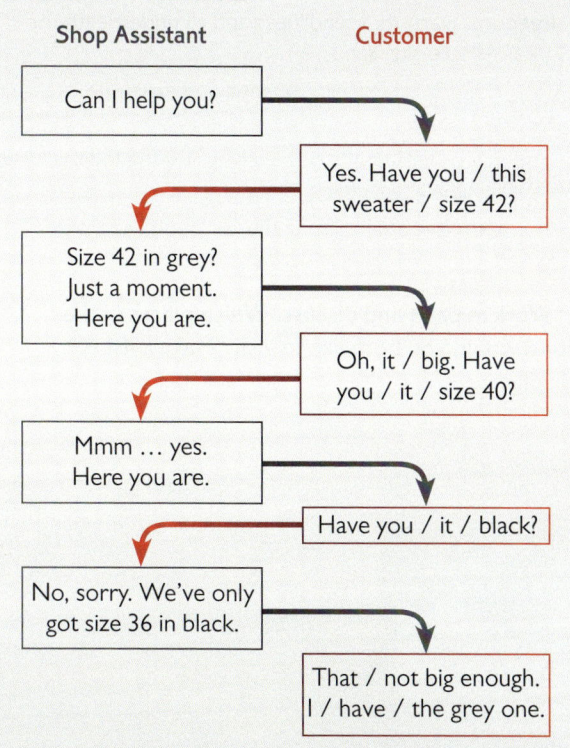

4.3

LEARN TO say *no* politely in a shop

5A Look at the three conversation extracts. Underline the phrases the customer uses to say *no* politely.

Extract 1:

4.4 FAVOURITE PLACES

DVD PREVIEW

1A Work in pairs. Look at photos A–E. Where are the places? Which countries are they in?

B Match the phrases 1–5 with photos A–E.
1 It's a romantic city with a lot of art galleries. C
2 There are beautiful views of mountains and beaches.
3 You can visit hundreds of temples and the shopping and the nightlife are great.
4 The colours are amazing. It's awesome!
5 It's a fantastic place to watch animals. You can see zebras, elephants, antelope, hippos and lions.

2 Work in pairs. Read the programme information and answer the questions.
1 How many places does this programme look at?
2 Which place do you think is number one?

BBC 50 Places To See Before You Die

There are so many places in the world to see, but if you want to visit fifty in your life, which do you choose? In this BBC programme, we look at five places: Bangkok, Cape Town, the Grand Canyon, the Masai Mara and Paris. Watch the programme and find out which is the number one place to see!

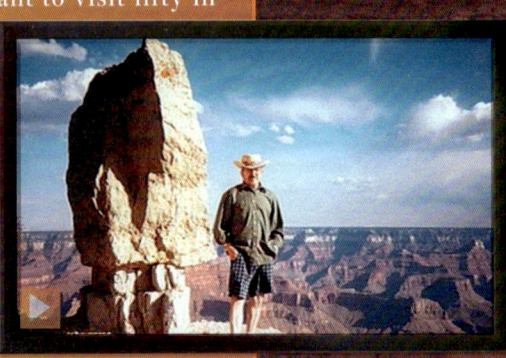

▶ DVD VIEW

3A Watch the DVD and check your answers to Exercise 2. Which place is number one?

B Watch again and underline the words you hear in the sentences.
1 'It's got lots of clubs, bars, shops, food. Everything you *need/want*, really.'
2 'Huge *open/big* spaces, fantastic animals, just wide open freedom, warmth, friendliness and all underneath the great African *sky/sun*.'
3 'To me, Paris is elegant, romantic and *expensive/exciting*.'
4 'Friendly people, loads of beaches, and the food is unbelievably *good/cheap*.'
5 'I remember actually sitting there … and I just *cried/looked*.'

C Work in pairs and discuss. Which places in the world would you both like to visit? Make a list of five places.

44

speakout a favourite place

4A Choose a favourite place: a place in the countryside, a town, a building or a room. The place can be famous or not. Look at the questions below and make notes about it:
- Where is it?
- How often do you go there?
- What do you do there?
- Why do you like it?

B ▶ 4.12 Listen to a man talk about his favourite place and answer the questions above.

C Listen again and tick the key phrases you hear.

key phrases
One of my favourite places is …
I go there every [day/year/summer/weekend] …
When I'm there, I usually …
I like it because it's …
It's a great place to …

D Work in groups and take turns. Tell each other about your place. Use the key phrases to help. Which places would you like to visit?

writeback a description

5A Read the description below and put the topics of the paragraphs in the correct order.
a) Why do you like it? _____
b) What's the name of the place and where is it? _____
c) How often do you go there and what do you do there? _____

26-09-11
traveller

Posting 1

1. My favourite place is my aunt's flat. She lives in the centre of the city, and she doesn't work so she's always at home.

2. I visit her once every month or two. She cooks lunch for me, and we chat about her life and my life. After lunch I usually sleep on her sofa for an hour, or we watch TV together. I sometimes take my work with me and sit in her living room and do it, or read a book.

3. I like it because when I'm there I remember my childhood. There's always a nice smell of her cooking. I always feel good there.

B Write a description of your favourite place. Use three paragraphs. Write about 100 words.

4.5 « LOOKBACK

FURNITURE AND ROOMS

1A Add the vowels to the furniture words.
1 rmchr   3 cpbrd   5 sf   7 lmp
2 bd   4 shlvs   6 wrdrb 8 dsk

B Think of a room in your flat/house. Write three objects that are in it.
I've got a TV, two armchairs and a sofa.

C Work in pairs and take turns. Student A: read out the objects. Student B: guess the room.

PLACES IN TOWNS

2 Write the places in the word puzzle and find the secret message.
(Hint: What have you got after you shop all day?)

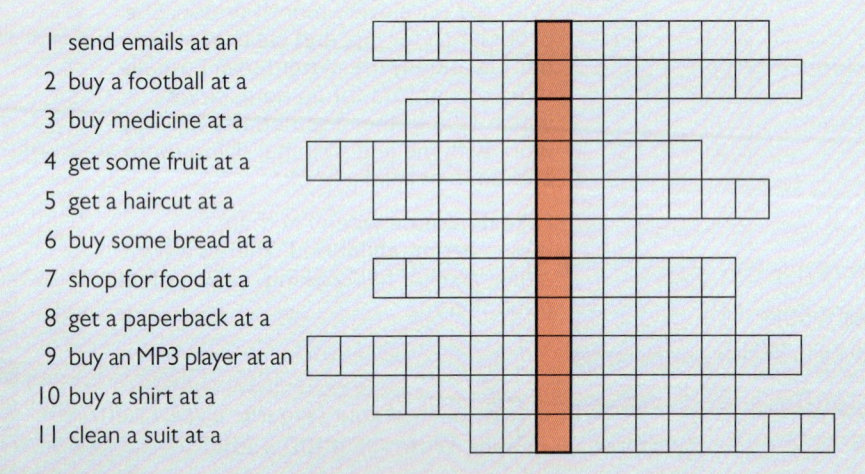

1 send emails at an
2 buy a football at a
3 buy medicine at a
4 get some fruit at a
5 get a haircut at a
6 buy some bread at a
7 shop for food at a
8 get a paperback at a
9 buy an MP3 player at an
10 buy a shirt at a
11 clean a suit at a

THERE IS/THERE ARE AND PREPOSITIONS

3A Read the sentences. Draw the things in the picture.
There's a newspaper on the chair and a shelf under the window. There's a flower on the shelf. There are two men on the left of the window.

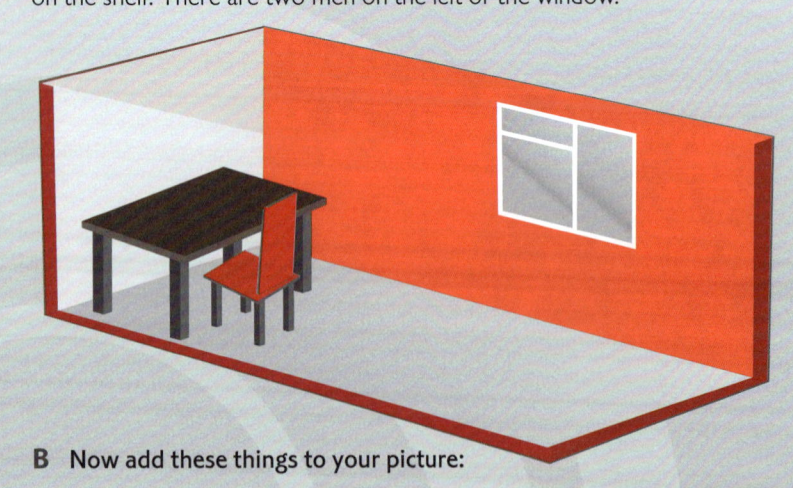

B Now add these things to your picture:
   a woman   a bottle of water   a sandwich   keys

C Work in pairs and take turns. Ask and answer *yes/no* questions about your pictures.
A: *Is there a sandwich on the table in your picture?*
B: *No, there isn't. It's on the shelf.*

CAN FOR POSSIBILITY

4A Put the words in the correct order.
1 buy / battery / can / for / Where / camera? / a / my / I
2 I / Where / smoke? / can
3 I / can / 'beautiful' / in / How / Italian? / say
4 they / match? / football / can / Where / watch / the
5 Can / the / come / friend / my / to / lesson?
6 centre? / can / the / What / do / in / sports / we

B Write answers to the questions above.
1 *At an electronics shop.*

C Work in pairs and take turns. Student A: say the answer to one of the questions above. Student B: ask the question.
A: *On the balcony.*
B: *Where can I smoke?*

SHOPPING

5A Correct the sentences below.
1 Have you got this shoes in size 36?
2 They aren't enough big.
3 Have you got in them size 34?
4 How much they are?
5 That's too very expensive.
6 I take them.
7 No, they're all right. Thanks anyway.
8 I'm not sure. I need think about it.

B Work in pairs. Choose four of the sentences above and write a conversation in a shop.

C Work in pairs. Role-play your conversation.

BBC VIDEO PODCAST
Watch people talking about their homes on ActiveBook or on the website.

Authentic BBC interviews

www.pearsonELT.com/speakout

UNIT 5

SPEAKING
- Talk about your eating and drinking habits
- Order a meal in a restaurant
- Describe a special dish

LISTENING
- Listen to people talk about food
- Learn to understand fast speech
- Watch an extract from a cookery programme about a famous chef

READING
- Read about eating and drinking habits

WRITING
- Use paragraphs to write a short report about your class
- Write a recipe

BBC CONTENT
- Video podcast: What's your favourite dish?
- DVD: Rick Stein's Seafood Odyssey

UNIT 5

food

- MyFridge.com p48
- A lifetime in numbers p50
- Are you ready to order? p52
- A Chef In Goa p54

5.1 MYFRIDGE.COM

▶ **GRAMMAR** | nouns with *a/an, some, any* ▶ **VOCABULARY** | food/drink ▶ **HOW TO** | talk about food/drink

VOCABULARY food/drink

1 Look at the fridges A–C and discuss.

1 Which fridge belongs to:
   a) a student
   b) a vegetarian
   c) a family?
2 Is your fridge at home similar to fridge A, B or C?

2A Look at the words in the box. Which fridge are the things in? Write fridge (A), (B) or (C) next to each item.

| eggs A   milk   a banana   an apple |
| cola   carrots   chicken   butter |
| water   a cucumber   sardines   bread |
| wine   grapes   yoghurt   leftovers |
| cheese   fruit juice   a hot dog |

B Write the words from the box in the correct word web below.

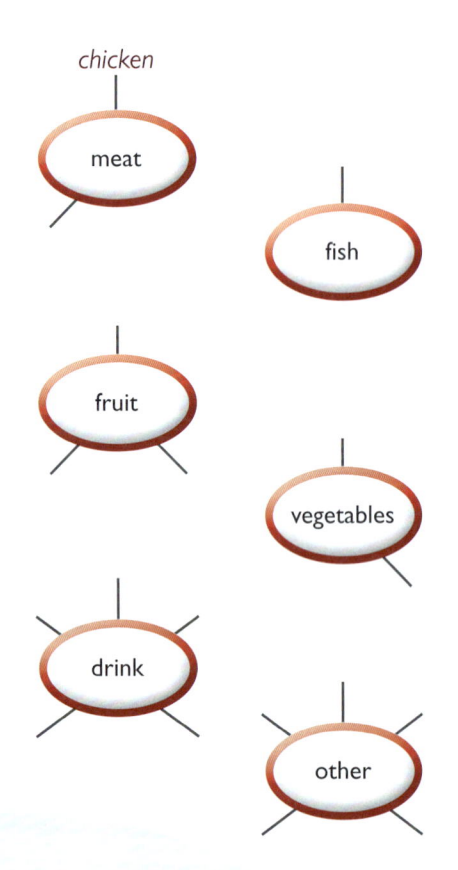

chicken
- meat
- fish
- fruit
- vegetables
- drink
- other

C Work in pairs and take turns. Look at the fridges. Student A: say a type of food or drink. Student B: say which fridge it's in.

A: *grapes*
B: *fridge C*

▶ page 157 PHOTOBANK

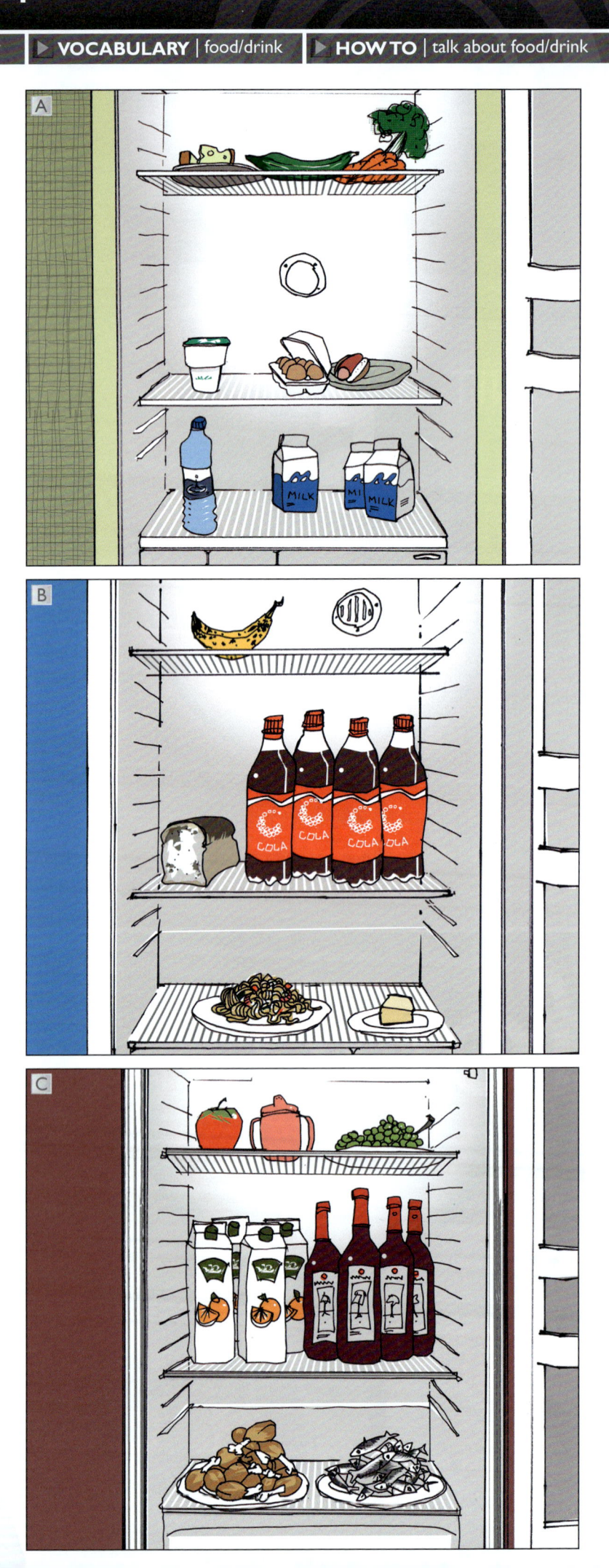

5.1

GRAMMAR countable and uncountable nouns

3A Write the words from Exercise 2A in the correct column below. Which word is always plural?

Words you can count		Words you can't count
Countable singular	Countable plural	Uncountable
a banana	eggs	milk

B ▶ 5.1 Listen and check. Then listen and repeat.

➡ page 136 **LANGUAGEBANK**

PRACTICE

4A Underline the correct alternative.
1 I love *cheese/cheeses*.
2 I really like *hot dog/hot dogs*.
3 I quite like *egg/eggs*.
4 I don't like *fruit/fruits*.
5 I really don't like *milk/milks*.
6 I hate *vegetable/vegetables*.

B Change the food/drink words to make the sentences above true for you. Then work in pairs and compare your answers.

> **speakout TIP**
> When you write a noun in your notebook, write (C) for countable or (U) for uncountable next to it, e.g. *a steak (C)*. Write five new words from the photo bank on page 157 in your notebook. Write (C) or (U) next to them.

LISTENING

5A ▶ 5.2 Listen and match each person with fridge A, B or C.

1 Luis ___   2 Amy ___   3 Mike ___

B Listen again. What is each person surprised about?

GRAMMAR nouns with a/an, some, any

6A ▶ 5.3 Listen and underline the correct alternatives in the sentences below.

I've got *a/some* cheese and *a/some* cucumber and *a/some* carrots. Of course, I haven't got *some/any* meat.

B Complete the table with *a/an*, *some* and *any*.

	Countable singular	Countable plural	Uncountable
We've got	___ apple	___ eggs	___ butter
We haven't got	___ banana	___ oranges	___ cheese

➡ page 136 **LANGUAGEBANK**

PRACTICE

7A Complete the text with *a/an*, *some* and *any*.

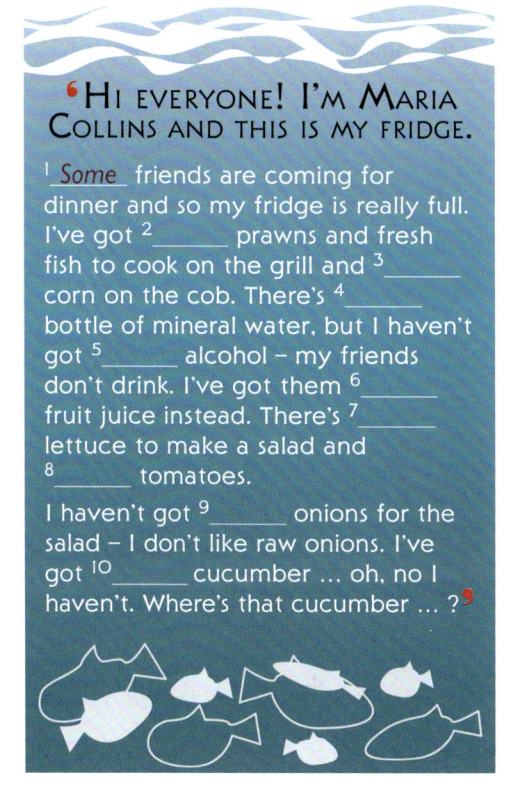

> 'Hi everyone! I'm Maria Collins and this is my fridge.
>
> ¹ *Some* friends are coming for dinner and so my fridge is really full. I've got ² ___ prawns and fresh fish to cook on the grill and ³ ___ corn on the cob. There's ⁴ ___ bottle of mineral water, but I haven't got ⁵ ___ alcohol – my friends don't drink. I've got them ⁶ ___ fruit juice instead. There's ⁷ ___ lettuce to make a salad and ⁸ ___ tomatoes. I haven't got ⁹ ___ onions for the salad – I don't like raw onions. I've got ¹⁰ ___ cucumber ... oh, no I haven't. Where's that cucumber ...?'

B Think about what's in your fridge. Write two types of fruit, two vegetables and two drinks that are in the fridge.

C Work in pairs and take turns. Ask your partner questions and guess what's in your partner's fridge.
A: *Have you got any milk?*
B: *Yes, I have! Are there any apples in your fridge?*
A: *No, there aren't. Have you got any oranges?*

SPEAKING

8A Complete sentences 1–6 about you.
1 For breakfast, I sometimes have …
2 For lunch, I never have …
3 In the evening, I usually drink …
4 My favourite vegetable is …
5 My favourite fruit is …
6 I really hate (a type of food/drink) …

B Work in groups. Ask and answer questions. Find out if any students have got similar eating habits to you.
A: *What do you usually have for breakfast?*
B: *Er … I often have muesli.*
C: *Do you? I usually have …*

49

5.2 A LIFETIME IN NUMBERS

▶ GRAMMAR | how much/many; quantifiers ▶ VOCABULARY | containers ▶ HOW TO | talk about quantities

VOCABULARY containers

1A Look at pictures A–K. What items can you see?

B Match pictures A–K to the words in the box below.

| bar A | bottle | bag | cup | can/tin |
| packet | jar | tube | mug | carton | roll |

C Work in pairs and take turns. Student A: point to one of the items above and say what it is. Student B: say the container.
A: *A. It's chocolate.*
B: *a bar of chocolate*

READING

2A Work in pairs. How do you say the numbers in the box below?

| 4½ | 21 | 61 | 845 | 1,200 | 4,300 |
| 10,000 | 35,000 | 60,000 | 75,000 |

B ▶ 5.4 Listen and check. Then listen again and repeat.

3A Read the article. Complete it with numbers from Exercise 2A.

B ▶ 5.5 Work in pairs and compare your answers. Then listen and check.

C Work in pairs and discuss the questions.
1 Which food in the article do you eat a lot? Which do you never eat?
2 What other food and drink do you eat or drink a lot?

---

1 **How much food does an average person eat in a lifetime? And how much do they drink? The answer is A LOT!!!**

2 Do you eat meat? Well, an average meat-eater eats ¹_____ sheep in their lifetime and ²_____ chickens. Does that sound quite a lot? The good news is that he or she only eats ³_____ cows. If you're a vegetarian, maybe you like beans? Well, on average, British and American people eat ⁴_____ cans of baked beans in their life.

3 And why is weight a problem for so many people? How many cookies does the average American eat? The answer is an amazing ⁵_____. And chocolate? Over ⁶_____ bars!

4 And how much water or tea do people drink in their lifetime? It's interesting that a person drinks about ⁷_____ litres of water and people in the UK drink about ⁸_____ cups of tea. Maybe it isn't surprising that people use ⁹_____ rolls of toilet paper a year! That's about ¹⁰_____ in their lifetime!

GRAMMAR how much/many; quantifiers

4A Complete the sentences below. Use the article above to help.
1 _____ food does an average person eat in a lifetime?
2 _____ cookies does the average American eat?

B Look at the sentences above. Underline the correct alternatives to complete the rules.

Rules:
1 Use *how much* with *countable/uncountable* nouns.
2 Use *how many* with *countable/uncountable* nouns.

C Match the words below with pictures A–D.

| not many | a lot/lots | none | quite a lot |

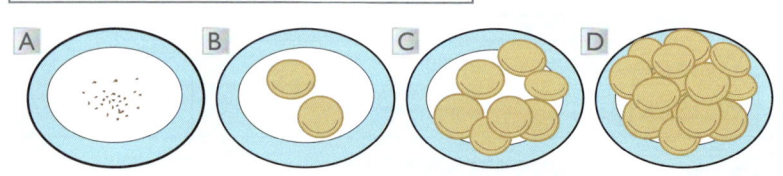

▶ page 136 LANGUAGEBANK

PRACTICE

5A Complete the questions.
1. How _many_ times does a six-year-old child laugh every day?
2. How _____ milk does a person drink in their lifetime?
3. How _____ shampoo do people use in their lifetime?
4. How _____ words does a woman say in a day?
5. How _____ times does a person laugh every day?
6. How _____ friends does a person make in their lifetime?
7. How _____ toothpaste does a person use in their lifetime?
8. How _____ words does a man say in a day?

B Work in pairs. Student A: turn to page 161 and find the answers to questions 1–4. Student B: turn to page 162 and find the answers to questions 5–8.

C Work in pairs and take turns. Student A: ask one of your questions and say both possible answers. Student B: listen and choose the correct answer.

A: *How many times does a six-year-old child laugh every day? a) about three hundred times or b) about a hundred times?*
B: *I'm not sure. I think a hundred times!*

SPEAKING

6A Work in groups. Ask and answer questions using the prompts below to complete the table. Use *a lot/lots, quite a lot, not much/many, none* and one extra piece of information in your answers.

In a week	You	Student 1	Student 2	Student 3
biscuits / eat?	Quite a lot. 5–10.	Not many. 1–2.	A lot! I love them!	
fruit / eat?				
vegetables / eat?				
water / drink?				
coffee / drink?				
exercise / do?				

A: *How many biscuits do you eat in a week, Julio?*
B: *Not many. Maybe one or two.*
A: *How about you, Yumi?*
C: *A lot! I love biscuits!*

B Discuss. Which students have a good diet/healthy lifestyle?
I think Julio has a good diet because he eats a lot of vegetables.

WRITING paragraphs

7A Look again at the article on page 50. Match topics a)–d) below with paragraphs 1–4.
a) drinks
b) introduction
c) sweet food
d) meat-eaters and vegetarians

B Read the sentences below. Underline the correct alternatives.

A paragraph is a group of *words/sentences* about *one/two* main topic(s) or idea(s). It can be short or long. When you finish the topic, start a new *sentence/paragraph*.

C Read the text below. How many paragraphs can you make? Draw a line between each one.

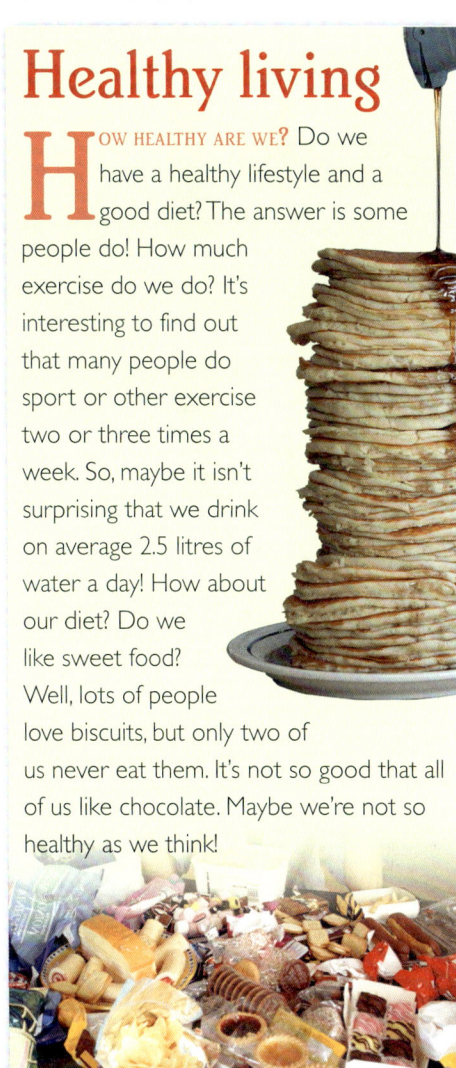

Healthy living

HOW HEALTHY ARE WE? Do we have a healthy lifestyle and a good diet? The answer is some people do! How much exercise do we do? It's interesting to find out that many people do sport or other exercise two or three times a week. So, maybe it isn't surprising that we drink on average 2.5 litres of water a day! How about our diet? Do we like sweet food? Well, lots of people love biscuits, but only two of us never eat them. It's not so good that all of us like chocolate. Maybe we're not so healthy as we think!

D Write a report about your group. Use your notes from Exercise 6A to help. Write three or four paragraphs.

5.3 ARE YOU READY TO ORDER?

▶ **FUNCTION** | ordering in a restaurant   ▶ **VOCABULARY** | restaurant words   ▶ **LEARN TO** | understand fast speech

VOCABULARY restaurant words

1A Work in pairs and discuss. Where do you go when you want to:
1 have a drink with a friend in the afternoon?
2 eat something fast before you go to the cinema?
3 have an evening meal in a good restaurant?

There's a very good café in … called …

B Work with another pair and compare your ideas.

2 Match each word to its meaning.

1	menu	a)	you pay this at the end
2	chef	b)	he/she brings the food
3	dish	c)	food cooked in a special way
4	bill	d)	a list of food with prices
5	order	e)	he/she cooks
6	tip	f)	ask for food
7	waiter/waitress	g)	extra money for service

FUNCTION ordering in a restaurant

3A Look at the phrases a)–k). Where do you usually hear them? Write restaurant (R) or fast food restaurant (FF).
a) Would you like something to drink? *R*
b) Small, medium or large?
c) Can we have the bill, please?
d) Are you ready to order?
e) Is that eat in or takeaway?
f) Thanks. Have a nice day!
g) Tonight's special is …
h) Afternoon. What can I get you?
i) Large fries with that?
j) Good evening. A table for two?
k) Anything else?

B ▶ 5.6 Listen and tick the phrases you hear.

C Number the ticked phrases in order. Then listen again and check.

4A ▶ 5.7 Listen and complete the sentences below.
1 Could _____ _____ an *orange* _____?
2 Can _____ _____ a _____ of mineral _____?
3 _____ like some _____, please.
4 The _____ for _____, please.

B Listen again and check your answers. What do the customers order?

▶ page 136 **LANGUAGEBANK**

5A Complete the conversation with the words in the box.

~~like~~   can   for   any   'd   could

              like
A: Good evening. Would you/something to drink?
B: Yes, we have two colas and some water, please?
A: Fine. Are you ready to order?
B: Yes. We like the fish and the chicken.
A: Would you like vegetables?
B: Yes, please.
A: We've got carrots, peas and beans.
B: I have some carrots and some peas?
C: The same me, please.

B Work in pairs and practise the conversation.

6A ▶ 5.8 Listen to the customers in a restaurant. Are they polite or impolite?

B Work in pairs and take turns. Student A: say customer sentences from Exercise 5A. Be polite or impolite. Student B: say if Student A is polite or impolite.

5.3

B Work in pairs and role-play the situation. Student A: you are the customer. Look at menu A on this page and order your food. Ask the waiter about any dish you don't know.

Student B: you are the waiter. Look at page 162. Answer the customer's questions. Take his/her order.
B: *Are you ready to order?*
A: *Can I ask about Today's Specials? What's the Garden delight?*

C Change roles. Student B: you are the customer. Look at menu B on this page. Student A: you are the waiter. Look at page 161.

LEARN TO understand fast speech

8A ▶ 5.9 Listen to the conversation in a fast food restaurant. What does the man order? Circle the correct answer.

B Listen again. Tick the phrases you hear in Exercise 3A.

speakout TIP

When one word finishes with a consonant and the next word starts with a vowel, the two words join and sound like one word, e.g. good‿evening, how much‿is‿it.

C Look at the example below. Then underline the key stressed words in the fast food phrases in Exercise 3A. Draw lines to show the linking.
After<u>noon</u>. What can‿I <u>get</u> you?

D ▶ 5.10 Listen and check. Then listen and repeat.

E Work in pairs. Choose one long sentence from audio script 5.6 on page 170. Try to finish the sentence faster than your partner.

SPEAKING

7A Look at the menus and discuss. Which dishes would you like to try? What food do you think is in today's special dishes?

A
STARTER
Onion soup
Melon

MAIN COURSE
Roast lamb
Thai chicken with rice
Fish of the day with chips or new potatoes
Served with seasonal vegetables

TODAY'S SPECIALS
Chef's Sunday special
Garden delight
Summer mix

DESSERT
Apple pie with ice cream or cream
Chocolate cake
Fresh fruit

B
STARTER
Tomato soup
Italian style grilled vegetables

MAIN COURSE
Cheese, tomato and mushroom pizza
Cheese, tomato, mushroom, olive and ham pizza
Pasta of the day
Served with a side salad

TODAY'S SPECIALS
Spring special
Fisherman's platter
Roman holiday

DESSERT
Ice cream
Fruit salad
Three cheese plate

53

5.4 A CHEF IN GOA

▶ DVD PREVIEW

1A Work in pairs and discuss.
1 Do you like cooking?
2 What's your favourite dish?
3 Do you like eating outside? Why/Why not?

B Look at the photo and read the text. Then answer the questions.
1 Who is Rick Stein?
2 What type of food does he like?
3 Which place does he visit in the programme?

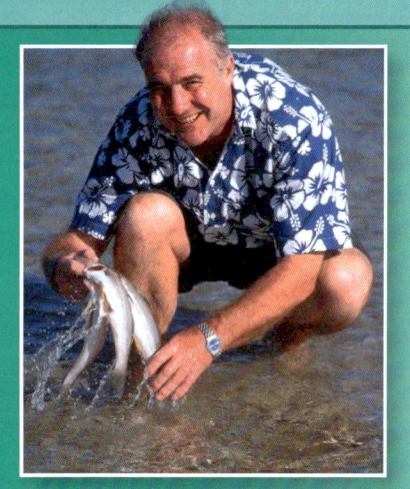

BBC Rick Stein's Seafood Odyssey

Rick Stein is an English chef who loves seafood. He travels around the world to find new dishes. He also meets and talks to the people who cook them. In this BBC programme, he visits Goa on the west coast of India. He buys some local fish at the market and cooks a simple dish on the beach.

▶ DVD VIEW

2A Watch the DVD. Tick seven things you see in the box below.

a market ✓   fruit   oil   a boat   the sea   a pan   a cat
meat   spices   fish   vegetables   a washing-up bowl

B Watch the DVD again and complete the sentences below with words in the box.

cheap   vegetables   spices   food   eight

This is Goa – a place I've known and loved for the best part of ¹_____ years. To buy ²_____ here is *a real joy. The variety of seafood, ³_____, ⁴_____ is quite *staggering and *incredibly ⁵_____.

* **a real joy** – something that makes you *very* happy
* **staggering** – very surprising | * **incredibly** – very very

C Match the verbs with pictures A–E.

stir   C   throw in   squeeze   drop   turn over

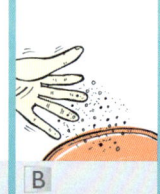

| A | B | C | D | E |

D Look at Rick Stein's instructions for cooking below. Number them in the correct order.
a) Put some flour into a washing up bowl. *1*
b) Cook for about three or four minutes.
c) Stir the fish around in some oil.
d) Put in some fish.
e) Squeeze some lime over the fish.
f) Drop the fish in the pan.
g) Add salt and spices.
h) Turn the fish over.

E Watch the DVD again and check your answers.

speakout a special dish

3A Work in pairs. Two other students are coming for dinner. Choose your ingredients from the list below:
- one kind of meat or fish
- two/three kinds of vegetables
- rice, pasta, noodles or potatoes
- three eggs
- oil, salt, pepper, soy sauce, spices or herbs

B Work in pairs and discuss. What can you make with your ingredients? Give your special dish a name.

4A ▶ 5.11 Listen to the students describe their dish. What ingredients are in their dish?

B Listen again and tick the key phrases you hear.

keyphrases
The name of [this/our] dish is …
It's [very easy/quite difficult] to make.
You need some prawns, some eggs …
It's [delicious/not too hot].
You'll love it!

C Prepare to tell your class about your dish. Use the key phrases to help.

D Tell your class about your dish. Listen to the other groups. Which dish would you like to try?

writeback a recipe

5A Read the students' recipe. Would you like to try it?

Italian special
SERVES FOUR

Ingredients: tiger prawns, a can of Italian tomatoes, a large onion, a red pepper, two celery sticks and some fresh pasta. A handful of herbs, some black pepper and some olive oil.

First, cut the vegetables into small pieces. Then heat the oil in a wok or a frying pan. Next drop in the vegetables and fry them for about two minutes. Add the prawns, tomatoes, pepper and herbs. Cook for about two minutes. Heat some water in a pan and then add the pasta. Cook for three minutes. Finally, take the pasta out of the water and mix with the sauce. Serve it immediately with some salad. It takes about twenty minutes to make and you'll love it!

B Look at the linkers underlined. Which ones can change places?

C Write the recipe for your special dish from Exercise 4D. Remember to use linkers.

55

5.5 « LOOKBACK

FOOD

1A Read the clues below and complete the food words.

1 It's green, it's a fruit and it starts with 'a'. _apple_
2 It's a drink and it starts with 'm'. _____
3 It's a vegetable and it starts with 'cu'. _____
4 It's a fruit, it's yellow and it starts with 'b'. _____
5 It's sweet and it starts with 'i'. _____
6 It's white, it's got four letters and it starts with 'r'. _____

B Write four more sentences to test your partner.
It's a drink and it starts with …

C Work in pairs and take turns. Student A: read out your sentences. Student B: say the name of the food.

NOUNS WITH A/AN, SOME, ANY

2A Look again at the three fridges on page 48. Complete the sentences below so that they are true. Use *be* and *a/an*, *some* or *any*.

1 There _isn't any_ milk in Mike's fridge.
2 There _____ carrots in Amy's fridge.
3 There _____ eggs in Luis's fridge.
4 There _____ beer in Luis's or Mike's fridge.
5 There _____ cucumber in Amy's fridge.
6 There _____ water in Amy's fridge.

B Write four questions about the things in the fridges.

Is there any chicken in Mike's fridge?
_____
_____
_____
_____

C Work in pairs. Ask and answer questions.

CONTAINERS

3A Find twelve words for containers.

cuppacketbagcartonbottlejartubemugrollicanbartin

B Work in pairs and take turns. Student A: start the phrase with a container. Student B: complete the phrase with the correct item.
A: A cup of …
B: A cup of coffee

HOW MUCH/MANY

4A Write the questions in full.

1 How / water / drink every day?
How much water do you drink every day?
2 How / chocolate / eat / every week?
3 How / brothers / have got?
4 How / people / be / there in your family?
5 How / sugar / have / in your coffee?
6 How / cola / drink / every week?
7 How / rooms / be / there in your flat/house?
8 How / salt / like / in your food?

B Answer the questions in Exercise 4A with numbers or phrases.
4 glasses, 2 bars, 3 …

C Work in groups. Try to guess the question for each number or phrase.
A: Eight
B: How many rooms are there in your flat?
A: Yes!

IN A RESTAURANT

5A Work in pairs. Look at the menu for a new restaurant. Write a description of dishes 1–3.

MENU

1 King's delight:

2 Winter warmer:

3 Light & tasty:

B Work in groups and role-play the restaurant situation. One student: you are the waiter. Tell the group the names of the dishes. The other students: ask about the dishes and order some food.
A: Good evening. Are you ready to order?
B: Nearly. Can I ask …

VIDEO PODCAST
Watch people talking about their favourite food on ActiveBook or on the website.

Authentic BBC interviews

www.pearsonELT.com/speakout

UNIT 6

SPEAKING
- Describe your favourite childhood things
- Talk about past events
- Interview a special person

LISTENING
- Hear about famous people's favourite things
- Learn to keep a conversation going
- Watch an extract from a documentary about a famous dancer

READING
- Read about 'time twins'

WRITING
- Link sentences with *because* and *so*
- Write your life story
- Write a profile about a special person

BBC CONTENT
- Video podcast: Did you go out last night?
- DVD: The Culture Show

UNIT 6

the past

▶ Favourite things   p58
▶ Time twins   p60 
▶ How was your weekend?   p62 
▶ Carlos Acosta   p64

6.1 FAVOURITE THINGS

▶ GRAMMAR | was/were ▶ VOCABULARY | dates and time phrases ▶ HOW TO | talk about the past

SPEAKING

1A Work in pairs and discuss. What do you know about the famous people in photos A–F?

Shizuka Arakawa is a Japanese figure skater. She is also an Olympic gold medallist.

B Match the famous people (A–F) with their favourite childhood things. Use your dictionary to help with new words.
1 Karate and radio-controlled cars __C__
2 Ballet and swimming ___
3 Football and the film *Gladiator* ___
4 The piano and Harrison Ford ___
5 Writing poems and dancing ___
6 John Cleese and Charlie Chaplin ___

C ▶ 6.1 Listen and check your answers.

GRAMMAR was/were

2A Find and underline the verbs in the sentences below. Are the verbs in the present or the past?
1 His favourite sport was football.
2 His favourite actors were John Cleese and Charlie Chaplin.

B Complete the past table below.

Present		
Shakira	is	Colombian.
Her CDs	are	very popular.

Past		
She	___	born in 1977.
Her favourite activities	___	writing poems and dancing.

C Look at the sentence below and complete the rule.

Skating wasn't her favourite sport.

> Rule: make the negative with was/were + _____.

D Make the sentence below into a question.
He was a quiet boy.
_____?

▶ page 138 LANGUAGEBANK

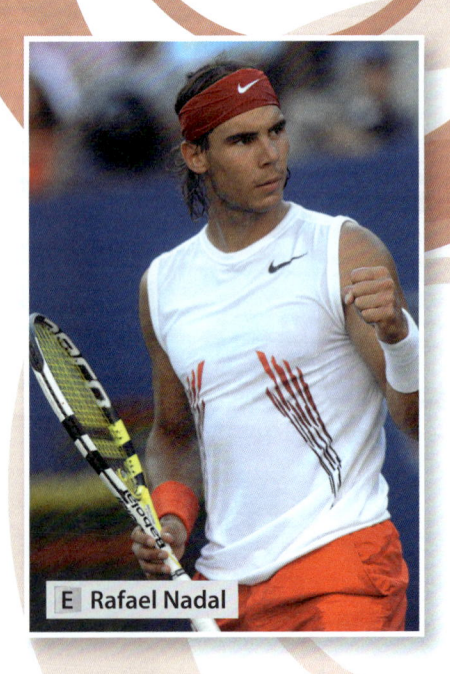

A Shakira
B Shizuka Arakawa
C Lewis Hamilton
D Cate Blanchett
E Rafael Nadal
F Rowan Atkinson

6.1

PRACTICE

3A ▶ 6.2 Listen to the sentences. Are they in the past or present? Write past (P) or now (N).

1 ___ 3 ___ 5 ___ 7 ___
2 ___ 4 ___ 6 ___ 8 ___

B ▶ 6.3 Listen and write the four sentences you hear.

1 _____
2 _____
3 _____
4 _____

C Listen again and underline the stress in each sentence.

D Circle the weak forms of *was* /wəz/ and *were* /wə/ in the sentences. Then practise saying the sentences.

4A Write the questions with prompts 1–8.

1 you / born before 1995?
   Were you born before 1995?
2 you / born in July?
3 you / a very quiet child?
4 you / afraid of the dark when you were a child?
5 your first English teacher / a man?
6 your parents / childhood friends?
7 your grandfather / born in another country?
8 your grandmother / a doctor or a nurse?

B Work in groups. Ask and answer the questions above.

A: *Were you born before 1995?*
B: *Yes, I was. I was born in 1985.*

SPEAKING

5A What were your favourite childhood things? Think of examples for each of the categories below:
- music/band
- activity/sport
- TV programme/film
- food/drink
- person/people

B Work in pairs and compare your ideas.
A: *Who was your favourite person?*
B: *My favourite person was my uncle Luciano. He was really funny.*

VOCABULARY dates and time phrases

6A ▶ 6.4 Listen and underline the years you hear.
1 1999 / 1990   3 1987 / 1997   5 1941 / 1951
2 2010 / 2003   4 2000 / 2002   6 1872 / 1972

B Work in pairs and take turns. Student A: say one of the years above. Student B: point to the year.

C Take turns to say the months of the year.
A: *January*
B: *February*

7A Match the dates A–H with the special occasions below. There are two extra dates.

A JUNE 3   B MARCH 2   C OCTOBER 31   D JANUARY 1
E APRIL 7   F DECEMBER 25   G JULY 4   H FEBRUARY 14

1 Christmas Day ___   4 Halloween ___
2 New Year's Day ___   5 World Health Day ___
3 Valentine's Day ___ 6 Independence Day (USA) ___

B ▶ 6.5 Listen and check your answers.

C Listen again. Write how you say these dates.

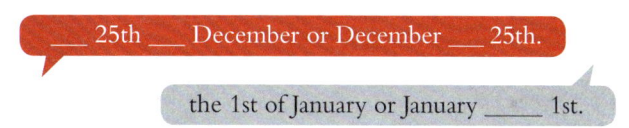

___ 25th ___ December or December ___ 25th.

the 1st of January or January _____ 1st.

D Write the numbers.

1st ___*first*___   4th _____   21st _____
2nd _____   5th _____   22nd _____
3rd _____   12th _____   30th _____

8 Work in pairs. Student A: go to page 165. Student B: go to page 160.

9A Complete the time phrases below with the words in the box.

| ~~yesterday~~ on in ago last |

1 *yesterday* morning, afternoon, evening
2 _____ night, Friday, weekend, week, month, year
3 _____ Saturday, Sunday, 12th June
4 _____ July, 1997, 2009
5 a week, ten days, ten minutes _____

B Choose five of the time phrases and write past sentences. Make them true for you.
I was at home last night.

C Work in pairs and take turns. Student A: say one of your past events, but don't say when it was. Student B: guess the time phrase.
A: *I was with some friends.*
B: *On Saturday?*
A: *Yes. That's right!*

59

6.2 TIME TWINS

▶ **GRAMMAR** | past simple   ▶ **VOCABULARY** | common verbs   ▶ **HOW TO** | talk about your life

READING

1A Look at the photos and discuss. Where do you think the women are from? Why are they time twins?

B Read about their lives. Then put the paragraphs in the correct order.

C ▶ 6.6 Listen and check your answers.

D Find two things that are the same and two things that are different between Lia and Carol.

They were born on the same day.

GRAMMAR past simple

2A Read the life stories again and circle the past form of the following regular verbs: *like, move, want, start, live, work, visit, stop.*

B Look at the verbs above and complete the rule.

> **Rule:** Make the past simple of regular verbs by adding _____ or _____ to the verb.

C ▶ 6.7 Listen to the pronunciation of the regular verbs below and write them in the correct place in the table.

| ~~finished~~   loved   hated   travelled   practised   decided |

/t/	/d/	/ɪd/
finished		

D Write the past form of the irregular verbs below. Use the life stories to help.
1. have ___had___
2. get (married) _____
3. make _____
4. buy _____
5. go _____
6. meet _____

E Complete the sentences with the negative form. Then complete the rule.
1. Lia _____ _____ any children.
2. Carol _____ _____ her children.

> **Rule:** Make the negative by adding _____ before the verb.

▶ page 138 **LANGUAGEBANK**

speakout TIP

The *Longman WordWise* Dictionary shows the past tense of a verb, e.g. *begin (began)*. In your notebook, always write (REG) for a regular verb or the past form for an irregular verb. Do this now with *find, finish, win* and *die*.

A Lia was born in Yugoslavia on the 14th of July 1931.

B She had sugar for lunch and dinner every day for three years.

C She got married at twenty-five. She didn't have any children, but children always liked her.

D In 1969, she moved to Lake Balaton in Hungary and made a lot of money selling ice cream with her sister. She bought a house with the money, and now she rents rooms there.

E She wanted to go to university, but there was no money, so she started working in a sugar factory at seventeen.

F She lived in a small village and went to school when she was seven. In 1944, her family moved from Yugoslavia to Hungary because of the war.

PRACTICE

3A Complete the sentences with the past form of the verb in brackets.
1. She ___lived___ in the city and always _____ to work (live/walk) C
2. The family _____ five days to get there. (travel)
3. Every day after work, she _____ for the five children. (cook)
4. They _____ her because she _____ to them. (love/listen)
5. They _____ their shop in 1969. (open)
6. She _____ being on the radio. (enjoy)
7. She _____ work when she was sixty-six. (stop)
8. She _____ to sell a lot of ice cream. (try)

B Write which sentences are about Lia (L) and which are about Carol (C).

60

6.2

A Carol was born in the USA on the 14th of July 1931.

B In 2002, they bought a house by the sea and now their children come and visit them.

C She went to a school for child actors in New York and at eight years old she had her own radio programme.

D Later, she worked in a bookshop in New York. She met her husband there in 1951. They got married and had five children.

E For a few years, she stopped going to school and studied at home with her mother. She became a well-known radio actress.

F In the 1990s, she didn't see her children very much because they lived abroad. She and her husband visited them sometimes.

4A Complete the sentences with the past form of the verbs in brackets.

1 I _____ a car. (not have)
2 I _____ a lot of sport. (do)
3 I _____ a lot of junk food. (eat)
4 I _____ to a great concert. (go)
5 I _____ a new mobile phone. (buy)
6 I _____ English. (not speak)
7 I _____ friends. (visit)
8 I _____ English classes. (start)

B Make the sentences above true for you last year.

C Work in pairs and compare your sentences. Find three things that are the same.

VOCABULARY common verbs

5A Read the texts again and underline six verbs in the past tense that you use for telling a life story.
Lia <u>was born</u> in Yugoslavia …

B Look at the irregular verbs on page 127 and find the past tense of these verbs: *begin*, *find*, *grow up*, *leave*, *learn*, *lose*, *win*.

6 Look at the sentences. What's different about the present and past question forms?
1 Do you live in New York?
2 Did you live in New York when you were a child?

▶ page 138 **LANGUAGEBANK**

7A Think about a friend you don't see now. Complete the questions below. Use the information in brackets to help.
1 Where and when _____? (you / meet)
2 Why _____ each other? (you / like)
3 _____ a lot of things together? (you / do)
4 How often _____ to each other? (you / speak)
5 When _____ him/her? (you / last / see)
6 What _____ then? (you / do)

B Work in pairs. Ask and answer the questions above.

SPEAKING

8A Think of three important events in your life.
2007 – met my wife, …

B Work in pairs and talk about the important events in your lives.
A: *2007 was a great year.*
B: *Why?*
A: *I met my wife!*

WRITING because and so

9A Complete the sentences with *because* or *so*.
1 Carol loved acting, _____ she went to a school for child actors.
2 Lia started working in a sugar factory _____ her family was poor.

B Complete the sentences about your life.
1 At school I liked _____, so I _____.
2 I started studying English because _____.

C Write your life story in 100 words. Remember to use *and*, *but*, *because* and *so*.

61

6.3 HOW WAS YOUR WEEKEND?

▶ FUNCTION | making conversation   ▶ VOCABULARY | weekend activities   ▶ LEARN TO | keep a conversation going

VOCABULARY weekend activities

1 Work in pairs and discuss. What's your favourite day of the week? Why? What do you do on that day?
A: *Why is Saturday your favourite day?*
B: *Because I can stay in bed all morning!*

2A Look at the word webs and cross out the phrase which does not go with the verb.

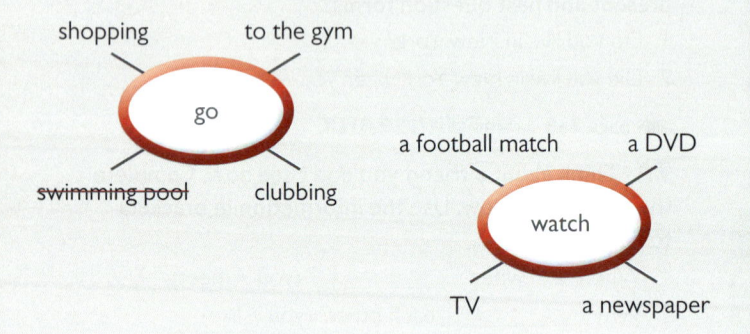

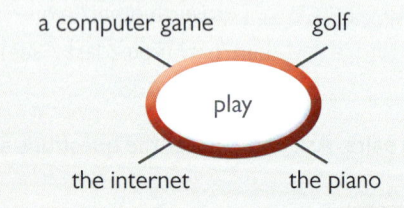

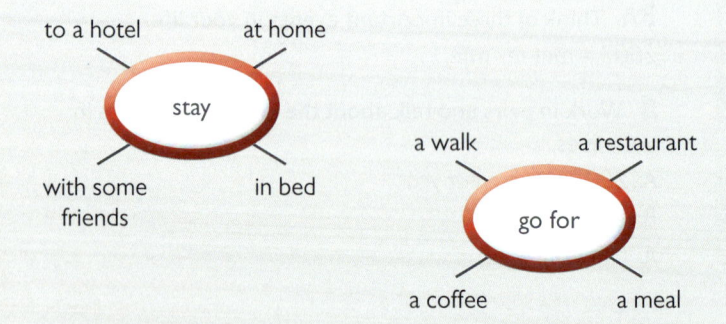

go: shopping, to the gym, ~~swimming pool~~, clubbing

watch: a football match, a DVD, TV, a newspaper

play: a computer game, golf, the internet, the piano

stay: to a hotel, at home, with some friends, in bed

go for: a walk, a restaurant, a coffee, a meal

B Look at the word webs again. Tick which activities you sometimes do at the weekend. Put a cross for activities which you never do.

C Add another activity you often do to each word web above.

D Work in pairs and take turns. Student A: use the verbs above and ask five questions about last weekend. Student B: answer the questions.
A: *Did you go out with friends?*
B: *No, I didn't.*
A: *Did you stay at home?*
B: *Yes, all Sunday!*

FUNCTION making conversation

3A ▶ 6.8 Listen to the conversation and underline the correct alternative.
1 Isabel went *for a walk/to the park*.
2 She went with *a girlfriend/her boyfriend*.
3 Marek *watched/played* football.
4 Marek's team *won/lost*.

B Look at the phrases. Write question (Q), answer (A), or show interest (I) next to each phrase.
1 Did you have a good weekend?   Q
2 How was your weekend?
3 Not bad/OK.
4 Nothing special.
5 What did you do?
6 It was great/terrible!
7 Who did you go with?
8 That sounds nice/good/interesting/terrible.
9 Where did you go?
10 Really?

C Listen again. Tick the phrases above you hear.

▶ page 138 LANGUAGEBANK

62

4A Complete A's part of the conversation.

A: How / your weekend?   *How was your weekend?*
B: It was terrible.
A: Why? What / do?
B: We went to the Saint Patrick's Day Festival. In Dublin.
A: Sound / good. / Who / go with?
B: Zena and Huan. They're students in my class.
A: So, why / it terrible?
B: It rained all weekend! We just stayed in the hotel!
A: Really? That / shame.

B Work in pairs and take turns. Ask and answer questions about your weekend. Use your own ideas and the photos to help.

LEARN TO keep a conversation going

5A Look at the extract. How many pieces of information does Isabel give in her answers? Why?

Marek: What did you do?
Isabel: I went for a walk. It was great!
Marek: That sounds nice. Who did you go with?
Isabel: With my boyfriend, Diego. He's a football player.
Marek: Oh. Where did you go?
Isabel: The river. It was really beautiful.

B Underline the extra pieces of information in Isabel's answers above.

speakout TIP

To have a good conversation, ask follow-up questions after your first question. When you answer, give extra information.

6A Complete the conversation with questions and extra information. Use your own ideas.

A: Did you go to Atsuko's party?
B: Yes, I did. It was ^{1}_____!
A: How many ^{2}_____?
B: Oh, a lot of people. They were all very ^{3}_____.
A: That sounds ^{4}_____! What time ^{5}_____?
B: After midnight. I left ^{6}_____. When I got home, I ^{7}_____.
A: Aren't you tired now?
B: Not really. I ^{8}_____, so I'm not very tired.

B Work in pairs and practise the conversation.

C Work in groups and take turns to say your conversation. Listen to the other pairs. Did everyone like Atsuko's party?

SPEAKING

7A Imagine that you had a perfect/terrible weekend. Write answers to questions 1–4.

1 Where did you go?
2 Who did you go with?
3 What did you do?
4 Why was it perfect/terrible?

B Work in groups. Take turns to tell each other about your weekend. Remember to show interest and to give extra information.

A: *How was your weekend?*
B: *Terrible. I had an awful weekend.*
C: *Really? Why?*

6.4 CARLOS ACOSTA

DVD PREVIEW

1A Read the text and answer the questions. What does Carlos Acosta do? Where is he from?

BBC The Culture Show

The Culture Show is an arts programme which profiles people from the world of theatre, music and dance. This programme is about Carlos Acosta – a famous dancer. He was born in Havana, but travels the world with his dancing. In the programme he talks about his home country and how important it is to him. He also talks about his family and childhood.

B Work in pairs and discuss. How are the photos connected to Carlos Acosta's life?

DVD VIEW

2A Watch the DVD. Were any of your ideas about Carlos Acosta correct?

B Watch again. Number the events in Carlos Acosta's life in the correct order.

a) He was born and grew up in Havana.   1
b) He was a champion break-dancer.
c) He won four dance competitions.
d) He often missed school.
e) He became famous.
f) He saw the Cuban National Ballet.
g) He travelled to Europe.
h) His father sent him to ballet school.

C Read what Acosta says about Cuba. Underline the correct alternatives.

> Cuba is always going to be my home. In my ¹*head/heart*, that's the only country, you know, because that's where all my ²*relatives/friends* are, my memories, you know, and this is the only place I'm never going to be ³*afraid/a foreigner*. You learn how to ⁴*speak/dance* first, then you learn how to ⁵*speak/dance*, you know, in Cuba. It's something that's been passed on through generation to generation. And it's also, you know, the ⁶*weather/heat* and the tropic, and the ⁷*sea/beach* and … it's almost that's what, er, it's asking for, dance and music and ⁸*happiness/love*.

D Watch the DVD again and check your answers.

64

speakout an interview

3A Work in pairs. Think of a hero or someone you admire, e.g. a famous person, a friend or someone in your family. Tell each other about the person. Why is he/she important to you?

B ▶ 6.9 Listen to an interview with Baruti Kaleb. What is one special thing about him?

C Listen again and tick the key phrases you hear.

keyphrases

Interviewer:

Can I ask you about [your childhood/mother/first wife/…]?

Where/When did you [decide to/first meet/…]?

That's very interesting.

What's your favourite [film/book/band/…]?

Are there any questions [from the audience/for …]?

Interviewee:

That's a good question.

Let me think about that.

D Work in pairs. Choose one of the special people from Exercise 3A and make a list of questions to ask them. Then write your interview.

E Work in groups and take turns. One pair: role-play your interview. Other students: make notes about the answers and ask follow-up questions.

writeback a profile

4A Read the profile about Baruti and number the paragraph topics in order.

a) A life-changing experience
b) His early life 1
c) Why I admire him
d) His work

A Special Person: Baruti Kaleb

1. Baruti Kaleb was born in Johannesburg in 1962. He was the fourth of eleven children. His father was a teacher and his mother worked as a cleaning woman for rich people.

2. When Baruti was at school, one of his friends lost his parents, and moved to an orphanage because he had no other family members to live with. Baruti visited his friend at the orphanage and felt very sorry for the children there. So he decided to work with orphans, to try to give them a good life.

3. Baruti met his wife Lerato in 1987, and they got married in 1990. They opened an orphanage in 1996 near Johannesburg, and they still work together. They started with eleven children and now they have sixty-three children living in the orphanage.

4. Baruti is a hero for me because he gives his life to helping children. He is an amazing man and I admire his work very much.

B Write a profile of a special person from Exercise 3D. Write about the events in his/her life and say why you admire him/her.

6.5 « LOOKBACK

WAS/WERE

1A Put the words in the correct order.
1 was / work / I / afternoon / at / yesterday
2 six / Where / o'clock / at / you / were?
3 evening / my / was / at / I / Wednesday / friend's / on
4 at / were / shops / you / the / When?
5 half / you / Were / home / at / twelve / at / past?

B Look at the table below. Where were you yesterday? Fill in the table.

Yesterday	
8.45	At home
12.30	
19.00	

C Work in pairs and take turns. Ask and answer questions about yesterday. Fill in the table when your partner says yes.

Yesterday	
8.45	
12.30	
19.00	

A: Where were you at 8.45 yesterday?
B: I was at home.
A: Were you in bed?
B: Yes, I was. / No, I wasn't.

DATES AND TIME PHRASES

2 Complete time phrases a)–h) so they mean the same as phrases 1–8.

Today is Monday 7th June, 2011.
Vicky is twenty-three.

1 When she was twenty
2 On Sunday afternoon
3 Last month
4 4th June
5 A week ago
6 Yesterday
7 In January
8 Last year

a) Three years ___ago___
b) _____ afternoon
c) _____ May
d) _____ Friday
e) _____ week
f) _____ 6th June
g) five months _____
h) _____ 2010

3A Write three things you can:

eat _a hamburger,_ _____

read _____

visit _____

watch _____

buy _____

play _____

B Work in pairs and take turns. Use the lists above to ask and answer questions.
A: When did you last eat a hamburger?
B: Last month./A week ago./When I was eighteen.

PAST SIMPLE

4A Make the sentences true for you. Use the positive and negative form of the verb.
1 I _____ lunch yesterday. (miss)
2 I _____ some friends at the weekend. (meet)
3 I _____ English yesterday evening. (study)
4 I _____ very well last night. (sleep)
5 I _____ breakfast for myself this morning. (make)
6 I _____ to this lesson by car. (come)

B Work in pairs and compare your answers. Add an extra piece of information.
I didn't miss lunch yesterday. I had a sandwich in the park.

PAST SIMPLE QUESTIONS

5A Look at the sentences and write questions to ask your partner. Add two of your own questions.
1 He/She was born in a hospital.
   Were you born in a hospital?
2 He/She grew up in a city.
   Did you grow up in a city?
3 He/She usually walked to school when he/she was ten.
4 He/She went abroad every summer when he/she was a child.
5 He/She played a lot of sports at school.
6 He/She liked mathematics at school.
7 _____?
8 _____?

B Work in pairs and take turns to ask and answer the questions.

BBC VIDEO PODCAST
Watch people talking about their social lives on ActiveBook or on the website.

Authentic BBC interviews
www.pearsonELT.com/speakout

66

UNIT 7

SPEAKING
- Talk about how you like to travel
- Compare places, transport, hotels and holidays
- Plan and talk about a long journey
- Give directions in the street
- Describe a town/city you know

LISTENING
- Understand directions
- Watch an extract from a travel show about Buenos Aires

READING
- Read an article about a bus ride from London to Sydney

WRITING
- Check and correct information about a holiday
- Write a short article about a town/city

BBC CONTENT
- Video podcast: How was your last holiday?
- DVD: Holiday 10 Best

UNIT 7

holidays

▶ Travel partners   p68
▶ The longest bus ride   p70 
▶ Can you tell me the way?   p72 
▶ Buenos Aires   p74

7.1 TRAVEL PARTNERS

▶ GRAMMAR | comparatives ▶ VOCABULARY | travel ▶ HOW TO | compare places and holidays

VOCABULARY | travel

1A Work in pairs. What places/things can you see in the photos? Make a list of adjectives to describe them.
Train: fast, comfortable …

B Match the adjectives in column A with the opposites in column B.

A	B
good	noisy
fast	empty
crowded	bad
expensive	boring
hot	cheap
comfortable	cold
interesting	uncomfortable
quiet	slow

C ▶ 7.1 Listen and underline the stressed syllable in each adjective. Then listen again and repeat.
*crow*ded

D Work in pairs and take turns. Student A: choose one of the photos A–D. Describe it using four adjectives from Exercise 1B. Student B: guess the photo.
A: *It's really comfortable and I think it's expensive. It's quite big and it isn't noisy.*
B: *Photo D?*

SPEAKING

2A Do the travel quiz below. Circle your answers.

B Work in pairs and compare your answers. Are you good travel partners? Why/Why not?

TRAVEL QUIZ

Going on holiday this year? Do the quiz and find your perfect travel partner …

1 How do you like to travel?
   a) By plane   b) By train

2 Where do you like to stay?
   a) In a hotel   b) In a self-catering apartment

3 What do you prefer to do?
   a) Go sightseeing   b) Relax on a beach

4 When do you like to go?
   a) In spring   b) In summer

5 What do you like to eat?
   a) Local dishes   b) The food I usually eat

6 What do you like to do in the evening?
   a) Go to a club   b) Go to a restaurant

7 How long is your perfect holiday?
   a) A week   b) A month

LISTENING

3A ▶ 7.2 Listen to two people doing the quiz. Answer the questions.
1 How many of their answers are the same?
2 Are they good travel partners?

B Listen again. Write man (M) and woman (W) next to the answers in the quiz in Exercise 2A.

C Work in pairs and discuss. Is the man or the woman a good travel partner for you? Why/Why not?

GRAMMAR comparatives

4A Look at audio script 7.2 on page 171 and complete the sentences.
1 Flying is fast____ _____ going by train.
2 Summer is hot____ _____ spring.
3 A hotel is _____ expensive _____ an apartment.

B ▶ 7.3 Underline the stressed words in the sentences above. Listen and check. Then listen again and repeat.

C Complete the table.

short adjectives	fast	fast**er**____	adjective + -_____
long adjectives	comfortable	_____ comfortable	_____ + adjective
irregular adjectives	good/bad	better/worse	

▶ page 140 **LANGUAGEBANK**

PRACTICE

5A Write comparative sentences. Use the adjectives in brackets.
1 cafés, restaurants (expensive)
   Restaurants are more expensive than cafés.
2 autumn, spring (romantic)
3 travelling by car, travelling by train (fast)
4 English, my language (easy)
5 shoes, trainers (comfortable)
6 water, coffee (good for you)
7 book, magazine (interesting)
8 city, beach (relaxing)

B Work in pairs and compare your answers.

6A Choose two places you know, e.g. cities, cafés, nightclubs. Which one do you like more? Write two sentences about each place using comparatives.
I like Edinburgh more than London because it's friendlier and cheaper.

B Work in pairs and take turns. Tell each other about your places.
A: *I like Edinburgh more than London.*
B: *Why?*
A: *It's friendlier and cheaper.*

SPEAKING

7A Write notes about a good/bad holiday you went on. Think about the questions below and use the photos to help.
- Where/When did you go?
- Who did you go with?
- Where did you stay? Was it good?
- What did you do? Did you enjoy it?
- Where did you eat? Did you like the food?
- Was it hot?
- Did you like it more than your town/city? Why/Why not?

B Work in pairs. Ask and answer the questions above.
A: *Where did you go?*
B: *I went to France …*

7.2 THE LONGEST BUS RIDE

▶ **GRAMMAR** | superlatives   ▶ **VOCABULARY** | places   ▶ **HOW TO** | talk about a journey

VOCABULARY | places

1A Work in pairs. Look at photos A–E. Which of the things in the box can you see?

| a mountain   a bridge   a village   a lake |
| a river   a jungle   a city   a market |
| a famous building   a desert |

B Work in pairs. Look at the words in the box above and write an example for each word. Use your country if possible.
A mountain: Mount Velino (Italy)

OZBUS an exciting way to travel from London to Sydney

The OZBUS is the longest bus ride in the world and the ultimate journey for backpackers. In twelve weeks it travels 16,000 kilometres through twenty different countries.

'Most people fly from London to Sydney at 40,000 feet and never see anything,' says Mark Creasey from Ozbus. 'On the Ozbus people can see the most beautiful places in the world. We go across Europe, through Turkey, India, China, Malaysia and Australia. We travel through deserts, mountains and jungles – it's amazing.'

Jeff Lane travelled on the Ozbus last summer. 'The best thing was the Taj Mahal,' he said. 'The most exciting place was the tiger reserve in the Himalayas, and I really enjoyed visiting the base camp of Mount Everest.' And what were the worst things? 'Well, in Tehran the bus broke down and we waited a whole day for a new one. That wasn't so good. And I didn't always enjoy camping at night. Sometimes I wanted to stay somewhere more comfortable!'

The Ozbus takes up to forty people of all ages. At night, the passengers usually stay in camps or sometimes in small hotels. Everyone takes turns to buy food in local markets and cook for the group.

The greatest journey in the world? Creasey thinks so: 'If you want a truly awesome experience, then the Ozbus is for you.'

READING

2A Read the introduction to the article about the Ozbus and answer the questions.
1 What is the Ozbus?
2 How many countries does it travel through?

B Work in pairs. What else would you like to know about the Ozbus? Write three questions using the words in the box to help.

| countries   price   sleep   people   food   sights |

How many countries does it visit?

3A Read the article. Did you find the answers to your questions?

B Read the article again. Are sentences 1–6 true (T) or false (F)?
1 The Ozbus travels through twelve countries in twenty weeks.
2 Ozbus passengers fly from London to Sydney.
3 Jeff Lane took the Ozbus in the summer.
4 He liked the Taj Mahal, the tiger reserve and camping.
5 Most Ozbus passengers are forty years old.
6 They stay in hotels and camps.

C Would you like to go on the Ozbus? Why/Why not?

7.2

PRACTICE

5A Make questions about the Ozbus trip. Use the prompts below to help.
1 What / cold / place you visited?
   What was the coldest place you visited?
2 What / hot / place?
3 What / friendly / place?
4 What / long / you travelled in one day?
5 What / beautiful / building you saw?
6 What / amazing / experience of the journey?

B Match answers a)–f) with questions 1–6.
a) The Red Desert in Australia.
b) The Taj Mahal
c) Seeing a tiger
d) 400 kilometres
e) Mount Everest
f) I can't say. We met so many fantastic people.

C ▶ 7.5 Listen to a conversation with an Ozbus passenger and check your answers.

SPEAKING

6A Work in groups. Plan a long journey to another country. Make a list of five places to visit: the most exciting, the most beautiful, the highest, etc.

B Prepare to tell the class about your journey. Use these phrases:
First we go to … then we visit the oldest/most famous … in …

C Work in pairs and take turns. Tell the class about your journey. Ask and answer questions about each journey.
A: *Where do you sleep at night?*
B: *In small hotels.*

D Discuss. Which journey is the most interesting?

WRITING checking and correcting

7A Read the student's homework below. Find and correct ten mistakes with:
• the spelling   • past tense forms   • singular and plural

> desert
> On Saturday we went by bus across the /dessert/. We meet a lot of peoples. The peoples in the villages was friendlyer than in the city. At night we staid in a camp. It was not very comftable, but it was more cheaper than the hotels. We buyed all our food in the market.

B Write four sentences about your last holiday.

C Work in pairs. Check each other's sentences. Use the list in Exercise 7A to help.

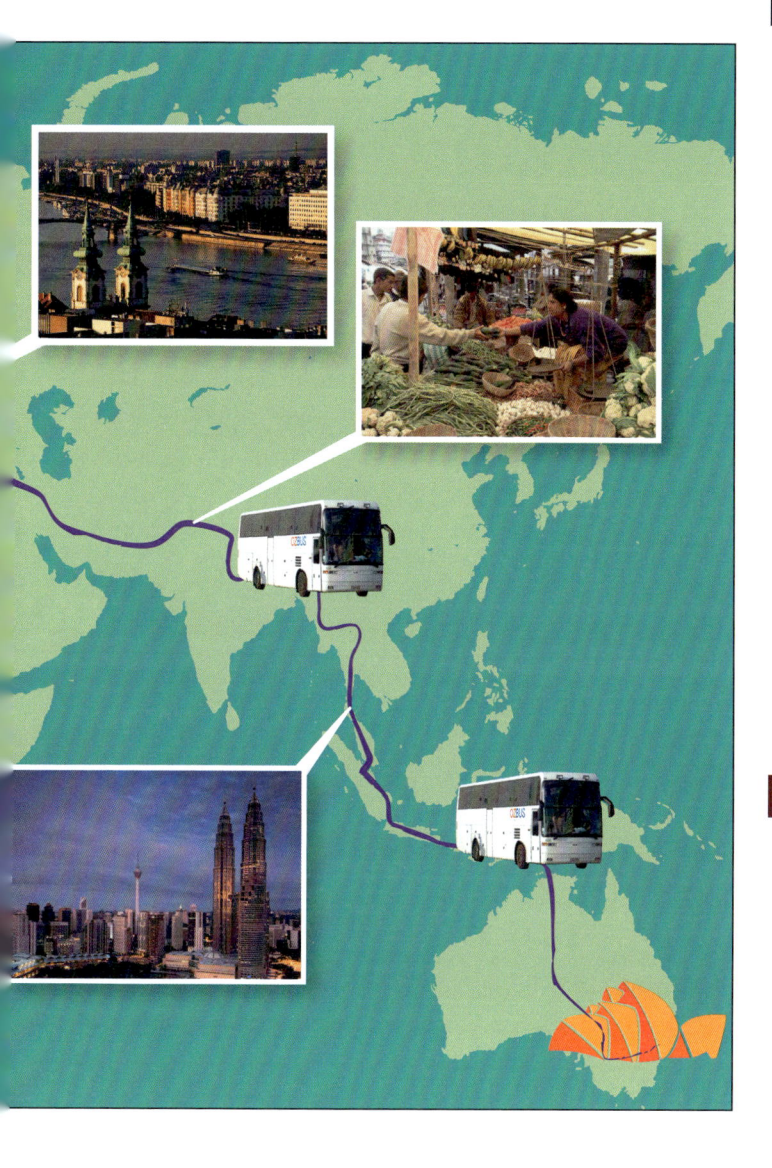

GRAMMAR superlatives

4A Complete the sentences with words from the article above.
1 The Ozbus is the _____ bus ride in the world.
2 People can see the _____ beautiful places in the world.
3 The _____ thing was the Taj Mahal.

B Underline other examples of superlatives in the article. Then complete the table below.

short adjectives	great	the greatest	the + adjective + _____
longer adjectives	exciting		
irregular adjectives	good		
	bad		

C ▶ 7.4 Listen to the pronunciation of *the* in the sentences in Exercise 4A. Then listen and repeat.

▶ page 140 **LANGUAGEBANK**

71

7.3 CAN YOU TELL ME THE WAY?

▶ **FUNCTION** | giving directions ▶ **VOCABULARY** | places ▶ **LEARN TO** | check and correct directions

VOCABULARY places

1A Read the leaflet below and look at the photos A–C. What can you see and do in Brighton? Would you like to go there? Why/Why not?

WELCOME TO BRIGHTON AND HOVE

Just 80km south of London on England's south coast, it is a great place to visit. Brighton is one of the most exciting cities in Britain – with its fantastic shopping, good-value restaurants, great arts and music and famous beach and pier – it's a popular place to visit or stay. It has even got its very own royal palace, the exotic Royal Pavilion.

B Look at the map of Brighton and find the places in the box below.

a bus station   a theatre   a car park
a Tourist Information centre   a pier
a museum   a clock tower
an art gallery   a park   a square
a library   a swimming pool

FUNCTION giving directions

2A Work in pairs and look at the map. Find three different routes from the Clock Tower to Brighton Pier.

B ▶ 7.6 Listen to the directions. Draw the route on the map.

C Listen again and complete the dialogue. Then listen and repeat.

A: Excuse me. Can you ¹_____ me the way to the ²_____, please?
B: Yeah … you ³_____ down West Street until the ⁴_____.
A: Straight ⁵_____?
B: Yeah. And then turn ⁶_____ and you'll see the Pier.
A: Thanks very much.

3A Match directions 1–8 to diagrams A–H.

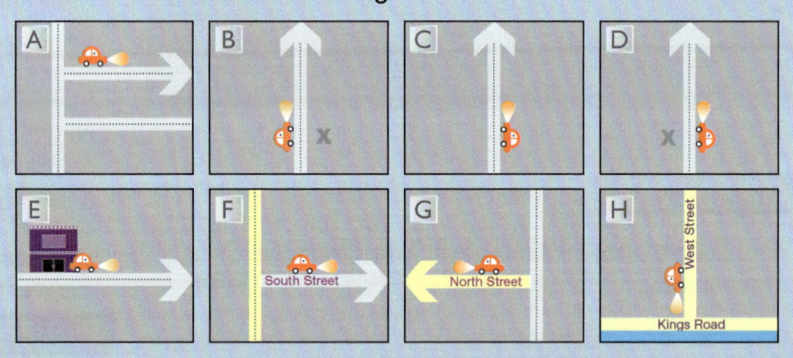

1 go straight on   C
2 turn left into North Street
3 turn right into South Street
4 go down West Street until the end
5 take the second right
6 go past the cinema
7 it's on the right
8 it's on the left

B ▶ 7.7 Listen and check. Then listen and repeat.

▶ page 140 **LANGUAGEBANK**

4A Choose two places in the box below. Write directions to them from the Clock Tower.

the Royal Pavilion   the Museum and Art Gallery   the swimming pool
Church Street car park   the Town Hall   the Theatre Royal

B Work in pairs and take turns. Student A: Read your directions. Student B: follow the directions. Where are you?

C Give directions for two more places.

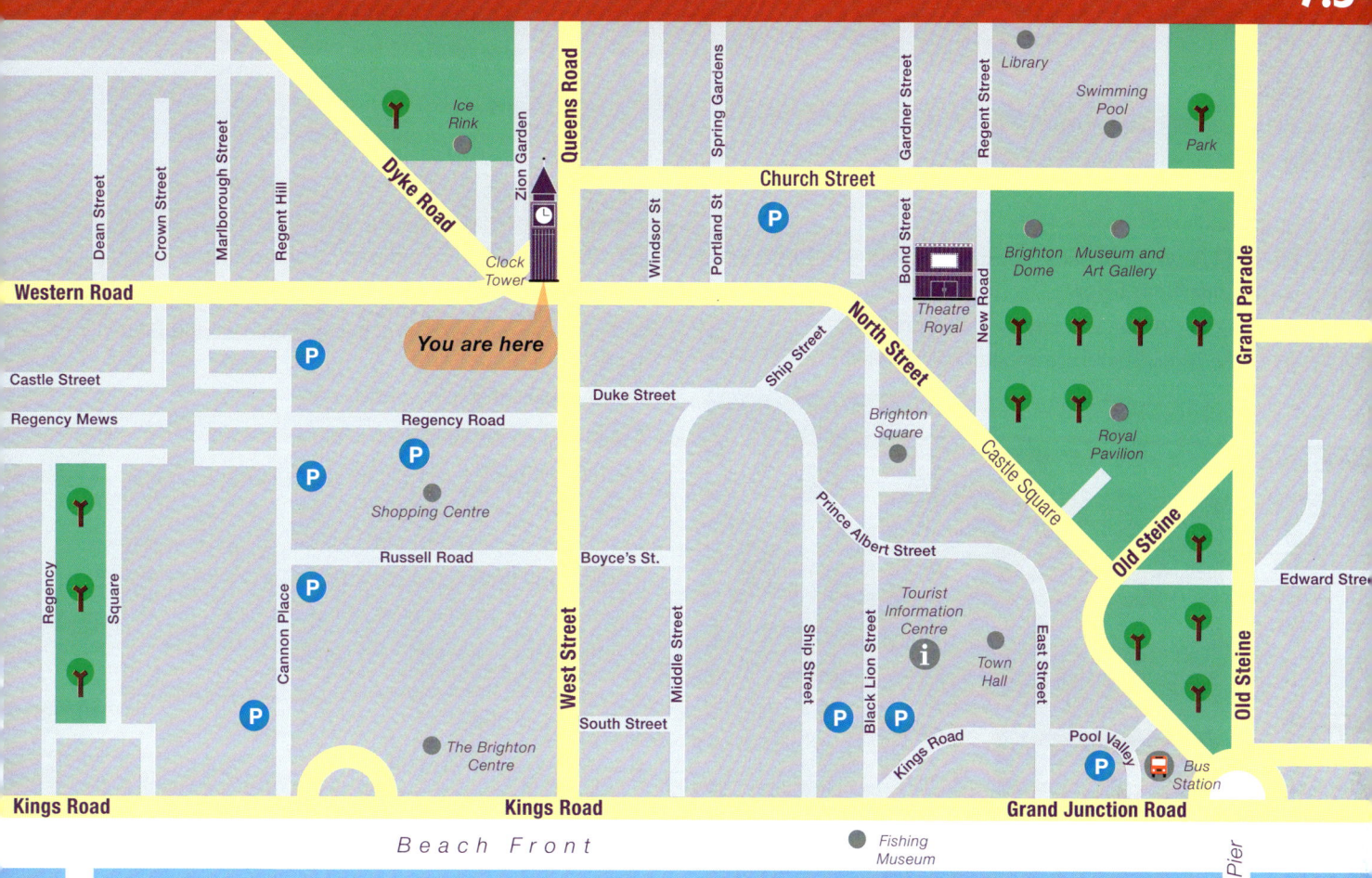

LEARN TO check and correct directions

5A ▶ 7.8 Find Church Street car park. Listen to the conversation and follow the directions. Where are you?

B Read the extract and listen again. How does the woman check the directions? Underline the phrases she uses.

A: You go out of this car park and turn right. So that's right into Church Street. Then take the third right, I think it's called New Road.
B: The first right?
A: No, the third right. And you go straight on until the end of the road and then turn left. After about one minute you'll see it on the left. You can't miss it!
B: So third right, erm, left at the end of the road and then … ?
A: It's on the left.
B: On the left.

C Work in pairs. Student A: read the part of A above, sentence by sentence. Student B: cover the extract. Listen to Student A and repeat to check you understand.
A: You go out of this car park and turn right.
B: Turn right?

6A ▶ 7.9 Look at the conversation extracts below. Listen and underline the stressed words in B's answers.

1 A: The first right?
  B: No, the third right.
2 A: So I turn left and then …
  B: No, you turn right.
3 A: So I go past the Pavilion and …
  B: No, past the Pier.
4 A: It's in Church Street.
  B: No, it's in Church Road.

B Listen again and repeat the man's answers.

speakout TIP

When you want to correct a mistake, you can use stress. Remember to say the correct word **higher**, **louder** and l o n g e r.
Is it fifty-two High Street?   No, it's **thirty**-two.

C Work in pairs and take turns. Student A: look at page 165. Student B: look at page 161.

SPEAKING

7 Work in pairs and take turns. Choose a starting point in your town/city that you both know. Student A: you are a tourist. Ask for directions to three places. Check you understand the directions. Student B: give directions and correct the directions if necessary.

73

7.4 BUENOS AIRES

DVD PREVIEW

1A Work in pairs. Look at the photos and answer the questions below.
1 What can you see/do in Buenos Aires?
2 What sports are popular in Argentina?

B Read the text and check your answers.

BBC Holiday 10 Best

In the last of ten programmes looking at exciting holidays, Nicki Chapman takes us on a quick tour of Argentina's capital. She starts her tour at the amazing Avenue 9th July, and then visits La Boca, where football legend Diego Maradona started his career. She also watches people dance the tango, tries the popular sport of polo and eats some famous Argentinian beef.

DVD VIEW

2A Watch the DVD. Number the photos in the order Nicki talks about them.

B Match the words/names below with descriptions a)–f).
1 the Avenue 9th July
2 La Boca
3 Diego Maradona
4 the tango
5 polo
6 Argentinian beef

a) is one of the poorest parts of Buenos Aires
b) is the best in the world
c) is the widest street in the city
d) is a famous dance
e) is a sport you do on a horse
f) is one of the most famous football players in the world

C Work in pairs and compare your answers.

D Watch the DVD again. Complete the extracts below with the words in the box.

famous   vegetables   south   football
widest   meat   emotion   career

The twenty-lane Avenue 9th July is the ¹_____ street on the planet and it cuts through the city from north to ²_____.

The people of La Boca share one of Argentina's greatest passions: ³_____. La Boca is where Diego Maradona, one of football's leading legends, began his ⁴_____.

We are also ⁵_____ for the tango. People started dancing the tango in the 1800s. It's a dance full of passion and ⁶_____.

You can't be a vegetarian, can you, with all this fantastic ⁷_____? If you want, we have very good ⁸_____ here! Very social, isn't it?

3 Work in pairs. Answer the questions.
1 What do you think are the two most interesting things to do or to see in Buenos Aires?
2 Do you think Buenos Aires is a good place for a holiday? Why/Why not?

speakout describe a town/city

4A Work in pairs. Choose a town/city you both know. Make a list of interesting facts and information about it. Think about:
- general information, e.g. where it is, how big it is
- important places
- famous people
- special food/local dishes

B Prepare to tell other students about the town/city. Use the key phrases to help.

> **keyphrases**
> We want to talk about …
> It's [the capital city/an old town] …
> It's got [a/some] …
> One of the most important places in … is …
> Here you can see …
> A famous person from … is …
> He/She's famous because …
> A typical food from [town/city] is …
> It's a (very) … place. You can … there.

C ▶ 7.10 Listen to two students talk about Rimini in Italy. Which things from Exercise 4A don't they talk about?

D Listen again and tick the key phrases you hear.

E Work in groups. Tell other students about the town/city. Which places would you like to visit?

writeback a travel article

5A Read the description of Rimini below. Divide the article into four paragraphs:
- a description of the place
- a famous person
- a typical food
- your opinion

> Rimini is an old city on the Adriatic Sea in Italy. It's famous for its beautiful beach and also for the cathedral and the Arch of Augustus. The Rimini nightlife is amazing. There are lots of places to dance and have fun. One of the most famous people from Rimini is the film director Federico Fellini. He made many films, for example *Amarcord*, *La Dolce Vita* and *La Strada*. His ideas for his films sometimes came from his childhood in Rimini. A typical food in Rimini is 'puntarelle'. This is a pasta dish with fresh vegetables. It's very simple but delicious. Rimini is also a good place to eat fish. I like travelling, and I like going to new places, but I go to Rimini every year because I love the beaches and the nightlife.

B Now write an article of 80–100 words about your town/city for a travel website. Use the ideas and phrases from Exercise 4 and the article above to help.

7.5 « LOOKBACK

COMPARATIVES

1A Look at the information below about two ways of travelling from Moscow to Beijing. Write eight sentences comparing them. Use the words in the box to help.

cheap fast expensive slow
crowded boring comfortable
interesting uncomfortable
exciting relaxing

Trans-Siberian Railway:
580 euros 2nd class,
7 days, 35 stops,
4 beds per compartment,
restaurant on train

China Airlines flight:
1,100 euros 2nd class,
7 hours 20 minutes, 0 stops,
2 meals, 2 movies

The train is cheaper than the plane.

B Work in pairs and discuss. Which way of travelling from Moscow to Beijing is better: the train or plane? Why?

VOCABULARY: PLACES

2 Work in pairs. Look at the words in the box below and find:

a mountain a village a city
a desert a jungle a lake
a market a river

1 two places where you can swim.
2 one place that has a lot of trees.
3 two places where people live.
4 one place where you can buy things.
5 one place that's hot in the day and cold at night.
6 one place that's very high.

SUPERLATIVES

3A Complete the quiz with superlatives of the adjectives in brackets.

City Quiz

1 *The friendliest* (friendly) city in the world is:
   a) Rio de Janeiro b) Cairo
   c) Kuala Lumpur
2 The world's _____ (big) city is:
   a) Seoul b) Mexico City
   c) Tokyo
3 _____ (good) place to live is:
   a) Zurich b) Vancouver
   c) Melbourne
4 _____ (safe) city in the world is:
   a) Istanbul b) Singapore
   c) Dublin
5 _____ (beautiful) city is:
   a) Cape Town b) Sydney
   c) Prague
6 _____ (popular) tourist destination in the world is:
   a) Spain b) The USA
   c) France
7 _____ (fast)-growing cities in the world are in:
   a) China b) Africa c) India
8 _____ (busy) shopping street is in the world is in:
   a) London b) Hong Kong
   c) Shanghai

Key: 1a 2c 3b 4a 5a 6c 7b 8a

B Work in pairs and do the quiz. Then check your answers in the key.

CHECKING AND CORRECTING

4A Complete the sentences with false information about you.
1 I spell my name …
2 I'm from …
3 I live in …
4 My teacher is …
5 I like …

B Work in pairs and take turns. Look at your partner's information and check statements with him/her.
A: So, you spell your name d-y-a-n-a.
B: No, my name's Diana! I spell my name d-i-a-n-a.
A: And, you're from Poland.
B: No, I'm from *France*.

GIVING DIRECTIONS

5A Put the words in order. Start with the underlined words.
1 Go / take / left. / and / down / the / Grand / first / Avenue
2 on. / bank / Turn / and / right / go / at / straight / the
3 turn / into / Park / right / Lane. / Take / the / right / then / third
4 's / left. / on / It / the
5 straight / turn / road / end / on / right. / and / of / until / Go / then / the / the
6 way / you / to / tell / the / Can / me / supermarket? / the

B Work in pairs and take turns. Student A: think of a place near where you are now. Give directions. Student B: guess the place.
A: *Go out of the main entrance and turn left …*

BBC VIDEO PODCAST

Watch people talking about where they went on their last holidays on ActiveBook or on the website.

Authentic BBC interviews

www.pearsonELT.com/speakout

UNIT 8

SPEAKING
- Talk about what people are doing
- Describe people's appearance
- Ask for and give recommendations
- Talk about an event

LISTENING
- Listen to a radio programme about ideas of beauty
- Watch an extract from a documentary about an English music festival

READING
- Read blog entries about what people are doing now

WRITING
- Write a blog about what you are doing
- Write a review of an event

BBC CONTENT
- Video podcast: What was the last film you saw?
- DVD: Inside Out

UNIT 8

now

▶ In the picture   p78
▶ Looking good   p80 
▶ What do you recommend? p82 
▶ Festival Highlights   p84

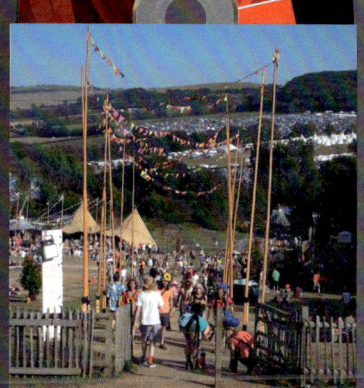

8.1 IN THE PICTURE

▶ GRAMMAR | present continuous   ▶ VOCABULARY | verbs + prepositions   ▶ HOW TO | talk about the present

SPEAKING

1A Read the sentences. Underline the alternative which is true for you.
1 I take photos *every day/on holiday/only on special occasions.*
2 I take photos with *my camera/my mobile/my camera and my mobile.*
3 I share photos with *my family/my friends/everyone.*
4 I put my photos *on a website/in a book/on my computer.*
5 My favourite subjects are *people/places/nature.*

B Work in pairs and compare your answers.

GRAMMAR present continuous

2A Look at the website page. Match sentences 1–5 below to photos A–E.
1 We're listening to live jazz.
2 I'm cleaning up after the party.
3 I'm lying on the beach in Cannes.
4 Patrizia's looking at paintings at the Hermitage.
5 He's singing *My Way* at a karaoke bar.

B Underline the verbs in sentences 1–5 above. Then complete the table.

I	___ ly _ing_	on the beach.
We	___ listen ___	to live jazz.
He	___ sing ___	*My Way*.

C Look at the sentences again and underline the correct alternative to complete the rule.

> **Rule:** Use the present continuous to talk about your life *every day/at this moment.*

D ▶ 8.1 Complete the questions with *is* or *are*. Then listen and check.
1 What ____ you doing?
2 What ____ he singing?

E Listen again and underline the stressed words. Then listen and repeat.

▶ page 142 **LANGUAGEBANK**

Cannes, 1p.m.

Caracas, 7.30a.m.

Singapore, 1p.m.

PRACTICE

3A Complete the sentences with verbs from the box.

| ~~dance~~ take read have swim chat feel make enjoy listen |

1 Some people *are dancing* to the music. We _____ to each other and _____ the band.
2 People _____ photos of the paintings.
3 I _____ about the film festival here in Cannes. Cath and Jim aren't here – they _____ in the sea, I think.
4 Everyone _____ to him sing – he's fantastic! We _____ a really good time!
5 It's a beautiful day, but I _____ really tired. Karen _____ some coffee and I really need it!

B Match photos A–E on the website page with sentences 1–5 above.

C Work in pairs. Cover the sentences above. Ask and answer questions about the people from the website.
A: *What's he doing? What are they doing?*
B: *He's …*

D Work in pairs and take turns. Write the names of three people you know. What do you think they are doing at the moment? Tell your partner.
My friend Julia lives in Sydney. I think she's getting up now or maybe she's having breakfast.

speakout TIP

Practise English in your head. When you do something, think of the sentence, e.g. *I'm walking, I'm doing my homework, I'm washing my hands …*

8.1

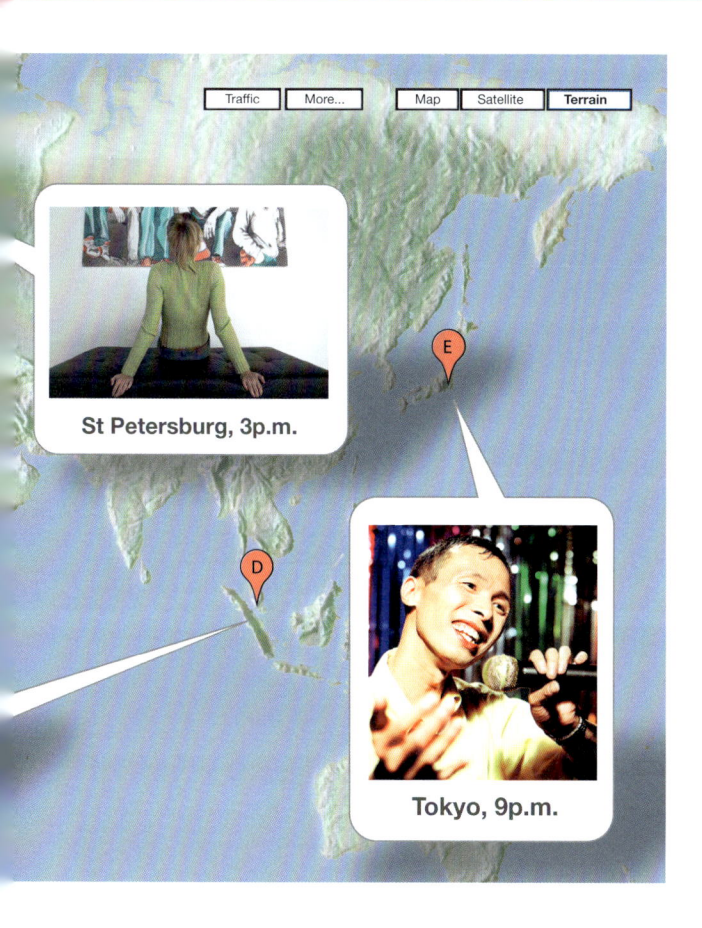

St Petersburg, 3p.m.

Tokyo, 9p.m.

VOCABULARY verbs + prepositions

4A Underline the correct alternative.

1 listen *with/to* the radio
2 take photos *of/about* a friend
3 wait *to/for* a train
4 read *on/about* a film star
5 lie *on/at* a bed
6 chat *to/from* my partner
7 be *for/on* the phone
8 look *on/at* a photo
9 think *about/on* your friend
10 ask *about/to* pronunciation

B ▶ 8.2 Listen and check. Notice the weak sound of the prepositions and articles. Then listen and repeat.

1 listen /tədə/ radio

C Work in pairs and take turns. Student A: say a verb from Exercise 4A. Student B: say the whole verb phrase. Then think of other possible nouns.

A: *listen*
B: *listen to the radio*
A: *listen to an MP3 player*
B: *listen to …*

SPEAKING

5 Work in pairs. Student A: look at page 163. Student B: look at page 166.

READING

6 Read the two blogs from WhatRUdoing.com. Write the number of the missing sentences from Exercise 3A in the correct places.

Next Blog >>

Jules

I'm having a great time here. I'm staying with my two best friends from college. I last saw **them** five years ago. **They**'re still the same – just a bit older. At the moment I'm relaxing and _____. Their apartment is only ten minutes from the festival. Yesterday we went to see our first film. Angelina Jolie was in **it**. I didn't like **it** much – but I thought **she** was very good!

Next Blog >>

Rafael

Hi, everyone. So what am I doing today? Not much! _____. We didn't get to bed until four in the morning, but it was great! Non-stop music and dancing, good food and all our friends. I think **they** enjoyed themselves. I got some fantastic presents: especially a digital camera. I used **it** to put a photo on WhatRUdoing.com. Take a look. That's me, with the dirty dishes!

WRITING pronouns

7A Look at the sentences below from the first blog. What does *them* refer to?

I'm staying with (my two best friends). I last saw **them** five years ago.

B Look at the pronouns in bold in the blogs. What do they refer to? Circle the pronouns and draw an arrow to the correct word.

C Read the blog entry below. Use pronouns to make four more changes.

Next Blog >>

Last night I went to Jazz Stop with Dan and Lisa.
                                         We
~~Dan, Lisa and I~~ saw Will Brown. Will Brown has got a new CD and Will Brown played songs from his new CD. Lisa and Dan danced a lot but I just chatted with Lisa and Dan between dances and took photos. I put one of the photos on WhatRUdoing.com. WhatRUdoing.com is my favourite website.

D Write your own blog entry. Write about a concert, a party, an art gallery or a karaoke bar. Use pronouns and include the names of two other students.

79

8.2 LOOKING GOOD

▶ GRAMMAR | present simple/continuous   ▶ VOCABULARY | appearance   ▶ HOW TO | describe people

SPEAKING

1A Work in pairs and discuss. Match the information with the film star.

She was in a lot of James Bond films.
He played Che Guevara in The Motorcycle Diaries.
She's American.
He also sings – he's a rapper.
He started acting in the 1950s.
She was born in Malaysia.

B What other information do you know about the film stars?
Sean Connery is Scottish.

C Do you think any of the film stars are good-looking? Why/Why not?

VOCABULARY appearance

2A Work in pairs. Look at the photos and answer the questions.
1 Which of the film stars has got:
  a) short grey hair?
  b) long blonde hair?
  c) dark curly hair?
  d) a beard and a moustache?
  e) brown eyes?
2 Which of the film stars is:
  a) black?
  b) in his/her seventies/eighties?
  c) in his/her twenties/thirties?
  d) wearing make-up?
  e) wearing earrings?

B ▶ 8.3 Listen to a man describing two of the film stars. Which two is he talking about?
1 _____
2 _____

C Listen again and write the questions. Use the prompts to help.
1 Is / man / or / woman?
2 What / she / look like?

D Work in pairs and take turns. Student A: choose one of the film stars and describe him/her. Student B: ask the questions in Exercise 2 and guess the film star.

▶ page 158 PHOTOBANK

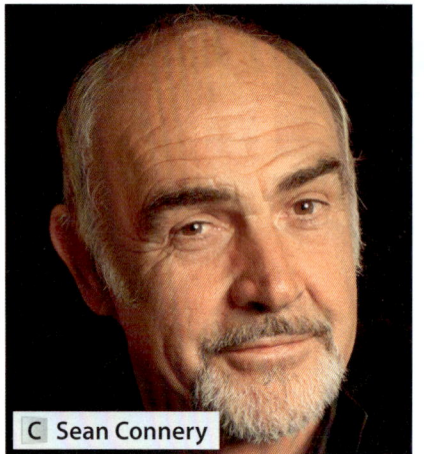

A Michelle Yeoh
B Scarlett Johansson
C Sean Connery
D Will Smith

LISTENING

3A ▶ 8.4 Listen to the first part of a radio programme. Is the programme about film stars, ideas of fashion or ideas of beauty?

B Read the information below. Then listen again and underline the words you hear.

Do men today *really* like women with [1]*blonde/black* hair and [2]*brown/blue* eyes? And do women like the James Bond look – tall, [3]*grey/dark* and very [4]*masculine/feminine*, or do they like something different now?

C ▶ 8.5 Listen to the second part of the radio programme. Which film stars do the people like?

D Listen again. What do the people talk about? Complete the table.

	height/build	hair/beard	eyes	other
Woman 1		beard		
Woman 2				nice smile
Woman 3				
Man 1				beautiful clothes
Man 2	slim			

E Work in groups and discuss. What's your idea of beauty?

8.2

E Gael García Bernal

F Judi Dench

GRAMMAR present simple/continuous

4A Look at the sentences and underline the verbs. Which tenses are they?
1 She always wears beautiful clothes.
2 He's wearing a white T-shirt.

B Underline the correct alternative to complete the rules.

> Rules:
> 1 Use the *present simple/present continuous* for something we do every day or usually.
> 2 Use the *present simple/present continuous* for something we're doing now or at this moment.

C Complete the table with the verb *wear*.

| What | _____ | you | usually _____ | to work/school? |
| What | _____ | you | _____ | now? |

| I | usually _____ | a suit. |
| Now, I | _____ | jeans and a sweater. |

▶ page 142 LANGUAGEBANK

PRACTICE

5A Look at the cartoons and discuss. What are the problems?

B Underline the correct alternatives below.

> In an office, men usually ¹*wear/are wearing* dark suits, ties and shoes, but Sam ²*wears/'s wearing* jeans, a T-shirt and trainers. He ³*doesn't wear/isn't wearing* a tie. Another problem is that he ⁴*wears/'s wearing* sunglasses and most businessmen ⁵*don't wear/aren't wearing* sunglasses at work.

C Complete the information about the second cartoon.

> Walkers ¹_____ (not) usually ²_____ skirts; they ³_____ trousers and walking jackets. Jenny's boyfriend ⁴_____ boots but she ⁵_____ high-heeled shoes – dangerous on a country walk. Another problem is that she ⁶_____ (not) a backpack. She ⁷_____ a handbag!

6 Work in pairs. Sit back to back and take turns. Student A: say six things you're wearing – four true and two false. Student B: say which things are false.
A: *I'm wearing a grey shirt.*
B: *True!*

SPEAKING

7A Work in pairs and discuss. What clothes do you usually/never wear for:
- a walk in the country?
- dinner at a friend's house?
- a job interview?
- meeting friends in a bar or club?
- a party?
- an exercise class?

B Work with a new partner. Student A: say the clothes you usually/never wear for the situations above. Student B: guess the situation.
A: *I usually wear jeans and a top. I never wear shorts.*
B: *A walk in the country?*

81

8.3 WHAT DO YOU RECOMMEND?

▶ **FUNCTION** | recommending   ▶ **VOCABULARY** | types of film   ▶ **LEARN TO** | link words to speak faster

SPEAKING

1A Complete the questionnaire below.

MOVIEWATCH

1. What was the last film you saw?
2. What's your favourite film?
3. Who is your favourite film actor?
4. Who is your favourite film actress?
5. Do you like watching films:
   a) *at home/at the cinema*?
   b) *on TV/on your computer*?
   c) *on your own/with someone*?
   d) *only once/more than once*?

B Work in pairs and compare your answers.

VOCABULARY types of film

2A Match the posters in pictures A–H with the types of film in the box.

> ~~romantic film~~ A   horror film   drama
> animated film   musical   action film
> comedy   sci-fi film

B Complete the sentences with the types of film.

1. People fall in love in a *romantic film*.
2. There's a lot of singing and dancing in a _____.
3. I laugh a lot when I watch a _____.
4. There are often UFOs and aliens from space in a _____.
5. A _____ can be too scary for me.
6. There are usually a lot of guns and car chases in an _____.
7. I sometimes cry when I watch a _____.
8. Drawings seem to move and talk in an _____.

C Work in pairs and discuss. Do you like the same films? Why/Why not? Which types of films <u>don't</u> you like? Why?

A: *Which types of films do you like?*
B: *I like musicals.*
A: *Oh, really? Why? …*

82

8.3

FUNCTION | recommending

3A ▶ 8.6 Listen to two conversations. Which types of film from Exercise 2A do the people talk about?

B Listen again. Do the people decide to watch the films? Why/Why not?

4A Put the words in the correct order.
1. you / do / recommend? / What
   What do you recommend?
2. French Kiss? / about / How
3. you / I'd / Do / it? / like / think
4. you'd / it / like / think / don't / I
5. I / French / like / that / film / you'd / think

B ▶ 8.7 Listen and check. Then listen and repeat.

➡ page 142 **LANGUAGEBANK**

5 Work in pairs and take turns. Look again at the film posters A–H. Student A: ask your partner to recommend a film. Student B: ask questions and recommend a film.

A: I want to watch a DVD this weekend. What do you recommend?
B: Hmm. What kind of films do you like?

LEARN TO | link words to speak faster

6A Read the flowchart and complete questions 1–5.

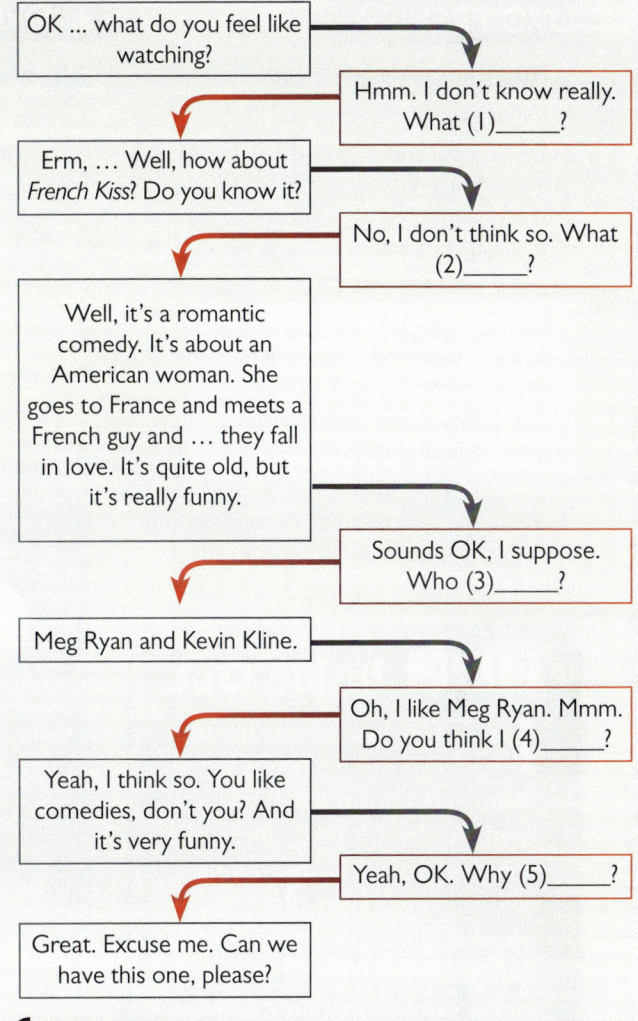

- OK ... what do you feel like watching?
- Hmm. I don't know really. What (1)_____?
- Erm, ... Well, how about *French Kiss*? Do you know it?
- No, I don't think so. What (2)_____?
- Well, it's a romantic comedy. It's about an American woman. She goes to France and meets a French guy and ... they fall in love. It's quite old, but it's really funny.
- Sounds OK, I suppose. Who (3)_____?
- Meg Ryan and Kevin Kline.
- Oh, I like Meg Ryan. Mmm. Do you think I (4)_____?
- Yeah, I think so. You like comedies, don't you? And it's very funny.
- Yeah, OK. Why (5)_____?
- Great. Excuse me. Can we have this one, please?

speakout TIP

Word linking can help your speaking sound more natural. Remember you can link the consonant at the end of one word and the vowel at the beginning of the next word, e.g. What's_it_about?

B ▶ 8.8 Listen and check your answers.

C Look at the questions in Exercise 6A and draw the links. Then practise saying them.

D Work in pairs and take turns. Cover the man's part and practise the conversation.

7A Work as a class and make a list of eight films. Write the titles in English or in your language.

B Work in pairs. Student A: choose one of the films and answer Student B's questions. Student B: ask questions 1–3 from Exercise 6A. Guess the film.

SPEAKING

8 Work with a new partner. Recommend one of your favourite films or a film you saw recently.
A: One of my favourite films is ... / Last week I saw ...
B: What's it about? Do you think I'd like it?

83

8.4 FESTIVAL HIGHLIGHTS

DVD PREVIEW

1 Work in pairs and discuss.
1 What type of music do you like?
2 Do you like concerts or music festivals? Why/Why not?
3 What do people often do at music festivals? Tick the activities in the box:

listen to music ✓   sleep in a hotel
dance   cook food   watch films
sleep in tents   go to bed early
play games   take their children
wear unusual clothes

2 Read the programme information and answer the questions. What is Bestival? When and where is it?

BBC Inside Out

Inside Out is a TV series that looks at surprising stories from well-known places around England. In this programme the presenter goes to Bestival, a music festival which takes place on the Isle of Wight every September. He finds out what types of people go to the festival, what they do when they are there and why they go.

▶ DVD VIEW

3A Before you watch, underline the alternative you think is correct.
1 A woman in a red dress is *singing/dancing*.
2 A man is carrying some *boots/socks*.
3 Some people are sitting outside on a *chair/sofa*.
4 A man is sitting and eating in front of a *beach hut/tent*.
5 A child is playing with a big *orange/white* ball.
6 Some people are putting up a *hut/tent*.
7 A band is playing *at night/in the afternoon*.
8 Families are *playing games/eating and drinking* in the tea tent.

B Watch the DVD and check your answers.

4 Why do people come to the festival? Watch the DVD again and listen to what the people say. Are the sentences true (T) or false (F)?
1 It's a holiday for the family.   T
2 People are away from their normal jobs.
3 People can buy music CDs.
4 Festivals are a playground for grownups (adults).
5 People can meet famous bands and singers.
6 Young people and old people can mix together.

5 Listen again and complete the sentences.

'It's like opening your back door, going down to the end of your ¹_____, getting in your shed with your baby and ²_____, and then calling it a ³_____.'

'Well, I suppose it gives everybody a chance just to be themselves, and just … be ⁴_____ … and be away from their normal ⁵_____.'

'The community getting together and the ⁶_____ mixing with the older ⁷_____. We make ⁸_____, we do pop festivals, we'll go anywhere, do anything.'

84

speakout describe an event

6A Think about a recent event you went to, e.g. a festival, a concert, a sports event, an exhibition, a play/dance or comedy show. Use the questions below to make notes about it.
- What was it?
- When and where was it?
- What did you do or see?
- What did you think of it?
- Do you recommend it?

B ▶ 8.9 Listen to someone talking about an event he/she went to recently. What was it? Did he/she enjoy it?

C Read the key phrases below. Then listen again and tick the ones you hear.

keyphrases
[Last week/month/year/Recently] I went to …
It was in (place).
I/We went because …
I think it was good for [children/families/teenagers/music lovers].
It cost … / It was free.
I thought it was [great/terrible].
I [really liked/really enjoyed/didn't really like/hated] it because …

D Work in groups and take turns. One student: talk about your event. Use the key phrases to help. Other students: listen and ask two questions about each event.

writeback a review

7A Read this web review from the Edinburgh Festival. What type of event is it?

26-09-11
listener
Posting 1
Last night we went to see Adam Hills at the Stand. We went because a good friend of mine recommended the show. Hills is a popular comedian from Australia and this is his first time in Europe. His show is called *Happy Feet* because he loves dance music from 1930s America. He's a very good story-teller – really funny. We never stopped laughing and one hour was too short. We wanted more! I really recommend the show – I thought Hills was great! Go and see him before he returns to Australia.

B Read the review again and put the topics in the correct order.
a) What was good/bad about it?
b) Why did you go?
c) What was it?
d) When and where was it? 1

C Write a review of 80–100 words about the event you talked about in Exercise 6D. Use phrases from the review above to help you.

8.5 « LOOKBACK

ACTIVITIES

1A Complete the puzzle with the verb phrases and find the hidden message.

1. take photos
2. l_ _ _ the beach
3. l_ _ _ _ jazz
4. h_ _ _ _ _ _ _ _ _ _ reat time (free time)
5. l_ _ k art
6. h_ _ _ _ _ _ ffee
7. r_ _ _ book

B Work in groups and discuss. Which two activities above do you usually do with other people/alone/outside?

PRESENT CONTINUOUS

2A Complete the sentences. Use the present continuous of the verb in brackets.

1. It _____ . (rain)
2. A plane _____ over the building. (fly)
3. Someone _____ and reading. (sit)
4. Students _____ . (talk)
5. Someone _____ on his/her computer. (work)
6. People _____ past the building. (drive)
7. Children _____ . (play)
8. Someone _____ a phone call. (make)

B Work in pairs. Which of the things above are happening outside your classroom at the moment?

DESCRIBING APPEARANCE

3A Use the prompts below to write complete questions.

1. man / woman? *Is it a man or a woman?*
2. he/she / dark hair? *Has he/she got dark hair?*
3. he/she / long hair?
4. he/she / tall?
5. he/she / black sweater?
6. he/she / in her/his twenties?
7. he/she / brown shoes?
8. he/she / blue eyes?

B Work in groups and take turns. One student: think of a student in the class. Answer questions with *yes* or *no*. The other students: ask the questions above and your own questions. Guess the name of the student.

CLOTHES

4A What are the clothes? Add the vowels.

1. tr*a*i ners
2. sh_ _s
3. s_cks
4. j_ _ns
5. tr_ _s_rs
6. sk_rt
7. T-sh_rt
8. j_ck_t
9. t_p

B Work in pairs and take turns. Student A: say an item of clothing. Student B: say the name of a person who is wearing it in the class.

PRESENT SIMPLE AND PRESENT CONTINUOUS

5A Write questions about students in your class. Use the present simple and present continuous.

1. wear glasses (*usually/today*)
   Does Mia usually wear glasses? Is she wearing them today?
2. use an electronic dictionary (*usually/now*)
3. chew gum (*often/at the moment*)
4. speak English (*always in class/now*)
5. wear black (*often/today*)

B Work in pairs and take turns. Ask and answer the questions.

RECOMMENDING

6A Write the conversation in full.

A: I want / read a good book. What / recommend?
B: What kind / books / you like?
A: Travel books and good stories.
B: I / got *Life of Pi* by Yann Martel. It / very good.
A: What / it about?
B: It / about a boy and a tiger on a boat.
A: you / think I / like it?
B: Yes, I do.
A: OK. Can / borrow it?
B: Sure.

B Ask three other students for book recommendations. Which of the books would you like to read?

BBC VIDEO PODCAST
Watch people talking about films and actors on ActiveBook or on the website.

Authentic BBC interviews
www.pearsonELT.com/speakout

UNIT 9

SPEAKING
- Talk about types of transport
- Apologise for being late
- Tell a long story
- Deal with problems when flying

LISTENING
- Listen to a museum tour
- Listen to a man talk about his problems getting to work
- Watch an extract from a documentary about a day at Heathrow airport

READING
- Read an article about Paris Citybikes

WRITING
- Write a story using linkers
- Write an email about your experience at an airport

BBC CONTENT
- Video podcast: How do you get to work?
- DVD: Airport

transport

▶ Travel in style   p88
▶ Citybikes   p90 
▶ Sorry I'm late   p92 
▶ Airport   p94

9.1 TRAVEL IN STYLE

▶ **GRAMMAR** | articles ▶ **VOCABULARY** | transport collocations ▶ **HOW TO** | talk about ways to travel

VOCABULARY transport collocations

1A Work in pairs. Which types of transport can you see in the pictures? Tick the correct words in the box.

> bus   plane   train   taxi   car   helicopter   bike
> horse   motorbike   foot

B Look at the word webs below and cross out the type of transport which does <u>not</u> go with the verb. Then add a correct type of transport to each word web.

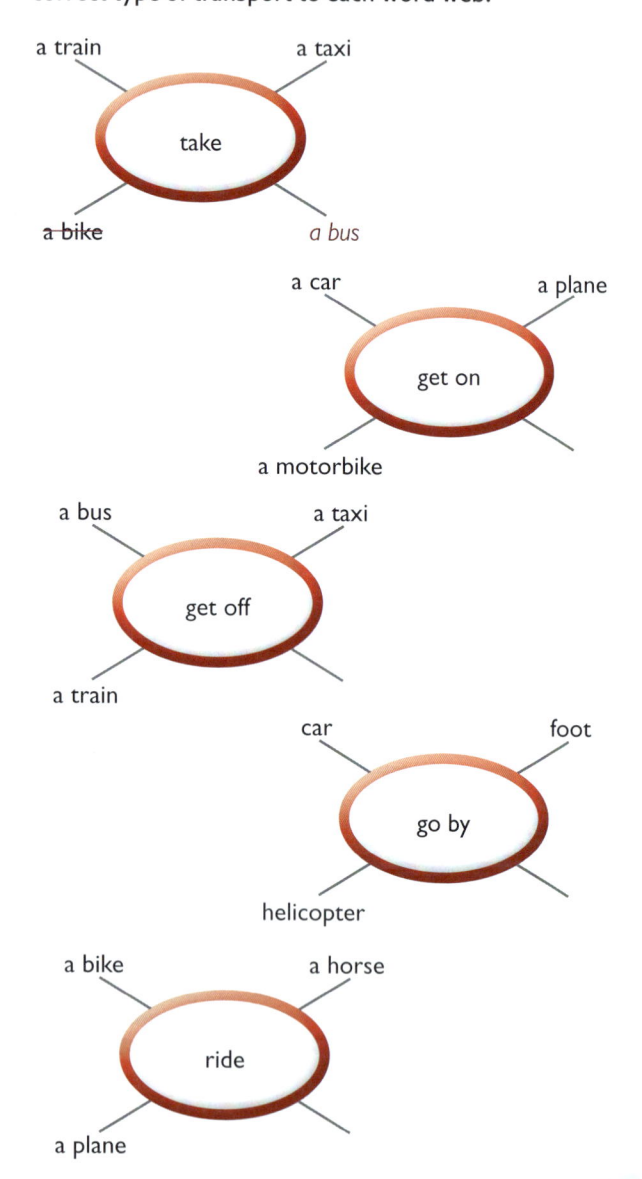

- take: a train, a taxi, ~~a bike~~, *a bus*
- get on: a car, a plane, a motorbike
- get off: a bus, a taxi, a train
- go by: car, foot, helicopter
- ride: a bike, a horse, a plane

⇒ page 159 **PHOTOBANK**

C Work in pairs and take turns. Student A: say a type of transport. Student B: say the verbs that can go with it.
A: *bike*
B: *go by bike, get on a bike, ride a bike …*

D Work in pairs and discuss.
1 How do you usually get to work/school?
2 What's your favourite type of transport? Why?
3 Which types of transport <u>don't</u> you like using? Why not?

LISTENING

2A Match pictures A–C with the titles below.
1 A monorail train from the World Fair in Seattle, USA, 1962
2 The 'Hiller Hornet' – a home helicopter, 1951
3 A plane with a car that comes off, 1948

B ▶ 9.1 Listen to a museum guide and answer the questions.
1 Which transport ideas from above does he talk about?
2 What are his favourite ways of travelling?

C Listen again. What's the problem with each transport idea?

D Work in pairs and discuss. What do you like about each idea? Which one was successful? Why?

88

GRAMMAR articles: a/an, the, no article

3A ▶ 9.2 Listen to an extract from the museum tour and complete the text with *a/an*, *the*, – (no article).

Look at this photo on ¹_____ left. It's from ²_____ World Fair in ³_____ Seattle. That was in 1962. ⁴_____ monorails were ⁵_____ very popular idea in ⁶_____ America at that time. ⁷_____ people wanted to leave their cars at ⁸_____ home and go to ⁹_____ work by ¹⁰_____ public transport.

B Find examples for rules a)–f) from the text above.

Rules:
a) Usually use *a/an* before singular nouns:
   I've got a car. __5__
b) Usually use no article before plural nouns:
   I love cars. _____
c) Usually use no article before cities and countries:
   Madrid is in Spain. _____
d) Use no article in some phrases: *by car, on foot, go to school, at work*. _____
e) Usually use *the* before nouns when there's only one:
   the sun. _____
f) Use *the* in some phrases: *in the morning, on the right, in the city centre*. _____

▶ page 144 **LANGUAGEBANK**

C ▶ 9.3 We usually pronounce *a* /ə/ and *the* /ðə/ in phrases/sentences. Listen and write the four phrases you hear. Then listen again and repeat.

1 _____
2 _____
3 _____
4 _____

D Listen again and check your answers. Then listen and repeat.

PRACTICE

4A Work in pairs and complete the sentences. Use *a/an*, *the* or – (no article).

1 There was __a__ big problem with each one.
2 There are some monorails in ___ world … but not very many.
3 Look at this photo. Is that ___ car under ___ plane?
4 People wanted to fly from ___ Los Angeles to ___ New York.
5 There was ___ engineering problem.
6 We laugh at this now, but ___ people were very serious about it.
7 People wanted to leave ___ home in ___ morning and go to ___ work by ___ private helicopter.
8 ___ helicopters are very difficult to fly.

B Check your answers in audio script 9.1 on page 173.

5A Look at questions 1–5. Choose one of the endings and write a short answer.

1 How do you get *to school / to work / home*?
   By car.
2 What are three things you *like / you don't like / you liked when you were a child*?
3 What's a famous city in *India / China / Africa*?
4 When do you *check your emails / do your homework / relax*?
5 What's the name of *the President of the USA / the student next to you / the teacher*?

B Work in pairs and take turns. Student A: read your answers to the questions above. Student B: close your book and guess the question.

A: *By car.*
B: *How do you get to school?*
A: *No.*
B: *How do you get to work?*
A: *Yes!*

speakout TIP

When you write a noun in your notebook, put it in a short phrase. This shows how to use the word with the articles *a/an*, *the* or no article. For example: *in the city centre, he's a doctor, I like cats*.

SPEAKING

6A Work in pairs. Look at the pictures of transport inventions below. Think of two problems with each invention.

The Horseless Sulky – it's difficult to turn.

B Work in pairs. Student A: look at page 164. Student B: look at page 161.

The Horseless Sulky

The Lightning Bug

9.2 CITYBIKES

▶ GRAMMAR | can/can't, have to/don't have to   ▶ VOCABULARY | adjectives   ▶ HOW TO | talk about transport

SPEAKING

1 Work in pairs and discuss.
1 Is there a lot of traffic where you live?
2 When is the worst time to travel?
3 Do you prefer to travel around your town/city by car, by public transport, by bike or on foot? Why?

VOCABULARY adjectives

2A Circle three adjectives to complete the sentence:

Cycling in the city is …

convenient   safe
fast
easy   inconvenient
comfortable   slow
dangerous   unhealthy
uncomfortable
polluting
difficult
green
healthy

B Match each adjective to its opposite.
fast – slow

C ▶ 9.4 Listen and check.

D Listen again and underline the stressed syllable.

speakout TIP

Look in your dictionary to find the pronunciation of new words. *Longman WordWise Dictionary* shows the word stress with a ' before the main stress, e.g. /ˈdɪfɪkəlt/ *difficult*. Find *dangerous* in your dictionary. How does it show stress?

3 Work in pairs and take turns. Student A: you like bikes. Student B: you like cars. Talk about which is better and why.
A: *Cars are faster.*
B: *Yes, but they're more dangerous!*

Paris by Citybike

With 20,000 bikes and 1,450 pick-up stations, *Vélib* is Paris's free bike scheme. Cyclists can take a bike from one pick-up station and leave it at any other station in the city.

Yves Guesnon, a businessman, loves travelling to work with the wind blowing in his hair. 'There's a station near my flat and another one twenty metres from my office, so it's perfect. I can get to work in ten minutes. It takes thirty minutes by metro.'

'The scheme is good for everyone, Parisians and tourists,' a city official said. 'The only condition* is that you have to be over fourteen and healthy.'

Users have to pay twenty-nine euros a year and give their credit card details. They don't have to pay for the first thirty minutes. After that, they have to pay one euro for the second half-hour.

The scheme is very popular, but there's one problem. Some people ride the bikes downhill in the morning and then take the metro home in the evening. 'I'm just not fit enough,' one man explained. 'I can't cycle up the hill to my flat.' So every evening, city workers have to bring the bikes back uphill in a lorry!

*condition = rule

READING

4A Look at the photos of Vélib, the citybike system in Paris. Write three questions with *how much*, *how many*, *who* or *where*.
1 How much *does it cost to use a bike* ?
2 How many _____ ?
3 Who/Where _____ ?

B Read the article. Did you find the answers to your three questions?

C Are the sentences true (T) or false (F)? Change the false sentences so that they are true.
1 You leave the bicycle in the same place you took it.
2 Yves Guesnon uses a bike because it's fast.
3 Tourists can't use the bikes.
4 Small children can use the bikes.
5 It costs one euro for one hour's cycling.
6 City workers ride the bikes uphill in the evening.

D Work in pairs and discuss. Is the Citybike system a good idea for your town/city? Why/Why not?

9.2

GRAMMAR can/can't, have to/don't have to

5A Underline the correct alternative. Then check your answers in the article.

1 You *can/can't* leave the bike at any station in the city.
2 A thirteen-year-old child *can/can't* use the bikes.
3 Users *have to/don't have to* be healthy.
4 Users *have to/don't have to* pay for the first thirty minutes.

B Match sentences 1–4 above with meanings a)–d).

a) It's necessary.
b) It's <u>not</u> necessary.
c) It's OK.
d) It's <u>not</u> OK.

C Complete the table below.

Tourists	*can*	use	the bikes.
Children	____	____	the bikes.
Users	*have* ____	give	their credit card details.
You	____ have to	____	for the first half hour.

D ▶ 9.5 Listen to sentences 1–4. Circle the correct pronunciation.

1 /kən/   /kæn/
2 /kənt/   /kɑːnt/
3 /hæftuː/ /hæftə/
4 /dəʊnthæftuː/ /dəʊnthæftə/

E Listen again and check. Then listen and repeat.

▶ page 144 **LANGUAGEBANK**

PRACTICE

6A Complete the sentences with *can/can't, have to/don't have to*.

1 You ___*can*___ go by underground, bus or taxi to get to the airport.
2 You _____ drive on the left in the UK.
3 You _____ drive in the town centre, so come by bus.
4 You _____ be sixteen or over to drive in Canada.
5 You _____ use your mobile when you drive. It's dangerous!
6 You _____ wear a seatbelt in your car – the driver <u>and</u> all the passengers.
7 You _____ wear a helmet on bikes but it's safer if you do wear one.
8 You _____ park here for free between 11 and 3. Other times you _____ pay.

B Work in pairs. Which sentences are true for your town/city?

SPEAKING

7A Work in groups. Student A: look at page 162. Student B: look at page 160. Student C: look at page 165. Complete the table below with information about each city's tourist card.

	'I love Amsterdam' card	The Madrid card	The Prague card
Price			
Transport			
Entry to museums etc.			
Other			

B Work in groups. Ask and answer questions to complete the information about the other cities. Which city has got the best tourist card system?

I think Prague has got the best system because it's the cheapest.

C Work in pairs. Talk about travelling in two or three towns/cities you know.

A: *What's the best way to get around your city?*
B: *You can buy a travelcard for buses and underground trains. But sometimes it's faster to walk!*

9.3 SORRY I'M LATE

▶ FUNCTION | apologising   ▶ VOCABULARY | excuses   ▶ LEARN TO | tell a long story

VOCABULARY excuses

1 Work in pairs and discuss. Are you often late for work, school or meetings? Why/Why not?

2A Work in pairs and match 1–5 to a)–e) below.

1 I lost	a) broke down.
2 I missed	b) my alarm clock.
3 My car	c) the train.
4 The traffic	d) my keys.
5 I didn't hear	e) was bad.

B Look at the collocations above and write sentences with the words in the box.

| the bus   my ticket   was terrible   the phone   didn't start |

FUNCTION apologising

3A Look at the cartoon and answer the questions. Who are the people? What's the problem? What do you think happened?

B Read the text and check your answers.

Train delays

Rail services on a busy commuter line into London were late on Tuesday morning when a train hit a cow. The animal got onto the line between two stations and the accident happened at about 7.40a.m. Train services between London and the south were seriously delayed.

4A What did the man say to his boss? Underline the correct alternatives in the sentences below.
1 Look, I'm *really/real* sorry I'm late.
2 I'm *terribly/terrible* sorry I'm late.
3 I feel *terribly/terrible* about it.
4 I'm *afraid/sorry* my train hit a cow!

B ▶ 9.6 Listen and check. Then listen and repeat.

C Look at the responses below. Is the boss happy (✓) or unhappy (✗) about the situation?
1 I don't believe you.
2 It's half past nine!
3 Don't worry about it.
4 That's OK. No problem.
5 Don't let it happen again.

▶ page 144 LANGUAGEBANK

5A Work in pairs. Complete the conversation between a student and a teacher.

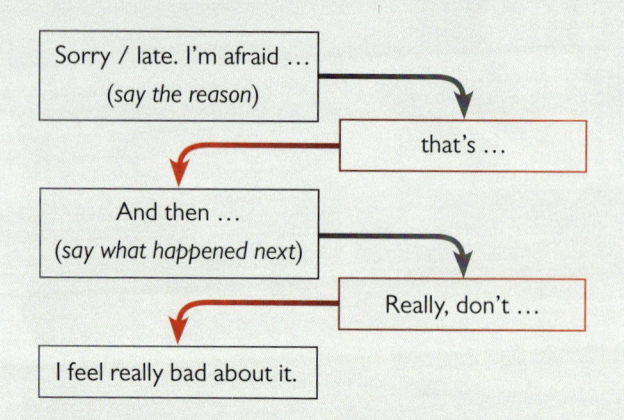

- Sorry / late. I'm afraid … (*say the reason*)
- … that's …
- And then … (*say what happened next*)
- Really, don't …
- I feel really bad about it.

B Work in pairs and have another conversation. Apologise for being late. Choose one of the pairs below.
- a student – a teacher
- a friend – a friend
- a worker – the boss
- a child – a parent

C Listen to other students' conversations. Guess their roles.

LEARN TO tell a long story

6A Look at the online diary extracts below. Why was the man late each day?
Day one: _____
Day two: _____
Day three: _____

Monday
The train left fifteen minutes late. But that wasn't the problem – it simply didn't go very fast. We really knew there was a problem when a man on a bicycle went faster than us! I was an hour late for work. The boss wasn't happy … but *she* doesn't take the train.

Tuesday
OK, I didn't hear my alarm so I woke up late and missed my train. I got the next one, but then the train stopped in the middle of nowhere … for twenty minutes! The guard said there was a signal problem and then the air-conditioning stopped working! Imagine, no air-conditioning in the middle of summer! I was two and a half hours late for work and really hot and sweaty. My boss was *very* unhappy.

Wednesday
Service: 0 points. Originality: 10 points. We stopped again, for no reason, but then there *was* a reason – not the signals, not the engine but a cow on the line! Poor thing, we didn't stop in time. This time, I was two hours late for work and my boss didn't believe me …

B ▶ 9.7 Listen to the man talk to a colleague. Which two days does he talk about?

C Listen again. Which two things are different from the online diary above?

7A Look at the linkers in the box and circle them in the listening extract below.

> ~~first of all~~   and   but   so   finally   because   then   after that

(First of all,) I got up late because I didn't hear my alarm, so I only woke up at 8.30. I ran to the train station – usually I walk – but I missed the train by two minutes! Then I waited for the next train, the 9.15, and everything was fine until we just stopped – just *stopped* – in the middle of nowhere. The guard said that there was a signal problem. After that, the air-conditioning stopped working. It was like an oven – at least a thousand degrees! Finally, after forty minutes, we started moving … very, very slowly.

B Work in pairs and discuss.
1 Which linkers do you use for the <u>beginning</u> and <u>end</u> of the story?
2 Which two linkers mean <u>next</u> in the story?

speakout TIP

Linkers join sentences in a story and help the listener to follow and understand the story better. When you next tell a story, practise using the linkers in Exercise 7A.

SPEAKING

8A Imagine you are late for an important event/situation, e.g. a wedding, a birthday party, an English lesson, a date with a boy/girlfriend, a meeting, a job interview, the doctor's. Make notes about five things that happened. Use the photos to help. Think about:
• When was it?
• Where were you?
• Who were you with?
• What happened?
• What did you do?
• What happened finally?

B Work in pairs and take turns. Student A: tell your story. Student B: show interest and ask follow-up questions.
A: *First of all, my car broke down …*
B: *Oh no! That's terrible! What did you do?*

9 Write your story using your notes above. Remember to use linkers.

9.4 AIRPORT

DVD PREVIEW

1 Work in pairs and discuss. What are the good and bad things about airports and flying?

2A Put the actions below in the correct order.
a) check in 1
b) the plane takes off
c) go through security
d) wait in the departure lounge
e) get on the plane
f) go to the departure gate
g) do some tax-free shopping
h) go through passport control

B ▶ 9.8 Listen and check. Then listen and repeat.

C Work in pairs and take turns. Student A: say one of the actions in Exercise 2A. Student B: say the next action.
A: You check in and then you … ?
B: Go through security and then you … ?

3 Read the programme information and answer the questions.
1 Why are the planes late at Heathrow Airport?
2 What do you think passengers do while they wait?

▶ DVD VIEW

4A Look at the sentences. Use a dictionary to check the meaning of any new words.
1 People are queuing.
2 Some men are making phone calls.
3 A woman is reading a newspaper.
4 Two men are playing chess.
5 People are sleeping everywhere.
6 A man is arguing at a check-in desk.
7 A family is eating pizza.
8 Some boys are skateboarding.

B Watch the DVD. Tick the activities above you see.

C Watch again and listen to four people talk about the situation. Match the person with the activity.

Woman 1 — is trying to get to Amsterdam.
Man 1 — wants to go to Berlin.
Woman 2 — is there with her grandmother and parents.
Man 2 — thinks everything is very calm, very 'Zen'.
can't find a place in a hotel.
is there with her son and daughter.

BBC Airport

Airport is a TV series about day-to-day life at one of the busiest international airports in the world, London Heathrow. In tonight's programme, there's a computer problem in the control tower and flights are delayed for hours. Hundreds of passengers have to wait in the crowded terminal so the programme looks at how people are feeling and how they spend their time waiting.

94

speakout deal with a problem

5A Work in pairs. Read problems 1–8 below and discuss. Which do you think are the three worst problems?

1 You want to check in, but there are no more seats on the plane.
2 Your baggage is too heavy. You have to pay 200 euros, but you don't have enough money.
3 Your flight is delayed by twenty-four hours. You want the airline to pay for a hotel.
4 You get on a long-distance flight. There's a screaming child in the seat next to you.
5 You ordered a vegetarian meal, but when your food arrives, it's chicken curry.
6 You're on the plane and very tired. The person next to you wants to talk … and talk.
7 You arrive and go to get your luggage. You see your bag but another passenger picks it up.
8 You arrive and go to pick up your luggage. It never comes out.

B ▶ 9.9 Listen to the conversation. Which problem does the passenger have?

C Listen again and tick the key phrases you hear.

key phrases

I'm sorry, but there's a (small) problem here.
I understand [the situation], but [it's very important that I get on this plane!]
I see, but …
Let me explain [one more time/again].
You don't understand.
It's your job to [find a hotel/bring me a meal/etc.].
Can I speak to the person in charge, please?

D Work in pairs. Choose a problem from Exercise 5A and role-play the situation. Use the key phrases to help.

writeback an email

6A Complete the email below.

To |

Hi ^{1}_____,
Well, I'm finally here in ^{2}_____, but the journey ^{3}_____! I arrived at the airport yesterday at ^{4}_____ but when I got there ^{5}_____, so I ^{6}_____.
At ^{7}_____ o'clock ^{8}_____ and so I ^{9}_____. Then I had a good idea. I ^{10}_____ and then I ^{11}_____.
After that I ^{12}_____. The plane finally ^{13}_____ at ^{14}_____!
On the plane, I thought everything was fine and then ^{15}_____. That made me really angry, so I ^{16}_____.
What a nightmare! I'm trying to get some sleep now. Speak to you soon, ^{17}_____

B Write an email to a friend. Tell them about a problem you had at an airport/on a plane.

95

9.5 « LOOKBACK

TRANSPORT

1A What are the adjectives? Add the vowels. Then match them with their opposites.

1 ch_e_ _a_ p	easy
2 _nh_ _lthy	fast
3 p_ll_t_ng	safe
4 d_ng_r__s	expensive
5 d_ff_c_lt	green
6 sl_w	healthy

B Work in pairs and take turns. Student A: choose a type of transport. Student B: guess the transport.
B: *Is it fast or slow?*
A: *Fast.*

2 Work in groups. Make a list of the things that:
1 you can ride   *a bike, …*
2 you can drive
3 you can get on and off
4 you do in an airport
5 can go wrong with transport to make you late for work/school

ARTICLES

3A Complete the sentences with *a/an*, *the* or no article (–).
1 Most of us have to use ___ alarm clock to wake up in ___ morning.
2 Two of us didn't have ___ breakfast this morning.
3 Three of us live in ___ town/city centre.
4 All of us think ___ bikes are better than ___ cars for travelling in the town/city centre.
5 One of us has got ___ motorbike.
6 Half of us took ___ taxi home last weekend.
7 None of us go ___ home by ___ train.

B Work in pairs. Write the questions and ask other students. Was the information above true or false?
A: *Do you have to use an alarm clock to wake up in the morning?*
B: *Yes, I do. I have to use two because I can't wake up!*

CAN/CAN'T, HAVE TO/DON'T HAVE TO

4A Complete the rules with the correct alternatives.
In a library …
1 You *can't/don't have to* talk on your mobile phone.
2 You *can't/don't have to* pay for a book before you take it out.
On a plane …
3 You *can/have to* wear a seat belt when the plane takes off.
4 You *can't/don't have to* smoke.
At home …
5 You *can/have to* do anything you want.
6 You *can't/don't have to* pay to eat.

B Choose three of the places below and write two sentences for each place. Use *can/can't*, *have to/don't have to*.

a restaurant    a classroom
_____   _____
_____   _____

a beach    a cinema
_____   _____
_____   _____

a hospital   a friend's house
_____   _____
_____   _____

C Work in pairs and take turns. Student A: read out your sentences. Student B: guess the place.

TELL A LONG STORY

5A Work in pairs and take turns. Student A: close your book. Student B: ask your partner to tell you words to put in the spaces 1–10. Write them in the spaces and then read the story.
B: *Tell me an adjective.*
A: *funny*

Today was a ¹_____ day. *(an adjective)*
First of all, I got up late because I didn't hear ²_____ knock *(a student's name)* on my door. Finally, ³_____ *(a celebrity's name)* phoned me on my mobile and woke me up. I went to the ⁴_____, *(a room in a house)* put on my ⁵_____ and *(a piece of clothing)* ⁶_____ and ran out of the *(another piece of clothing)* door. Then my ⁷_____ *(a type of transport)* didn't start, so I took a ⁸_____. But I got on the *(another type of transport)* wrong one and it went all the way to ⁹_____. I phoned my *(the name of a city)* boss from there, but he didn't believe my story, so I lost my job. That's OK – I never liked working as a ¹⁰_____. *(a job)*

B Work in groups. Read your story to the other students. Which is the funniest?

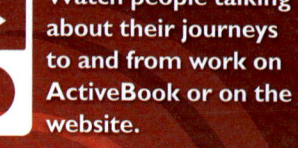

BBC VIDEO PODCAST
Watch people talking about their journeys to and from work on ActiveBook or on the website.

Authentic BBC interviews
www.pearsonELT.com/speakout

UNIT 10

SPEAKING
- Talk about your future plans/wishes
- Make predictions about situations
- Make suggestions and learn to say *no* politely

LISTENING
- Listen to a radio interview with lottery winners
- Watch an extract from a documentary about the wettest place in Europe

READING
- Read an extract from an instruction book about survival
- Read an article with tips on things to do with your friends

WRITING
- Improve your use of linkers and write a short story
- Write a message board notice about your country

BBC CONTENT
- Video podcast: What are your plans for the future?
- DVD: Wild Weather

the future

▶ Life's a lottery   p98
▶ Survive!   p100 
▶ Let's do something   p102 
▶ Wild Weather   p104

10.1 LIFE'S A LOTTERY

▶ **GRAMMAR** | be going to; would like to   ▶ **VOCABULARY** | plans   ▶ **HOW TO** | talk about future plans/wishes

LISTENING

1A Look at the photo below and read the newspaper extract. What's surprising about the story?

Big Mac couple's lotto win

A couple who work together at McDonald's say they have no plans to stop working after winning £1.3 million on the lottery.

Elaine Gibbs, twenty-eight, and Aled Bevan, twenty-three, from Cardiff, met four years ago at work and learnt about their big win last Thursday. 'We're going to stay here. It's an enjoyable job and they treat us well,' said Aled.

B Work in pairs and discuss. How do you think the couple plan to spend their money?

C ▶ 10.1 Listen to a radio interview and check your ideas. Tick the couple's plans.
- move house
- stop work
- get married
- buy a car
- travel around the world
- have a holiday
- buy some clothes
- start a family

D Discuss. What do you think of Elaine and Aled's plans?

GRAMMAR be going to; would like to

2A Look at the sentences. Then underline the correct alternative to complete the rules below.
1 We're going to get married.
2 I'd like to learn to drive.

Rules:
1 Use *be going to* when you *have/don't have* a definite plan.
2 Use *would like to* when you want to do something or when you *have/don't have* a definite plan.

B Look at audio script 10.1 on page 174 and complete the table with the correct forms of *be going to* and *would like to*.

I'____		buy	some new clothes.
We'___	going ____	look for	a house.
He ___		buy	a car.

| I'____ | like ____ | learn to drive. |
| We'___ | | move. |

| What | ____ you | going ____ | do? |
| | | like ____ | |

C ▶ 10.2 Listen and check your answers.

D Circle the correct pronunciation of *going to* and *would*. Then listen again and repeat.
1 going /tuː/   going /tə/
2 /wʊd/   /wʊld/

▶ page 146 **LANGUAGEBANK**

PRACTICE

3A Write the sentences in full. Use *be going to* or *would like to*.
1 I / like / move into a big flat / city centre.
   I'd like to move into a big flat in the city centre.
2 I / like / drive / sports car.
3 I / go / have / holiday / in the Caribbean.
4 I / not / go / buy / any presents / my family and friends.
5 I / like / move / to another country.
6 I / go / buy / a boat.
7 I / like / start / my own business.
8 I / not / go / keep / all the money for myself.

B Imagine you won the lottery yesterday. What are your plans? Change the sentences so that they are true for you.

C Work in pairs and compare your answers.

10.1

VOCABULARY plans

4A Complete the collocations with verbs from the box.

| have | buy | go for | get | move |
| start | do | go | learn | stay |

1. _have_ a holiday, a barbecue, a party
2. _____ married, a new suit, a job
3. _____ nothing, a course, a lot of exercise
4. _____ shopping, clubbing, jogging
5. _____ in, with friends, at a hotel
6. _____ Spanish, to drive, to swim
7. _____ a walk, a bike ride, a drink
8. _____ a new job, a family, a new business
9. _____ to another country, house, into a flat
10. _____ a present for a friend, a boat, some jeans

B Work in pairs. Student A: say the verb. Student B: say the phrases that go with the verb.

C Look at the collocations in Exercise 4A again. Add a new phrase to each verb.

speakout TIP

When you study, make lists of words that go together. Cover all the verbs, and try to remember them. Then cover the other words and try to remember the full phrases.

SPEAKING

5A What are you going to do/would you like to do in the future? Complete the table using your own ideas or the photos to help.

	You	Student 1	Student 2
this weekend	shopping	basketball	
next week			
next year			

B Work in groups. Ask and answer questions about your plans/wishes for the future. Make notes in the table.

A: Rafael, what are you going to do this weekend?
B: Well, I'm going to watch a basketball match …

C Tell the class about someone in your group. Can they guess who it is?

A: This weekend, he's going to watch a basketball match and next month he's going to do a course in sports education. Next year he'd like to go to the USA.
C: Is it Rafael?

10.2 SURVIVE!

▶ **GRAMMAR** | will, might, won't ▶ **VOCABULARY** | phrases with get ▶ **HOW TO** | make predictions

VOCABULARY phrases with get

1A Work in pairs. Look at the four photos and discuss.
1 Where are the people?
2 Which situation is the most dangerous? Why?

B Look at sentences 1–5 below and discuss. Which ones can happen at sea (S) and which can happen in the desert (D)? Which can happen in both (SD)?
1 You don't have enough water so you get thirsty. S D
2 Sharks are swimming around.
3 There are snakes and insects.
4 You fall off your raft.
5 You're hot and you sweat a lot.

C Complete the sentences to make phrases with *get* and the words in the box below.

~~hot~~ wet hungry thirsty bored sunburnt lost tired

1 When I exercise in the gym I get very ___hot___.
2 I didn't drink anything all day so I got _____.
3 I stayed up too late and I got really _____.
4 I forgot my umbrella yesterday and I got _____.
5 I didn't eat breakfast so I'm getting _____.
6 I didn't have a map so I got _____.
7 I stayed out in the sun and I got _____.
8 This exercise isn't very interesting! I'm getting _____.

speakout TIP

The verb *get* has more than twenty meanings in English! It can mean 'become' (*get hungry*), 'arrive' (*get home*), 'obtain' (*get a job*), 'buy' (*get a new car*) and is in many phrases: *get up, get on a plane, get dressed*. When you hear or see the word *get*, think about which meaning it has.

Which meaning does *get* have in these phrases: *get to the airport, get a new haircut, get better, get some chocolate*?

READING

2A Read the survival tips below. Cross out the incorrect alternatives.

B Work in pairs and compare your ideas.

C Work in pairs. Student A: read the text on page 165. Student B: read the text on page 162. Were your ideas correct? Tell your partner.

SURVIVE!

Imagine your boat sinks and you are alone on a raft in the middle of the sea. Or your car breaks down in the desert and you're far away from the nearest town. Could you survive? Here are some tips to help!

At sea:
1 Do/~~Don't~~ sit in the bottom of the raft.
2 Do/Don't sleep a lot.
3 Do/Don't drink sea water.
4 Do/Don't put rubbish in the water.
5 Do/Don't move around too much on the raft.

In the desert:
6 Do/Don't sleep on the ground.
7 Do/Don't take off your shirt.
8 Do/Don't travel in the day.
9 Do/Don't wear shoes.
10 Do/Don't wear gloves.

100

10.2

GRAMMAR will, might, won't

3A Look at the sentences and complete the rules.

1 You'll get wet.
2 You won't get sunburnt.
3 You might sweat too much.

> Rules:
> 1 Which sentence do we use when we think something in the future:
> a) is certain to happen? ____
> b) is possible? ____
> c) is certain not to happen? ____
>
> 2 What are the full forms of 'll and won't?
> ____ ____

B ▶10.3 Listen to the sentences 1–3 above. Then listen and repeat.

C ▶10.4 Listen and underline the sentence you hear.

1 You'll get too hot. / You get too hot.
2 We'll fall into the water. / We fall into the water.
3 They'll sweat too much. / They sweat too much.
4 I'll get hungry. / I get hungry.

➡ page 146 **LANGUAGEBANK**

PRACTICE

4A What can you remember? Complete the sentences below with 'll, won't or might.

1 Don't sit in the bottom of the raft. You 'll get wet.
2 Don't drink sea water. You _____ get thirstier after you drink it.
3 Don't put rubbish in the water. Sharks _____ come because for them it's food.
4 Don't move around on the raft. You _____ fall into the water.
5 Don't sleep on the sand. You _____ get too warm.
6 Always use sun cream. You _____ get sunburnt with it on.
7 Travel at night. You _____ sweat so much.
8 Always wear shoes. You _____ step on a snake, so it's safer to have them on.

B Read the texts on pages 162 and 165 again to check your answers.

SPEAKING

5A Work in pairs. Look at the cartoon below and discuss.
1 What happened to the plane? Why did it crash?
2 How are the people from the plane feeling?
3 What problems might they have?

B Work in pairs. Choose three objects from the box below that might help the people from the plane. Give reasons for your choice.

| ~~chocolate~~ | a radio | a box of matches | a mobile phone |
| sun cream | a knife | a bottle of water | playing cards |

I think chocolate is useful because they might get hungry.

C Think of three other objects that might be useful. Use your dictionary if you don't know the word.

D Work with another pair and compare your objects. Decide which five objects will help the people in the cartoon.

WRITING too, also, as well

6A Look at the sentences. What is the position of *too*, *also* and *as well* in the sentences?

1 Your body loses a lot of water when you sweat, so relax and try to sleep a lot, **too**.
2 Fish is your most important food and it's **also** easy to catch.
3 Most fish are safe to eat and you can drink water from fish eyes **as well**.

B Put *too*, *also* and *as well* into the story.

> We walked all morning and we walked for five hours in the afternoon, *too*. We had a short break for lunch. We stopped for a rest in the afternoon. In the evening, Sam taught us how to kill a snake and how to cook it. I didn't like the smell, but I ate some and Sam ate some.

C Finish the story with your own ideas. Use *too*, *also* and *as well*.

10.3 LET'S DO SOMETHING

▶ **FUNCTION** | making suggestions   ▶ **VOCABULARY** | adjectives   ▶ **LEARN TO** | respond to suggestions

VOCABULARY | adjectives

1A Look at the adjectives in the box. Do they all mean *OK* or *very good*?

> ~~brilliant~~ wonderful amazing fantastic
> great awesome excellent cool lovely

B How many syllables are in each adjective? Write the adjectives in the correct column in the table.

O	Oo	Ooo	oOo
		brilliant	

C ▶ 10.5 Listen and check. Then listen and repeat.

speakout TIP

Some adjectives are very informal, e.g. *cool* and *fantastic*. The *Longman WordWise Dictionary* shows this as:

> **cool** *adjective spoken informal*

Use these words with friends, and not in formal situations, e.g. a job interview.

READING

2A Work in pairs and complete the sentences.

1 When I meet my friends, we usually do
 a) the same old things.
 b) something different each time.
2 We like doing things
 a) indoors.
 b) outdoors.
3 At weekends, we meet
 a) for just a few hours.
 b) for the whole weekend.
4 We need new ideas for things to do.
 a) true
 b) false

B Read the article about how to spend time with friends. Tick five activities that you think are good ideas.

C Work in pairs and compare your ideas.

We're all super-busy these days so it's important that friends make the most of their time together. If you're stuck for ideas, we've got some suggestions …

① Get some exercise! Go swimming or play tennis or go for a walk in the park.

② Enjoy a 'movie marathon'. Rent some DVDs, get lots of snacks and spend the day being film critics.

③ Paint a room in your flat. Invite your friends to help you.

④ Go to a club or a concert or a music festival.

⑤ Go to the zoo. Show each other your favourite three animals.

⑥ Go to the theatre. Read the play together first.

⑦ Do some internet shopping. Buy something for each other.

⑧ Go for a bike ride and have a picnic lunch.

⑨ Play a card game. First, look in a book of card games (or on the internet) for a new game.

⑩ Cook something, e.g. a cake, or dinner. Try a new recipe together. Invite some friends and have a food tasting.

⑪ Play a computer game together or watch a fitness DVD and practise aerobics or yoga.

⑫ Go to an art gallery. Find a painting you like and talk about why you like it.

10.3

FUNCTION making suggestions

3 ▶ 10.6 Listen to two conversations. Which activities from the article do the friends decide to do?

4A Look at the sentences. Underline four phrases for making suggestions.
1 How about going to an art gallery?
2 What about having a 'movie marathon'?
3 Let's cook something.
4 Why don't we invite Augusto and Carla for lunch?

B ▶ 10.7 Complete the suggestions below. Then listen and check.
1 How _____ _____ to the zoo?
2 What _____ _____ something more relaxing?
3 Why _____ _____ _____ some internet shopping?
4 _____ _____ to the theatre.

C Listen to the sentences again. Does the speaker sound positive? Does his/her voice start high or low?

D Listen again and repeat.

5A Complete the suggestions.
1 How about _____ swimming?
2 What about _____ a new recipe?
3 Why don't we _____ a picnic lunch?
4 Let's _____ to the cinema.

B Work in pairs and take turns. Student A: make a suggestion. Student B: say *OK* if your partner sounds positive or *no thanks* if he/she doesn't.

LEARN TO respond to suggestions

6A ▶ 10.8 Listen to the conversations again. Match the suggestions 1–5 with the responses a)–e) below.
1 visiting an art gallery
2 cooking
3 inviting friends for lunch
4 a bike ride
5 going to see a play

a) Ah, fantastic!
b) I don't really feel like doing that.
c) Sounds lovely.
d) That sounds a bit tiring.
e) Brilliant!

B Look at the phrases a)–e) above and decide if they are positive (+) or negative (-).

▶ page 146 LANGUAGEBANK

7 Work in pairs and take turns. Student A: choose three weekend activities and make suggestions. Student B: respond to the suggestions. When you respond negatively, give a reason.
A: *Why don't we go for a walk in the park?*
B: *Mmm. I don't really feel like doing that. It's too cold!*

SPEAKING

8A Complete the table with three activities you would like to do. Write a place and a time next to each activity.

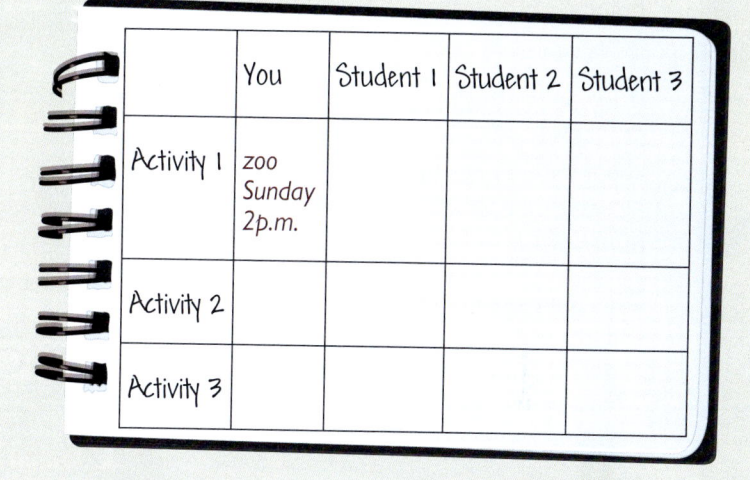

	You	Student 1	Student 2	Student 3
Activity 1	zoo Sunday 2p.m.			
Activity 2				
Activity 3				

B Work in pairs and take turns. Student A: phone your partner and suggest an activity for tomorrow. Student B: respond and suggest another activity. Use the flowchart to help you role-play the conversation. Add your partner's information to the table above.

- Phone your friend.
- Answer the phone. Ask how he/she is.
- Suggest an activity.
- You don't want to do this. Why not? Suggest another activity.
- Agree. Suggest a time to meet.
- Agree.
- Confirm plans and say goodbye.
- Finish the call.

C Phone two more students and suggest activities. Add their information to the table above.

D Work in groups. Tell the other students about your plans.
I'm going to play tennis with Alfonso and then I'm going to …

10.4 WILD WEATHER

DVD PREVIEW

1A Match phrases 1–6 with pictures A–F.
1 It's stormy.
2 It's windy.
3 It's snowing.
4 It's sunny.
5 It's cloudy.
6 It's raining.

B Work in pairs and take turns. Student A: point to a photo and ask about the weather. Student B: reply.
A: *What's the weather like?*
B: *It's raining.*

2A Complete the weather forecast with the words from the box.

| ~~hot~~ | warm | cool | cold | wet | dry |

In Dublin today, it'll be ¹ _hot_ and sunny with temperatures up to twenty-five degrees Celsius. Tomorrow will be cloudy but quite ² _____, with a high of twenty. Things will change on Friday night: it'll be a ³ _____ night with rain from midnight to early next morning. The temperature will fall to ten so it'll feel quite ⁴ _____, but the rain will stop so we'll have a ⁵ _____ day all Saturday. Sunday will be windy and cloudy ... and very ⁶ _____, so make sure you wear your winter coat!

B ▶ 10.9 Listen and check your answers.

▶ DVD VIEW

3A Read the programme information. Which places do you think the presenter visits for each of the four programmes?

BBC Wild Weather

In *Wild Weather* the presenter, Donal MacIntyre, looks for the wildest weather in the world. He travels to different places and finds answers to the questions: Where does the weather come from? How does it work? There are four programmes: *Hot*, *Wet*, *Wind* and *Cold*. Follow his journey as he finds and experiences dramatic moments of amazing weather.

B Watch the DVD and answer the questions.
1 Which programme is it: *Hot*, *Wet*, *Wind* or *Cold*?
2 The presenter talks to two people. Where do they work?

C Watch the DVD again. Underline the correct alternative.
1 In Bergen it rains *one / two / three* out of three days.
2 There are *two / three / four* types of umbrellas.
3 They sell Bergen rain to tourists in *bottles / cups / cans*.
4 In one year, *105 / 125 / 225* tonnes of rain fall on a family house.
5 The longest period of rain in Bergen was in *1990 / 1992 / 1995*.
6 It rained for *73 / 83 / 93* days.

speakout the weather

4A Make sentences with the prompts below.
1 What / favourite / kind / weather? Why?
2 What / kind / weather / hate? Why?
3 What / be / weather / like on your last holiday?
4 What / favourite / season? Why?
5 What / like / do in (spring/summer/autumn/ winter)?
6 What / best / season / visit your country or city? Why?

B ▶ 10.10 Listen to people answer the questions above. Number the questions in the order you hear the answers.

C Look at the key phrases below. Listen again and tick the ones you hear.

keyphrases
I love/hate [stormy] weather.
I really [don't like/like/love/hate] it when it [rains/'s hot].
The best time to visit [country/city/town] is [month/season] because …
That's when …
It's the perfect time to …
It [rained/was sunny] every day, [but/and] we had a [great/awful] time.

5A Work in pairs. Interview each other using the questions in Exercise 4A. Make notes on your partner's answers.

B Work in groups and compare your answers. What did you find out?

C Tell the rest of the class. How many people talked about the same place?

writeback reply on a message board

6A Read the message from a travel website. Write the name of your town/city/country.

Message Board — 02-Feb-09 12.26 pm
I want to visit _____ for two weeks.
What's the best time of year to come?
What about clothes?
Posted by: **Lars, Sweden**

Reply   < Previous Message | Next Message >

B Write a reply. Use the phrases in brackets to help.

Message Board — 03-Feb-09 11.55 pm
Hi Lars, I'm from _____ and I live
               (country)
in _____. The best time to visit is _____
   (town/city)   (month/season)
because _____ and also you can _____.
        (weather)   (activity)
You _____, too. Bring _____ and
    (give another idea)   (clothes)
_____ as well, or you'll be too _____.
(clothes)   (adjective)

Posted by:

Reply   < Previous Message | Next Message >

105

10.5 ◀◀ LOOKBACK

VERB PHRASES

1A Complete the questions with the correct verbs.
1 On your next holiday, do you want to:
  • st_ay_ at home or g___ abroad?
  • st___ in a hotel or with friends?
2 You have a free Saturday. Do you want to:
  • g___ shopping or g___ ___ a walk?
  • in the evening, st___ in and d___ nothing, or h___ a party and then g___ clubbing?
3 Time for some big changes. Do you want to:
  • g___ married or go travelling?
  • m___ to an English-speaking country or stay in your country?

B Work in pairs and take turns. Ask and answer the questions.

GOING TO; WOULD LIKE TO

2A Look at the list. Write sentences using *be going to* and *would like to*.
1 I'd like to have dinner with Gemma, but I can't – she's busy.
2 I'm going to Oxford. I've got my bus ticket.

```
Weekend wish list
1 dinner with Gemma – she's busy!
2 go to Oxford (bought bus ticket) ✓
3 go to the U2 concert – no tickets!
4 meet Andy for drink (he said OK) ✓
5 Watch 'Gone with the Wind' on DVD (borrowed it from Cindy) ✓
6 sleep a lot – no time!
```

B Make your own 'Weekend wish list'. Then look at the list and tick the things that are possible. Write reasons for the things that aren't possible.

C Work in pairs and take turns. Tell your partner about your plans for the weekend.

PREDICTIONS

3A You and some friends are going to spend the weekend in a hotel on a high mountain. Read the information.

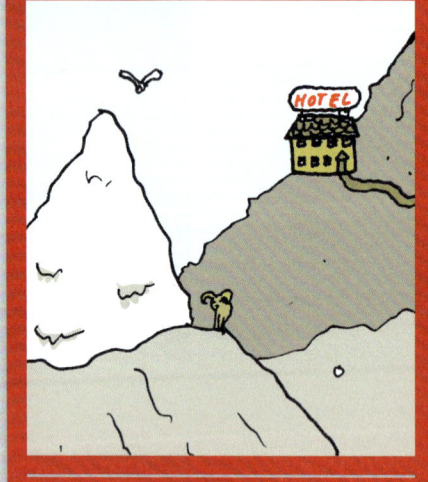

- It's a beautiful, quiet place.
- It always rains at this time of year.
- Walking in the mountains is beautiful, but very dangerous.
- There are ten beds.
- The hotel has a very good kitchen. Their restaurant can serve meals for twenty-five people maximum.
- Not all the students like 'mountain life'!

B Complete the sentences with *might*, *might not*, *'ll* or *won't*.
1 It _____ rain.
2 We _____ get bored.
3 Someone _____ get hurt.
4 Some people _____ like it. I think I _____ like it.
5 There _____ be enough beds for all of us.
6 The food _____ be very good.
7 There _____ be enough food.
8 It _____ be very peaceful.

C Work in pairs and compare your answers.

D Discuss. Would you like to go on this kind of weekend break? Why/Why not?

MAKING SUGGESTIONS

4A Correct the sentences.
1 Why we don't have a party in the school garden?
2 Let's to have 90s music.
3 What about start at 7 o'clock?
4 That a great idea!
5 Sound good.
6 That might be problem.

B Work in groups. Make suggestions for a class party/celebration. Think about the place, food, music, etc. Use the phrases above to help.

C Tell the other groups about your party/celebration. Which one would you like to go to?
We're going to have a barbecue in the park. We're going to bring beef and …

THE WEATHER

5A Rearrange the letters to complete the sentences.
1 When it's _sunny_ (nusny) I often go to the beach.
2 When it _____ (irsan) I usually go running.
3 When it's _____ (dulcoy) I always feel depressed.
4 When it _____ (swons) I never go out.
5 When it's _____ (dinyw) I like going for a walk.
6 When it's _____ (roymts) I feel quite nervous.

B Write four sentences about you and the weather. Begin each sentence with: *When it … I …*

C Work in pairs and compare your ideas.

BBC VIDEO PODCAST
Watch people talking about their ambitions for the future on ActiveBook or on the website.

Authentic BBC interviews
www.pearsonELT.com/speakout

UNIT 11

SPEAKING
- Talk about what to do when you don't feel well
- Discuss cures for the common cold
- Give advice and offer help
- Ask for help in a pharmacy

LISTENING
- Listen to a radio programme about colds and flu
- Watch an extract from a sitcom about a shopping experience

READING
- Read and do a quiz about how fit you are
- Read about a social experiment

WRITING
- Make your stories more interesting
- Write some advice for a health message board

BBC CONTENT
- Video podcast: Do you have a healthy lifestyle?
- DVD: The Two Ronnies

health

▶ My head hurts   p108
▶ Never felt better   p110 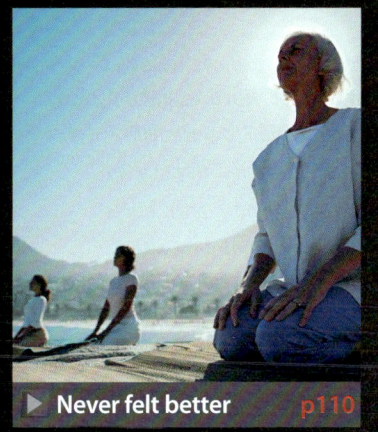
▶ Help!   p112 
▶ The Optician   p114

11.1 MY HEAD HURTS

▶ **GRAMMAR** | should/shouldn't   ▶ **VOCABULARY** | the body; health   ▶ **HOW TO** | give advice

VOCABULARY   the body

1A Look at photos A–E. How many parts of the body can you see and name?

➡ page 158 **PHOTOBANK**

B ▶ 11.1 How do you pronounce: *throat, stomach, mouth, shoulder, thumb, toes*? Listen and repeat.

C Work in pairs and take turns. Student A: say a part of the body. Student B: point to it in photos A–E.

LISTENING

2A Work in pairs and discuss.
1 What do you do when you've got a cold? Do you go to work/school, stay at home and rest or go to the doctor/take medicine?
2 When was the last time you were ill? What was the problem? What did you do about it?

B Look at the health problems in the box. Which can you see in photos A–E?

| a runny nose   his/her legs hurt   a sore throat   a cough   a headache |
| a temperature (= a high temperature)   his/her arms hurt   stomach ache |

C Look at the problems above and write the problems in the correct place in the table.

Cold	Flu	Both
a runny nose		

D ▶ 11.2 Listen to a radio programme and check your answers.

E Listen again. Underline the correct alternatives you hear.
1 Flu starts *suddenly/slowly*. You *can/can't* work.
2 A cold starts *suddenly/slowly*. You *can/can't* work.

speakout TIP

Many words in English have a very different pronunciation from their spelling. You can underline problem letters and write the sound underneath, e.g. *cou̲gh ac̲he*
                              /f/   /k/
In your notebook, do the same for *thumb* and *stomach*.

3A Look at the sentences below. Cross out the incorrect alternative. Then add one more word to each group.
1 I've got an *earache* / *a backache* / ~~a throatache~~   a stomach ache
2 I've got a sore *cough* / *throat* / *eye*.
3 My *runny nose* / *head* / *back* hurts.
4 I feel *tired* / *temperature* / *better*.

B Work in pairs and take turns. Student A: choose a problem and mime it. Student B: guess what's wrong.

11.1

cold cures around the world

This month, we asked readers from around the world, 'What's the best thing to do when you've got a cold?' Here are some of their answers:

Jean from France: 'You should drink lots of water and get lots of sleep. Nothing else helps.'

Sun-Do from Korea: 'We eat kimchi – a dish made from cabbage. You should try it. The cabbage is full of vitamin C and the spices in kimchi also help.'

Sam from South Africa: 'No medicine – you shouldn't take antibiotics for a cold – that's crazy. Your body can fight the cold virus.'

Ana-Maria from Spain: 'You should eat fruit, lots of it, especially things like oranges.'

Mary from Scotland: 'You should drink herbal tea with honey and lemon in it and you should relax. You shouldn't go to work.'

Doug from the USA: 'That's easy. You should have a bowl of my grandmother's chicken soup. That's the perfect cure. I don't care what anybody says – there's nothing better.'

READING

4A Read the article about cold cures. Which ideas in the text are in the pictures?

B Read the article again. Which person do you agree with most? What do people do in your country when they've got a cold?

C Work in pairs and compare your ideas.

GRAMMAR should/shouldn't

5A Look at the sentences and underline the correct alternative to complete the rules.
1 You should get lots of sleep.
2 You shouldn't go to work.

> Rules:
> 1 Use *should* for something that is *necessary/a good idea*.
> 2 Use *shouldn't* for something that is *unnecessary/ a bad idea*.

B Complete the table. Use the article to help.

You	should	_____	lots of water.
		_____	fruit.
	_____	take	antibiotics.

C ▶ 11.3 Listen and check. Then listen and repeat.

▶ page 148 LANGUAGEBANK

PRACTICE

6A Look at problems 1–4 and advice a)–h). For each problem, write advice with *should/shouldn't*.
1 I'm tired.
  You should get more sleep.
  You shouldn't go to bed so late.
2 I'm hungry.
3 It's raining and I have to go.
4 I feel ill.

a) be here in the lesson
b) eat something
c) ~~get more sleep~~
d) go home
e) go out now
f) ~~go to bed so late~~
g) take an umbrella
h) miss breakfast

B Work in pairs and take turns. Cover the advice a)–h) above. Student A: say one of the problems. Student B: give advice with *should/shouldn't*.

SPEAKING

7A Work in groups. What are your 'five tips for good health'? Make a list. Think about the things in the box.

> sleep   food   exercise   drink   smoking   other

You should go to bed early.

B Work with another group. Compare your lists and decide on the top five tips.

109

11.2 NEVER FELT BETTER

▶ **GRAMMAR** | adverbs of manner ▶ **VOCABULARY** | common verbs ▶ **HOW TO** | talk about how you do things

Healthy body, healthy mind

1 Can you __swim__ 100 metres in a pool?
   a) Yes, easily.   b) Yes, but only slowly.   c) No chance!
2 Can you _____ 400 metres without stopping?
   a) Yes, easily.   b) Yes, I can, but not very fast.   c) No, I can't.
3 Can you _____ up four sets of stairs?
   a) Yes, no problem.   b) Yes, but it's really hard!   c) I always take the lift.
4 Can you _____ a car number from fifty metres?
   a) Yes, clearly.   b) Yes, just.   c) No, I have to wear glasses.
5 Can you _____ and _____ someone talking to you in a noisy room?
   a) Yes, easily.   b) Yes, but not very well.   c) If they speak _very_ loudly.
6 Can you _____ on something (e.g. your homework) for thirty minutes without a break?
   a) Yes, I can.   b) Yes, but not easily.   c) No, I can't.
7 Do you _____ everything you ate the day before yesterday?
   a) Yes, perfectly.   b) Yes, but not easily.   c) No, not really.
8 Do you often _____ your bank PIN number or a computer password?
   a) No, never.   b) Not often, but sometimes.   c) All the time!

KEY
a = 3 points   b = 2 points   c = 1 point

16–24 points:
Well done! You are very fit and healthy in mind and body. You do regular exercise, you eat well and get enough sleep, so your mind and memory are clear. Don't stop! And tell your friends how they can do things to feel better.

9–15 points:
You are quite fit and healthy in mind and body. Do you want to be fitter? Then maybe you should do more exercise. Thirty minutes three times a week keeps your mind and body young. Eat more fruit and vegetables and have oily fish once a week. Join a brain gym or look for one on the internet.

1–8 points:
Maybe you should do some exercise for your body and mind. Start small! You don't have to go to the gym. Walk more. You can get off the bus or tram one stop before work/school and walk the rest of the way. Try to eat healthily, too and get enough sleep – this will help your mind as well as your body.

VOCABULARY common verbs

1A Complete the quiz with the verbs in the box.

| ~~swim~~ run remember forget hear |
| understand read climb concentrate |

B Work in pairs. Ask and answer the questions. Add up your partner's score and read the results in the key.

C Work in pairs and take turns. Student A: say a verb from Exercise 1A. Student B: say the verb phrase. Then think of other possible nouns.
A: _forget_
B: _forget your PIN number_
A: _forget people's names_
B: _forget ..._

▶ page 127 **IRREGULAR VERBS**

GRAMMAR adverbs of manner

2A Look at the sentences and the rule. Underline the correct alternatives to complete them.
1 Can you swim 100 metres? Yes, but only _slow/slowly_.
2 Can you run 400 metres? Yes, _easy/easily_.

Rule: Use adverbs of manner to say _how/when_ we do something.

B Complete the table. Use the quiz and key to help.

Adjective	Adverb
easy	easily
slow	
clear	
fast	
loud	
perfect	
good	
healthy	

▶ page 148 **LANGUAGE BANK**

11.2

PRACTICE

3A Complete the sentences and make them true for you. Use the correct form of one of the words in brackets.
1 It's _easy_ for me to remember new words in English. (*easy/hard*)
2 I like it when the teacher speaks English _____. (*quick/slow*)
3 I think I speak English _____. (*good/bad*)
4 I've got a _____ memory. (*good/bad*)
5 When I have lunch or dinner, I usually eat _____. (*fast/slow*)
6 I think I usually eat _____. (*healthy/unhealthy*)
7 I can't concentrate when it's _____. (*quiet/noisy*)
8 I'm usually quite _____. (*lazy/energetic*)

B Work in pairs and compare your sentences.

WRITING adverbs in stories

4A Look at pictures A–D. What do you think happened? Put them in the correct order. Use the prompts 1–4 to help.

1 Saturday / Ken / get up / have breakfast / got on / bike
2 he / ride / down the road / not / look / ahead / cat / run / in front / him
3 he / fall off / bike / broke / arm  
4 evening / he / sit / at home / with / broken arm

B Use the prompts to write the story. Remember to use linkers.
1 On Saturday, Ken got up, had breakfast and …

C Change the adjectives in the box below into adverbs. Then use three to add to your story in Exercise 4A.

| quick careful careless dangerous early fast |
| late sad slow |

On Saturday, Ken got up late, had breakfast quickly …

D Write the next part of the story with three more adverbs. Start with '*Six weeks later, on Saturday morning, Ken got up …*'

E Work in pairs and exchange your stories.

SPEAKING

5A Work in pairs and discuss. Look at two pages from Julie's diary. Did she have a healthy weekend? Why/Why not?

Saturday 20
- woke up late – 10 hours sleep, felt better (difficult week at work!)
- big breakfast – not very healthy!
- watched DVDs all afternoon – popcorn and coke for lunch …
- pizza for dinner with friends – cake for dessert VERY late night – not very good!

Sunday 21
- fruit, cereal and coffee for breakfast
- went swimming
- lunch – big salad and sandwich
- met brother in city centre – more coffee!
- new recipe for dinner – very healthy
- early night – work tomorrow!

B In your notebook, write a 'health diary' for last weekend. Make notes about:
- food and drink
- exercise
- sleep
- relaxing

C Work in groups and compare your answers. Who had the healthiest weekend? What three things can you do differently next weekend?
Last weekend I didn't have a healthy weekend because …

111

11.3 HELP!

▶ GRAMMAR | offering to help ▶ VOCABULARY | problems ▶ LEARN TO | thank someone

VOCABULARY problems

1A Look at the photos above and discuss the questions.
1 What are the problems?
2 In each situation, what can you say to offer to help?

B Work in pairs. Read the questions below and discuss.
1 Do people usually help when someone **can't lift** heavy luggage?
2 Do people usually help when an older person is **standing** on a train or bus?
3 Do people usually help when someone **drops** some files or papers?
4 Do people usually help when someone is **pushing** a car?
5 Do people usually help when someone suddenly **falls** to the ground?
6 Do people usually help when someone **cuts** his/her hand?

READING

2A Read the article quickly. Number pictures A–C in the correct order.

B Read the article more carefully. In which situation does the person get help?

When someone sees a person in trouble, do they stop and help, or just 'walk on by'?
BBC reporter Michael Coombes wanted to find out. With his assistant, Kitty Dann, he chose three situations to test how quickly people help or if they help.

In the first situation, Kitty dropped some papers. After a few seconds, Brian McCann came and helped her. He said 'I saw her drop everything and I wanted to help her. Most people don't help these days.'

In the next situation, Kitty tried to move a heavy sign on the street outside a shop. She pushed and pulled it, but no one helped her.

In the final situation, Michael fell to the ground in the street. He stayed there for several minutes, but no one came to help.

Later, he asked some people why they didn't help. One woman, Claire, said, 'I thought maybe you were drunk or dead. People are afraid of helping these days because they don't know what's going to happen to them.'

Eighty-two-year-old Paul Weston said, 'You don't know if it's real or not. You have to be very, very careful these days. The world is different now.'

11.3

FUNCTION offering to help

3A ▶ 11.4 Listen and match each conversation with pictures A–C.

B Listen again and complete sentences 1–3 below.
1 _____ me help.
2 _____ I call an ambulance?
3 I _____ do that for you.

C ▶ 11.5 Listen to the pronunciation of the offers. Then listen and repeat.

4A Match problems 1–5 with offers a)–e).
1 I can't open the window.   a) I'll get it for you.
2 I'm hungry.   b) Let me carry it.
3 I can't reach the dictionary. c) I'll make you a sandwich.
4 I can't lift this bag.   d) Shall I open the window?
5 It's hot in here.   e) Let me try … Ooh, it's stuck.

B Work in pairs and take turns. Student A: say a problem. Student B: offer to help.
A: I can't open the window.
B: Let me try … Ooh, it's stuck.

speakout TIP

When you see someone who needs help, you often start the conversation with *Are you OK?* or *Are you all right?* and then offer to help.

LEARN TO thank someone

5A Look at audio script 11.4 on page 175 and complete the sentences.

Conversation 1:
Man: Here, let me help. What a mess!
Woman: Thank ¹_____.
Man: No ²_____.

Conversation 2:
Woman: Are you all right? Shall I call an ambulance?
Man: No … Yes … Uh … Thanks ³_____.
Woman: That's ⁴_____.

Conversation 3:
Man: Oh, look. I'll do that for you. Where do you want it?
Woman: Just over here, in front of the window … Thanks ⁵_____. That's ⁶_____.
Man: You're ⁷_____.

B Underline the ways of thanking someone. How can you respond when someone thanks you?

➡ page 148 **LANGUAGEBANK**

6A Look at the flowchart below and put the conversation in the correct order.

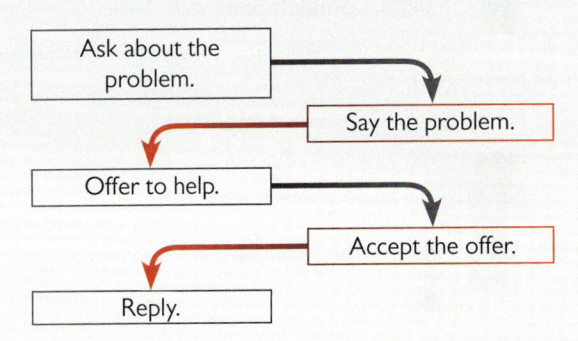

Ask about the problem. → Say the problem. → Offer to help. → Accept the offer. → Reply.

1 A: That's OK.
2 B: Thanks a lot.
3 A: I'll make you a sandwich.
4 A: Are you OK?
5 B: No, I'm really hungry.

B Work in pairs and take turns. Student A: look at page 166. Student B: look at page 164. Use the flowchart to help and role-play the conversation.

SPEAKING

7A ▶ 11.6 Listen to the situations. What's happening?

B Work in pairs. Listen again and offer to help.
1 _____
2 _____
3 _____
4 _____
5 _____
6 _____

11.4 THE OPTICIAN

DVD PREVIEW

1A Look at the photos A–F. What does each person do?
Photo A is an optician. He/She checks someone's eyes.

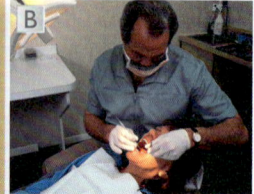

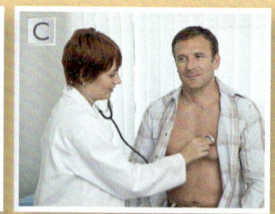

B Work in pairs. Look at the phrase and discuss. Do you think it's good advice?

> Never go to an optician who wears glasses.

C Work in pairs. Complete sentences 1–5.
1 Never go to a hairdresser who ___hasn't got any hair___.
2 Never go to a doctor who _____.
3 Never go to a fitness instructor who _____.
4 Never go to a dentist who _____.
5 Never go to an accountant who _____.

D Work in groups and compare your answers.

▶ DVD VIEW

2A Read the programme information. Why is the programme called *The Two Ronnies*?

BBC The Two Ronnies

The Two Ronnies are the stars of one of the longest-running comedy shows on British television. They both wear glasses, they're both called Ronnie and together they can make a simple situation very complicated … and very funny! In this sketch, Ronnie Corbett (the short one) has a problem and goes into a shop to ask for help from Ronnie Barker (the tall one).

B Watch the DVD and answer the questions.
1 Where is the man?
2 Where does he think he is?
 a) at a greengrocers
 b) at a baker's
3 What's the problem with both of the men?
 a) they can't hear very well
 b) they can't see very well
4 Which letter <u>doesn't</u> the man say?
 a) Y.
 b) H.
5 Why are the two men happy at the end?
 a) They don't need glasses..
 b) They can both see better.

3 Watch the DVD again. Number the sentences below in the order you hear them.
a) Hello. Anybody there? *1*
b) Is that better or worse?
c) Could I have two pounds of potatoes, please?
d) What do you see with?
e) No, you're reading all the furniture!
f) They're mine! They're mine!
g) Try the next line on your own.

114

speakout at a pharmacy

4A Work in pairs and answer the questions.
1. Do you go to a pharmacy, a doctor's, a dentist's or a hospital in these situations?
   a) You ate some fish last night. This morning you've got an awful stomach ache.
   b) You broke a glass and cut your thumb badly.
   c) You woke up this morning with earache.
   d) Your eyes are really sore.
   e) You've got terrible toothache.
   f) You stayed out in the sun too long this morning. Now you've got bad sunburn.
2. Can you remember a time when you had any of these problems? Where were you? What did you do?

B ▶ 11.7 Listen to the conversation in a pharmacy. What's the problem? What does the pharmacist advise?

C Look at the key phrases below. Listen again and tick the phrases you hear.

key phrases
Can you help me? I've got [bad toothache/a problem with my eye].
Have you got anything for [a headache/an earache/sore eyes]?
When did it start?
Take [this medicine/these tablets/some painkillers].
Put [these drops in your …/this cream on your …].
You [should see a doctor/shouldn't go out in the sun].

D Work in pairs. You are on holiday in another country. Choose a problem from Exercise 4A or use your own idea and role-play the situation. Use the key phrases to help.

E Work in groups and take turns. One pair: role-play your conversation. Other students: listen and guess the problem.

writeback a website message

5 Work in pairs. Read the two questions from a health message board. Choose one and complete Message 3 to give some advice. Use the key phrases to help.

Message 1 < posted yesterday >

Help! I started working from home three weeks ago. Now I've got terrible backache and my eyes hurt. I'm on the computer for about eight hours every day. Any advice?

Posted by: **YuchenChi, China**

Reply   < Previous Message | Next Message >

Message 2 < posted yesterday >

I stopped smoking a year ago and now I'm overweight. I often feel stressed and unhappy. I think I might start smoking again but I don't want to. What can I do?

Posted by: **Great Amigo, Mexico**

Reply   < Previous Message | Next Message >

Message 3 < posted today >

Hi, _____. The same thing happened to _____. Don't worry! The best thing is to _____. Also you should _____. Why don't you _____ as well? Don't _____ and you shouldn't _____.
All the best, _____.

Reply   < Previous Message | Next Message >

115

11.5 « LOOKBACK

HEALTH PROBLEMS

1A Complete the poems.

A: What's the matter? What's wr_ _ _ with you?

B: I've got a terrible co_ _ _,
– a runny n_ _ _, a bad s_r_ thr_ _ _ …
I can't stay here. I'm off!

A: My a_ _ _ hurt, my l_ _ _ hurt,
I think I've got the fl_.

B: Have you got a t_mp_r_t_ _ _?

A: Yes, what can I do?

A: I've got an awful h_ _d_ _ _ _.

B: My f_ng_ _ _ hurt a lot.

A: My e_ _ _ are t_r_d.

B: My b_ck_ _ _'s bad.

A & B: We don't know what we've got!

B Work in pairs. Read the poems.

ADVERBS

2A Write the opposite adverbs.

1 calmly *angrily*
2 loudly
3 slowly
4 badly
5 carelessly

B Complete the sentences with the words in the box below and your own ideas.

speak(s)   eat(s)   talk(s)
drive(s)   walk(s)

1 I _____ too _____ (adverb).
2 My teacher sometimes _____ too _____ (adverb).
3 My closest friend _____ too _____ (adverb).
4 Everyone _____ too _____ (adverb).

C Work in groups and take turns. One student: say one of your sentences. Other students: give advice or say your opinion using *should/shouldn't*.

A: *Everyone talks too loudly on their mobiles.*

B: *Yes, they should speak quietly.*

COMMON VERBS

3 Work in pairs. Match phrases 1–6 with a)–f). Then ask and answer the questions.

1 Can you read   c)
2 Do you remember
3 Did you hear
4 Can you concentrate
5 Do you understand
6 Did you ever climb

a) with the TV or radio on in the same room?
b) trees when you were younger?
c) music?
d) the first day of this English class?
e) films in English?
f) the news this morning?

SHOULD/SHOULDN'T

4A Read the situations and make a note of what the person *should/shouldn't do*.

A
My arm hurts so I can't use my computer. I have to finish a report by tomorrow.

B
I've got a terrible backache. I'm going on holiday tomorrow and I've got two heavy bags to carry.

C
I've got a headache and a bad sore throat. I've got an important interview for a new job tomorrow.

D
My leg hurts so I can't walk very far. I'm going out tomorrow night and I want to dance.

B Work in pairs and take turns. Role-play the four situations using your ideas above.

OFFERING TO HELP

5 Work in pairs. What can you say in each situation?

1 You're at a friend's house and she breaks some glasses.
2 You're walking down the street and someone falls off his bicycle.
3 You're on a train and a woman next to you becomes ill.
4 You're in a restaurant and the waiter pours hot coffee on your friend's clothes.
5 Your friend is cutting vegetables and cuts his finger badly.
6 Your friend wants a coffee, but she doesn't have enough money to buy one.

6A Complete the conversation with the words in the box.

~~I'll~~   Shall   me   a   're   you (x2)

A: Good morning. Can I help you?

B: Yes, the shower in my room doesn't work.

A: I'll send someone to look at it.

B: Thank. And when does the City Museum open?

A: Let look on the computer … It opens at 10.00 today.

B: Thanks. And can get me a taxi … to go to the museum?

A: No problem. I phone for one now?

A: In about an hour, please.

B: Certainly.

A: Thanks lot.

B: You welcome.

B Work in pairs. Practise the conversation.

BBC VIDEO PODCAST

Watch people talking about their lifestyles on ActiveBook or on the website.

Authentic BBC interviews

www.pearsonELT.com/speakout

UNIT 12

SPEAKING
> Talk about unusual experiences
> Describe movement from one place to another
> Phone someone about a problem

LISTENING
> Listen to people talking about their experiences
> Watch an extract from a documentary about sharks

READING
> Read about a dangerous job

WRITING
> Write a postcard
> Write about an exciting/frightening experience

BBC CONTENT
- Video podcast: What's the most exciting thing you've ever done?
- DVD: Shark Therapy

UNIT 12

experiences

▶ Unforgettable   p118
▶ Afraid of nothing   p120
▶ I've got a problem   p122
▶ Shark Therapy   p124

12.1 UNFORGETTABLE

▶ **GRAMMAR** | present perfect   ▶ **VOCABULARY** | outdoor activities   ▶ **HOW TO** | talk about experiences

VOCABULARY outdoor activities

1A Complete the phrases below with the words in the box. Use the photos to help you.

| ride | swim | go | sail | climb | watch |

1 _____ an elephant / a horse
2 _____ a volcano / a mountain
3 _____ a small boat / down the Nile
4 _____ fishing / camel trekking
5 _____ in a river / in a thermal spa
6 _____ an opera / a play outdoors / birds

B Work in pairs. Look at photos A–E and discuss the questions.
1 Which of the activities above can you see in the photos?
2 Which activities would you like to do? Why?
3 Which activities would you not like to do? Why not?

LISTENING

2A ▶ 12.1 Listen to a survey. In what order do people talk about the activities in photos A–E? Which two activities don't they talk about?

B Listen again. Tick the activities the speakers have done.

	Speaker 1	Speaker 2	Speaker 3
ridden elephants			
sailed down the Nile			
climbed a volcano			
swum in a thermal spa			

118

GRAMMAR present perfect

3A Look at the sentence and underline the correct alternatives to complete the rules.

I've been to Guatemala and I've climbed that volcano.

Rules:
1 Use the present perfect to talk about past events when you know the exact time/*don't know when* the event happened.
2 Use the present perfect to emphasise *what*/*when* the action happened.

B ▶ 12.2 Listen and complete the table.

| I | _____ haven't | sailed _____ | down the Nile. to Iceland. |

| _____ No, | you ever I | ridden | an elephant? _____ . |

C Listen again and check. Then listen and repeat.
▶ page 150 LANGUAGEBANK

PRACTICE

4A Complete the table with the correct infinitive.

infinitive	past participle
1 drive	driven
2 _____	flown
3 _____	had
4 _____	met
5 _____ / _____	been
6 _____	seen
7 _____	slept
8 _____	swum

B Use four of the past participles above to write sentences about you. Two sentences should be false.
I've driven a Ferrari.

C Work in pairs and take turns. Student A: say your four sentences. Student B: guess which two are false.

speakout TIP

Many past participles are similar. Look for patterns to help you remember. In your notebook, complete the verb patterns and add another verb to each group:
meet – met, keep …
speak – spoken, break …
grow – grown, know …
drive – driven, give …
swim – swum, drink …

SPEAKING

5A Complete the questions with your own ideas.
1 Have you ever been to _____?
2 Have you ever slept in a _____?
3 Have you ever had _____?
4 Have you ever _____?
5 Have you ever met _____?

B Work in groups. Ask and answer the questions above. Who has done most things in your group?
A: *Have you ever been to a festival?*
B: *Yes, I have.*
C: *No, I haven't, but I'd like to.*
D: *No, I haven't and I don't want to.*

WRITING postcard phrases

6A Read the postcard from Oliver and Kristina. Which country are they visiting?

Luxor, 12th May
Hi everyone,
Having a great time. It's very hot here in the day and cold at night. We sleep in tents, or sometimes on the boats and every day we get up at 6 o'clock and have breakfast next to the river. We've seen the temples in Kom Ombo and Edfu and we've taken lots of pictures. We haven't seen the Pyramids – that's Saturday. Must go now! See you soon.
Wish you were here!
Oliver and Kristina

The Wilson Family
434 Church Street
Pleasantville,
NY 10570
USA

B Look at the postcard again and complete the information.
1 Write the *name* and _____ on the right-hand side.
2 You can write the _____ and _____ at the top.
3 You can start a postcard with _____.

C Underline four typical postcard phrases in the postcard. What's missing from each phrase? Write the phrases in full.
We're having a great time.

D Cross out words to make more postcard phrases.
1 ~~We're~~ staying in a fantastic hotel.
2 I have to stop now.
3 I'll speak to you soon.
4 I hope you're all OK.

7 Work in pairs. Write a postcard to your class. Use the ideas above to help. Don't write the name of the place. Then exchange postcards with another pair and guess the place.

12.2 AFRAID OF NOTHING

▶ **GRAMMAR** | present perfect and past simple   ▶ **VOCABULARY** | prepositions   ▶ **HOW TO** | talk about past experiences

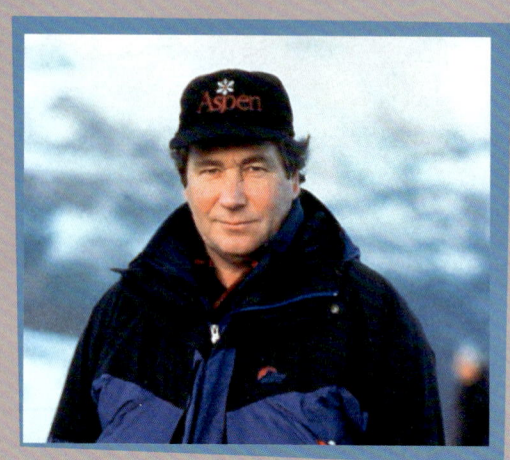

Vic ARMSTRONG is afraid of nothing. He has fallen out of windows, jumped off bridges, ridden a motorcycle through fire, climbed up the outside of a skyscraper and driven into a wall – because that's his job.

Vic is a stunt double in films and does things that most of us think are crazy.

Vic was Harrison Ford's stunt double in all three early Indiana Jones films. He has also worked on many James Bond films including *Die Another Day*. 'A job on a Bond film is the most fun for a stuntman – I try out the cars,' says Vic.

His most famous stunt was when he jumped from a horse onto a German tank in one of the Indiana Jones films. Movie viewers voted this 'one of the ten best stunts of all time'.

Vic has broken some bones, but he says that it's part of the job.

He now spends more time as a stunt director, directing other stuntmen. In 2002 he worked on *Gangs of New York* with one of his favourite directors, Martin Scorsese. Vic says it was 'great fun'.

Now, after forty years of stunt work, the man without fear feels the same way. Vic still thinks it's the best job in the world: 'I enjoy my work now as much as when I started,' he says. 'And now, as a stunt director, I tell other people to fall and jump. And the money is very, very good.'

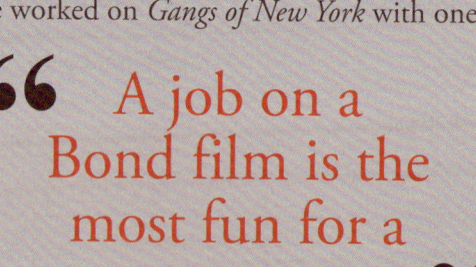

> " A job on a Bond film is the most fun for a stuntman ... "

READING

1A Read the definition of *stunt* below. Can you think of any famous stunts?

> **Stunt¹** /stʌnt/ *noun*   A dangerous thing that someone does to entertain people, especially in a film: *There's a great stunt in which his car has to jump across a 15 metre gap.*
>
> From Longman Wordwise Dictionary.

B Read the article and list the stunts the man has done.

C Read the article again. Are sentences 1–7 true (T) or false (F)?

1 Vic played Indiana Jones when Harrison Ford was ill.
2 He likes working on Bond films because he can drive the cars.
3 Steven Spielberg is one of his favourite directors.
4 He started doing stunt work over forty years ago.
5 Vic has sometimes hurt himself in his job.
6 He doesn't like working on films very much any more.
7 Vic gets a lot of money for his work.

D Find five movement verbs in the first paragraph of the text. Write the verb, past simple and past participle.

(fallen) – fall   fell   fallen

12.2

GRAMMAR present perfect and past simple

2A Look at the sentences. Underline the correct tense of the verbs.
1 He has worked on many James Bond films.
 (*past simple/present perfect*)
2 In 2002 he worked on *Gangs of New York*.
 (*past simple/present perfect*)

B Underline the correct alternatives.

> Rules:
> 1 With the present perfect, you *say/don't say* the exact time.
> 2 With the past simple, you *say/don't say* the exact time.

➡ page 150 **LANGUAGEBANK**

PRACTICE

3A Write the questions in full. Use the present perfect.
1 meet / a famous person?
 Have you ever met a famous person?
2 break / your arm?
3 eat / anything unusual?
4 watch / a live football match?
5 make / something to wear?
6 go / to a really hot or cold country?

B Work in pairs and take turns. Ask and answer the questions above. Remember to ask and answer follow-up questions using the past simple.
A: *Have you ever met a famous person?*
B: *Yes, I have. I met a famous actor last year.*
A: *Really? Who did you meet?*

4A Work in pairs. Write the past participles of the verbs in the box next to the correct sound below.

| sleep sing speak drive buy meet |
| write think fly win read do give |
| choose bring |

/e/	/ʌ/	/əʊ/	/ɪ/	/ɔː/
sl**e**pt	s**u**ng	sp**o**ken	dr**i**ven	b**ou**ght

B ▶ 12.3 Listen and check. Then listen and repeat.

VOCABULARY prepositions

5A Look at the pictures below. What is the man doing?

B Match the prepositions in the box with the pictures A–J.

| down   through   up   out of   under   towards |
| away from   across   over   into |

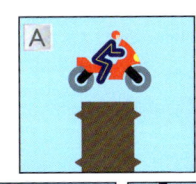

C Some of the prepositions have opposites. Look at the pictures again and find the opposites of these prepositions: *down, over, away from, out of*.

6 Complete the situations with a preposition of movement. More than one might be possible.
1 going *up/down* the outside of a building in a glass lift
2 walking _____ a big dog
3 going _____ a bridge when a train is going _____ the bridge
4 walking _____ a big park alone
5 riding a bike fast _____ a big hill
6 walking _____ customs at an airport
7 driving _____ a very long tunnel
8 walking _____ a room full of new people

SPEAKING

7A Work in pairs. Make a list of some dangerous/exciting/scary situations.

B How do you feel about the situations? Write one of the phrases in the box below next to each one.

| I love it.   It's not a problem. |
| I really don't like it.   I'm afraid of it. |
| I've never done it.   I'm not keen. |

C Work in pairs and discuss your answers.
A: *How do you feel about going across a river on a rope bridge?*
B: *I really don't like it.*
A: *Why? Have you had a bad experience?*
B: *Yes, two years ago I was …*

12.3 I'VE GOT A PROBLEM

▶ **FUNCTION** | telephoning ▶ **VOCABULARY** | telephoning expressions ▶ **LEARN TO** | say telephone numbers

SPEAKING

1 Work in pairs and take turns. Ask and answer questions 1–5.
1 Have you ever lost your keys/passport/credit card/mobile phone? What happened?
2 Have you ever locked yourself out of your house or car? What happened?
3 Have you ever missed the last train or bus home? What happened?
4 Have you ever been very late for a meeting/appointment? What happened?
5 Have you ever got lost in a city? What happened?

VOCABULARY telephoning expressions

2A Complete the sentences with phrases from the box.

~~take a message~~   leave a message   call   answer   ring back

1 You answer the phone. It's a call for Patricia but she's not in the office today so you __take a message__ for her.
2 You phone Mark but he's not at home so you _____ on his answerphone.
3 You want Mark to _____ you _____ this evening.
4 It's the evening. You _____ Mark, but he's having a shower.
5 Ten minutes later the phone rings and you _____ it. It's Mark.

B Work in pairs and compare your answers.

FUNCTION telephoning

3A ▶ 12.4 Listen to three conversation extracts. Which situations from Exercise 1 are they?

B Listen again. In which conversation(s) do the people know each other?

4A ▶ 12.5 Complete the extracts with words from the box. Then listen and check.

| ~~it's~~   check   moment   tell   ask   there   ring |
| number   message   back   leave   speak   call |

Extract 1
B: Hi, Sean. ¹ __It's__ Debbie.
A: Hi, Debbie. What's up?
B: ²Is Kevin _____?
A: No, he's not. He went out about ten minutes ago.

Extract 2
B: ³Could I _____ a _____ for him?
A: Of course.
B: ⁴Just _____ him to _____ me.

Extract 3
B: Hello. ⁵Could I _____ to customer services, please?
A: ⁶Just a _____.
C: Customer services.
B: Hello, I've got a problem.

Extract 4
B: ⁷Could you _____ me back?
C: Of course. ⁸Could you give me the _____ there?
B: Just a moment … It's 34 for Spain, 91 for Madrid, then 308 5238.
C: ⁹Let me _____ that. 34 91 308 5238.
B: That's right.
C: Fine. Put the phone down – ¹⁰I'll call you _____ straight away.

B Match the conversation extracts 1–4 with descriptions a)–d) below.
a) Asking someone to call back 4
b) Calling a business
c) Calling a friend
d) Leaving a message

C Underline the key stressed word in telephoning phrases 1–10 in Exercise 4A.

D ▶ 12.6 Listen and check. Then listen and repeat.
▶ page 150 LANGUAGEBANK

12.3

LEARN TO say telephone numbers

6A ▶ 12.7 Complete the phone number. Then listen and check.
3114020 = Three _____ one four _____ two _____

B Listen again. Draw a line between the words where you hear a short break.

speakout TIP

In telephone numbers:
- say 'oh' for the number zero.
- when there are two of the same number, e.g. 77, say 'seven seven' or 'double seven'.
- say the last seven numbers of a telephone number in two groups. First, three numbers and then four, e.g. 926 5173.

7A Work in pairs. Practise saying the numbers.
1 7996072
2 9954270
3 8013005
4 5807713

B Work in pairs and take turns. Student A: look at page 161. Student B: look at page 166.

SPEAKING

8A Work in pairs. Choose a situation from Exercise 1. Write key words for your conversation in the flowchart below. Then practise together.

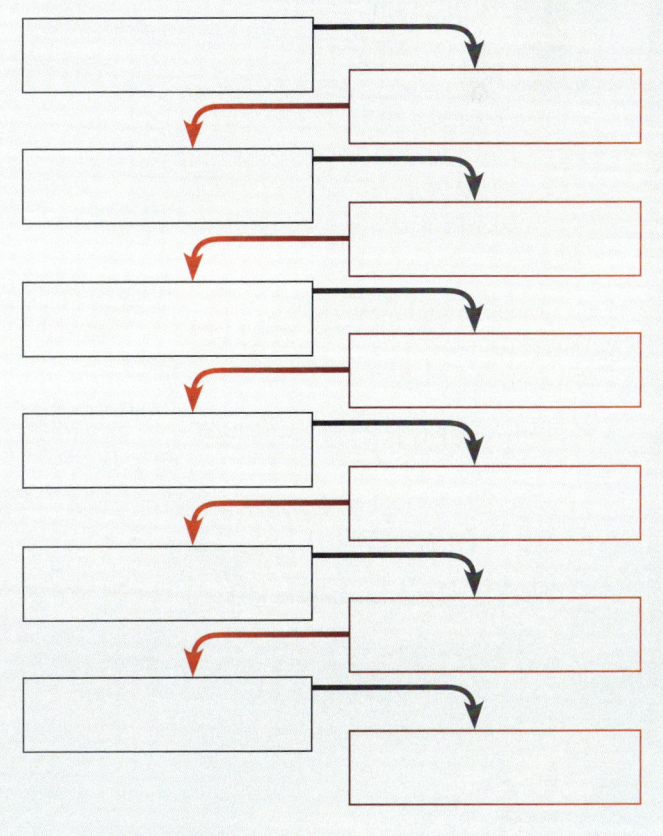

B Work with another pair. Exchange flowcharts and act out their conversation.

5A Work in pairs. Look at the flowchart and write the conversation in full.

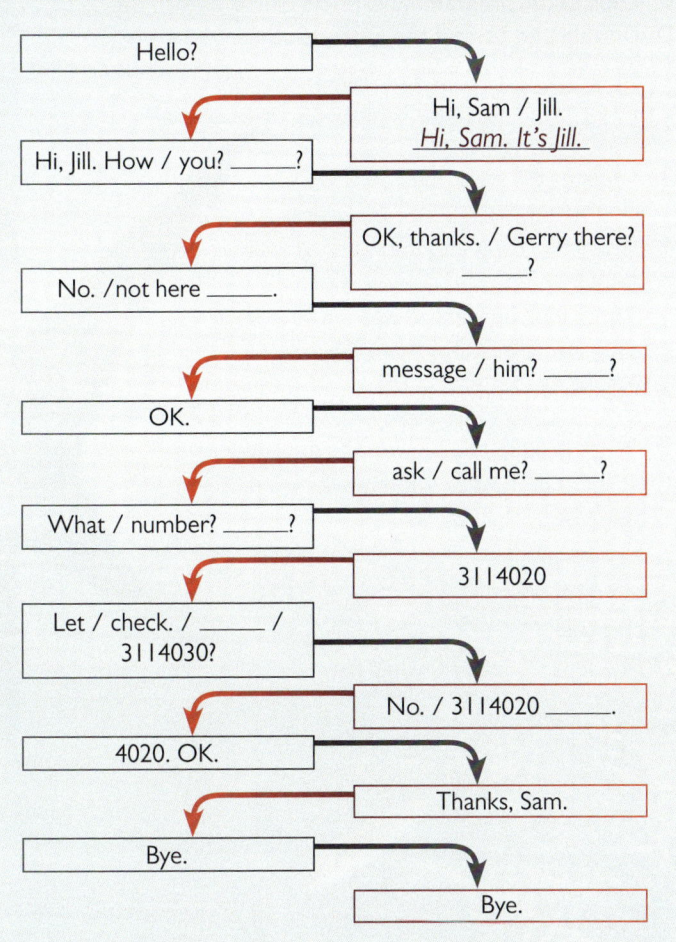

- Hello?
- Hi, Sam / Jill. Hi, Sam. It's Jill.
- Hi, Jill. How / you? _____?
- OK, thanks. / Gerry there? _____?
- No. / not here _____.
- message / him? _____?
- OK.
- ask / call me? _____?
- What / number? _____?
- 3114020
- Let / check. / _____ / 3114030?
- No. / 3114020 _____.
- 4020. OK.
- Thanks, Sam.
- Bye.
- Bye.

B Work in pairs. Read out your conversation.

123

12.4 SHARK THERAPY

DVD PREVIEW

1 Work in pairs. Look at the photos and answer the questions.
1 Are you afraid of any of these animals? Which ones? Why?
2 How do most people feel about sharks? Is it safe to swim with them?

2A Complete the sentences with words from the box.

> ~~frightened~~   proud   excited   afraid
> nervous   embarrassed

1 Some people are <u>frightened</u> or _____ of the dark.
2 When you are positive and happy before your birthday or a party, you feel _____.
3 When you are happy about something you've done, often something difficult, you feel _____.
4 Before an exam or going to the dentist, you feel _____.
5 When other people see you do something stupid, you feel _____.

B Complete sentences 1–6.
1 I'm afraid of _____.
2 I get very excited before _____.
3 I'm not frightened of _____.
4 I felt very proud when I _____.
5 I often feel nervous when I _____.
6 I feel embarrassed when I _____.

C Work in pairs and compare ideas.

▶ DVD VIEW

3A Read the programme information. Why does Tanya go to the Bahamas?

BBC Shark Therapy

Tanya Streeter is a world-famous diver but she's got one *big* problem. She's afraid of sharks! To overcome her fear, she needs help or 'therapy' and travels to the Bahamas to get it. Here, she learns how to swim with them … and comes face to face with the dangerous tiger shark.

B Watch the DVD. Underline the correct alternatives.
1 It's safer to wear a *black/green/shiny* swimsuit.
2 Tanya uses a *knife/stick/gun* to protect herself from the sharks.
3 *No/One/Two* shark(s) try to bite Tanya.

C Look at the programme extracts below. Watch the DVD again and correct the mistakes.
1 'At first, it isn't ~~difficult~~.' *easy*
2 'I didn't think that they were going to be … quite so … friendly.'
3 'I noticed the mask and I think we should change the mask completely.'
4 'Jim throws meat into the water to attract the sharks.'
5 'Tanya, look behind you over on your right.'
6 'That was frightening! Tanya did great.'
7 'I've started to overcome my very real feeling.'

D Work in pairs and answer the questions.
1 At the end of the programme do you think Tanya was:
   a) frightened?
   b) embarrassed?
   c) proud?
2 Would you like to try what Tanya did? Why/Why not?

speakout a frightening experience

4A Think about an exciting or frightening experience you've had. Look at the questions below and make notes:
- How old were you?
- Where was it?
- What happened? (write the verb phrases)
- How did you feel?
- What happened in the end?
- How did you feel in the end?

B ▶ 12.8 Listen to a man talk about an experience. Was it exciting or frightening? What happened?

C Listen again and tick the key phrases you hear.

> **keyphrases**
> This happened in [time/place] when I was (age).
> One day, … Then, … After that, …
> I felt [excited/afraid/frightened] …
> In the end, …
> It was (one of) the most [exciting/frightening] experiences I've ever had.

D Work in groups and take turns. One student: talk about your experience. Use the key phrases and your notes to help. Other students: listen and ask two questions about each event.

writeback a story

5A Before he talked about his experience, the man made some notes. Look at the notes below and number the events in the correct order.

> went for a walk   1
> one dog bit my arm
> didn't move, didn't look at the dogs
> remembered advice
> dogs ran towards me
> heard some dogs
> realised I didn't know where I was
> dogs jumped and barked

B Work in pairs and compare your answers.

C Use your notes from Exercise 4A and write about your experience in 80–100 words. Remember to use some of the key phrases to help.

12.5 « LOOKBACK

OUTDOOR ACTIVITIES

1A What are the activities? Add the vowels.

1 g_ tr_kk_ng
2 r_d_ an _l_ph_nt
3 sw_m _n a r_v_r
4 cl_mb a m_ _nt__n
5 g_ sc_b_ d_v_ng
6 t_k_ a b__t d_wn the N_l_
7 w_tch a pl_y __td__rs
8 g_ f_sh_ng
9 sw_m _n a th_rm_l sp_
10 cl_mb a v_lc_n_
11 w_tch b_rds
12 r_d_ a h_rs_

B Work in pairs and discuss.

1 Which activities above can you do in your country? Where can you do them?
2 Which activities above do you think are fun/boring/exciting?
3 Which activities above do you want to do/try? Why?

PRESENT PERFECT

2A Write the sentences in full.

1 I / never / eat / fish eyes.
2 I / never / go to / an art gallery.
3 I / never / see / a sunrise.
4 I / never / drive / a Mercedes.
5 I / never / drink / tea with milk for breakfast.
6 I / never / play / golf.
7 I / never / cook / dinner for my parents.
8 I / never / speak / English on the phone.
9 I / never / be / to an outdoor festival.
10 I / never / hear / Oasis live.

B Change the last part of each sentence so that it is true for you.
I've never eaten cabbage.
I've never been to an art gallery, but I'd like to.

C Work in pairs and compare your answers.

PRESENT PERFECT AND PAST SIMPLE

3A Complete the questions. Use the correct form of the verb in brackets.
Have you ever …

1 *ridden* a horse? (ride)
2 _____ an overnight train? (take)
3 _____ in a small plane? (fly)
4 _____ across a river? (swim)
5 _____ a long distance? (cycle)
6 _____ on a train? (sleep)
7 _____ a mountain? (climb)

B Work in pairs and take turns. Ask and answer the questions in Exercise 3A and ask follow-up questions.
A: *Have you ever … ?*
B: *Yes, I have.*
A: *Oh, when was that?*

PREPOSITIONS

4A Look at the word webs and cross out the place/thing which does *not* go with the preposition.

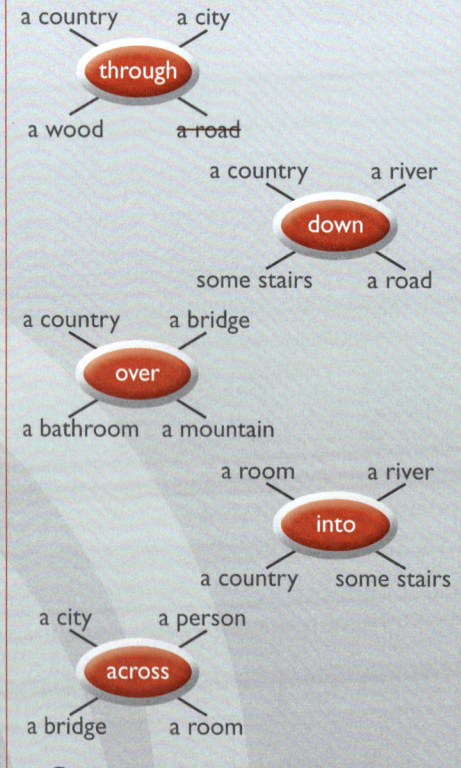

through: a country, a city, a wood, ~~a road~~
down: a country, a river, some stairs, a road
over: a country, a bridge, a bathroom, a mountain
into: a room, a river, a country, some stairs
across: a city, a person, a bridge, a room

B Work in pairs. Student A: choose one of the prepositions. Say three things that can come after it. Student B: guess the preposition.
A: *A country, a building, a bridge*
B: *Over?*

ADJECTIVES

5A Unjumble the letters and find six adjectives below.
pypha = happy

1 dupor
2 xeectid
3 fiarda
4 onreuvs
5 amebearrssd
6 freghtinde

B Find five more words from Unit 12. Write them as jumbled words.

C Work in pairs. Exchange papers and unjumble the words.

TELEPHONING

6A Complete the telephone conversation.

A: Hello, the Learn English Centre.
B: Hello, [1]_____ Sofia Mitsotakis. [2]_____ my teacher, Rachel, please?
A: Just a moment. [3]_____ check … I'm afraid she's in class at the moment. [4]_____ in about half an hour?
B: Oh, that's difficult. [5]_____ a message for her?
A: Sure. Go ahead.
B: Could you [6]_____ me this afternoon?
A: Yes, could you [7]_____ number?
B: It's 0853 58230.
A: Fine. [8]_____ her to call you. And it's Sofia … ?
B: Mitsotakis. Thank you very much.

B Work in pairs and role-play the conversation. Student A: you want to speak to your English teacher. Phone the school. Student B: you are the receptionist. The teacher can't come to the phone. Continue the conversation with your ideas.

BBC VIDEO PODCAST
Watch people talking about recent experiences on ActiveBook or on the website.

Authentic BBC interviews

www.pearsonELT.com/speakout

IRREGULAR VERBS

VERB	PAST SIMPLE	PAST PARTICIPLE
be	was	been
become	became	become
begin	began	begun
bite	bit	bitten
blow	blew	blown
break	broke	broken
bring	brought	brought
build	built	built
buy	bought	bought
catch	caught	caught
choose	chose	chosen
come	came	come
cost	cost	cost
cut	cut	cut
do	did	done
draw	drew	drawn
drink	drank	drunk
drive	drove	driven
eat	ate	eaten
fall	fell	fallen
feel	felt	felt
find	found	found
fly	flew	flown
forget	forgot	forgotten
freeze	froze	frozen
get	got	got
give	gave	given
go	went	gone
grow	grew	grown
have	had	had
hear	heard	heard
hide	hid	hidden
hit	hit	hit
hold	held	held
hurt	hurt	hurt
keep	kept	kept
know	knew	known
learn	learned/learnt	learned/learnt
leave	left	left

VERB	PAST SIMPLE	PAST PARTICIPLE
lend	lent	lent
let	let	let
lie	lay	lain
lose	lost	lost
make	made	made
mean	meant	meant
meet	met	met
pay	paid	paid
put	put	put
read	read	read
ride	rode	ridden
ring	rang	rung
run	ran	run
say	said	said
see	saw	seen
sell	sold	sold
send	sent	sent
shine	shone	shone
show	showed	shown
shut	shut	shut
sing	sang	sung
sit	sat	sat
sleep	slept	slept
smell	smelled/smelt	smelled/smelt
speak	spoke	spoken
spend	spent	spent
spill	spilled/spilt	spilled/spilt
stand	stood	stood
swim	swam	swum
take	took	taken
teach	taught	taught
tell	told	told
think	thought	thought
throw	threw	thrown
understand	understood	understood
wake	woke	woken
wear	wore	worn
win	won	won
write	wrote	written

1 LANGUAGE BANK

GRAMMAR

1.1 Present simple: *be*

Positive

+			
	I	am / 'm	fine, thanks.
	You/We/They	are / 're	students.
	He/She/It	is / 's	in class 3A.

Use contractions in speaking, e.g. *I'm …* NOT *I am …* ' = a missing letter, e.g. *You aren't …* NOT *You are not*

You is singular (1 person) or plural (2+ people).

Don't use contractions in positive short answers, e.g. *Yes, she is.* NOT *Yes, she's.*

Negative

–			
	I	'm not	very well.
	You/We/They	aren't	students.
	He/She/It	isn't	here.

When speaking, it is also possible to use *You/We/They're not* and *He/She/It's not*.

Questions and short answers

?						
	Am	I	married?	Yes, / No,	I	am. / 'm not.
	Are	you/we/they	tourists?	Yes, / No,	you/we/they	are. / aren't.
	Is	he/she/it	OK?	Yes, / No,	he/she/it	is. / isn't.

It *is* good.   *Is* it good?

Use *be* + subject (*I/You/He,* etc.) for the question.

Use *be* to say who a person is or what an object is: *I'm James. It's a pen.*

Use *be* to say where a person or a thing is from: *She's American. Spaghetti is Italian.*

Use *be* to talk about people's jobs: *I'm a student. My mother's a teacher.*

Use *be* to talk about a person's age: *I'm eighteen. Mark's twenty-four.*

Use *be* to say where something is: *The Eiffel Tower is in France.*

Use *be* to say how much something is: *It's twelve euros.*

1.2 *this/that, these/those*

	near	far
singular	this bag	that bag
plural	these bags	those bags

possessive *'s*; *mine/yours*

It's	Akira's	bag.
They're	Chris's	magazines.
These are	the student's	books.

Use *Akira's bag* NOT *the bag of Akira.*

It is also possible to say *Akira's* without repeating the noun: *Is this John's bag? No, it's **Akira's**.*

Use *my/your* + noun: *my/your **magazine***

We use *mine/yours* + no noun in short answers: *Is this Ben's **mobile**? No, it isn't Ben's. It's **mine**.*

1.3 making requests

Can	I	have	a sandwich, please?
			one of those batteries, please?
Could		send	a package, please?
		change	these dollars for yen, please?

Use *Can/Could* + I + infinitive to make requests.

Note: *could* is often more formal than *can*.

When speaking, reply: *Yes, of course. / Here you are.*

LB 1

PRACTICE

1.1

A Complete the sentences with positive forms of *be*. Use contractions.
1. I _____ Sonia D'Angelo.
2. They _____ at university.
3. It _____ Tuesday today.
4. Julio _____ on holiday.
5. We _____ from the BBC.
6. You _____ in my class, Yasmin.

B Complete the conversation. Use the correct forms of *be*.
Farah: ¹_____ you Cindy?
Jenny: No, I ²_____. I ³_____ Jennifer.
Farah: ⁴_____ you a student?
Jenny: No, I ⁵_____ the teacher! ⁶_____ you a student?
Farah: Yes, I ⁷_____.
Jenny: OK, please sit down.

C Put the words in the correct order. Start with the underlined word.
1. in / <u>Debra</u> / the / café / isn't.
2. name / your / <u>Is</u> / Khan?
3. at / Mrs / aren't / <u>Mr</u> / airport / and / Cabrera / the.
4. friend / is / Paolo / <u>This</u> / my.
5. their / <u>What</u> / names / are?
6. centre / 's / <u>Where</u> / health / the?

1.2

A Complete the conversations. Use *this, that, these* or *those*.

Conversation 1
A: Brigitte, _____ is Phil.
B: Hello, Phil. Nice to meet you.
A: And _____ are my children. _____ is Tom and _____ is Chris.
B: Hi!

Conversation 2
A: Is _____ your car over there?
B: Yes, it is. It's great! And very fast!

Conversation 3
A: One of _____ cakes, please.
B: _____ one here?
A: No, _____ one there.

B Underline the correct alternative.
1. It's the *laptop of Megan/Megan's* laptop.
2. Are those *your/yours* sunglasses?
3. This is my newspaper. That's *your/yours*!
4. These are *John/John's* keys.
5. Where's *my/mine* wallet?
6. This is Angela's book. *My/Mine* is here.

C Change the conversations so they don't repeat the nouns.

Conversation 1
A: Hey! That's my pen!
B: No, it isn't. It's ~~my pen~~ *mine*. Your pen is over there.

Conversation 2
A: I think these are Stefan's books.
B: No, they aren't Stefan's books. Maybe they're Daniela's books.

Conversation 3
A: Is this your mobile?
B: No, it's Jason's mobile. My mobile is black.

Conversation 4
A: Thanks for a lovely evening!
B: Thank you for coming. Is this your coat?
A: No, it isn't my coat. It's Sam's coat. This is my coat.

1.3

A Complete the conversation with the words in the box.

exchange That's please could For change Can euros

A: ¹_____ I help you?
B: Yes, ²_____ I change these dollars for ³_____, please?
A: Yes, of course.
B: What's the ⁴_____ rate today?
A: It's 1 dollar to 0.651 euros. So that's 65.1 euros.
B: Oh. Could I ⁵_____ these pounds too, please?
A: ⁶_____ euros?
B: Yes, ⁷_____.
A: ⁸_____ 25 euros.
B: Thank you.

2 LANGUAGE BANK

GRAMMAR

2.1 present simple: I/you/we/they questions and short answers

| ? | Do | I/you/we/they | drink
like | coffee?
tennis? | +
− | Yes,
No, | I/you/we/they | do.
don't. |

Use *Do* + subject + verb for a question. **Do** you **have** lunch at home?
In short answers, use *Yes, I do* and *No, I don't*. NOT ~~Yes, I like~~ or ~~No, I don't like~~.

present simple: I/you/we/they positive and negative statements

| + | I
You
We | love
go
take | films.
running every day.
a lot of photos. |
| − | They | don't read | books. |

Use the present simple to talk about:
- things which are always true: *I **come** from Spain. I **like** cats.*
- habits and routines: *We **take** a lot of photos.*

In the negative, use *don't* + verb: *I **don't like** working at the weekend.*
When speaking, use the contraction *don't* (= do not).

2.2 present simple: he/she/it positive and negative statements

| + | He
She
It | comes
watches
does
flies
has | from Japan.
TV.
everything.
to the USA.
lunch | verb + -s
verb ending in -ch, -sh, -s, -x + -es
do and *go* + -es
verb ending in a consonant + -y,
change -y to -ies
have change to *has* |

| − | He/She/It | doesn't like | cats. |

In the negative, use *doesn't* + verb:
*He **doesn't want** to come.*
When speaking, use the contraction *doesn't* (= does not).

present simple: he/she/it questions and short answers

| ? | Does | he/she/it | come | from Italy? | +
− | Yes,
No, | he/she/it | does.
doesn't. |

Use *Does* + subject + verb to make a question: **Does** she **get** home late?
In short answers, use *Yes, it does* and *No, it doesn't* NOT ~~Yes, it comes~~ or ~~No it doesn't come~~

2.3 asking for information

What time When			start? finish?
Where	does	it the tour	leave from?
How much			cost?

| Do | you | take | credit cards? |

The answers to *what time/when* questions are times/time phrases. Use *in*, *at* and *on* with these time phrases:

in	at	on
the morning the afternoon the evening	9 o'clock, 7.30 midnight night the weekend	Saturday Sunday

130

PRACTICE

2.1

A Put the words in the correct order to make questions.
1 you / Do / classes / like / English / your ?
 Do you like your English classes?
2 running / every day / go / they / Do ?
3 chat / you / friends / Do / with / a lot ?
4 junk / like / you / Do / food ?
5 TV / on / watch / they / football / Do ?
6 cinema / the / to / go / you / Do / a lot ?

B Look at the short answers to the questions above and correct the mistakes.
1 Yes, I ~~like~~. *do*   3 Yes, we do chat.   5 No, they not.
2 No, they don't.   4 No, I don't like.   6 Yes, we go.

C Complete the sentences with the correct form of the verbs in the box.

~~go~~   eat   read   watch   listen to   drink   work

1 I *don't go* running because I'm not very active!
2 We _____ sport on TV a lot because we really like it.
3 I _____ junk food because I don't like it.
4 They _____ on Sundays – just relax all day!
5 I _____ books in English because it's good practice.
6 We _____ coffee late at night. We have milk or tea.
7 You _____ music a lot. What's your favourite band?

2.2

A Write the *he/she/it* form of the verbs.
1 eat *eats*   3 understand   5 wash   7 write   9 play
2 study   4 take   6 chat   8 have   10 do

B Complete the texts with the verbs in the box. Use the present simple in the correct form.

go   listen to   watch   study   get up   drink   read
meet   work   start   have   finish   relax   talk

Simona is a student. She ¹_____ late, at 10a.m., ²_____ some black coffee and then ³_____ to classes at the university. In the afternoon, she ⁴_____ in the library. In the evening, she ⁵_____ TV or ⁶_____ music.

Beatrice is a businesswoman. She ⁷_____ breakfast at 6a.m. and ⁸_____ work at 8. In the morning, she ⁹_____ her emails and ¹⁰_____ to people on the phone. Beatrice's husband ¹¹_____ near her office, so they ¹²_____ and have lunch together. She ¹³_____ work at 6p.m. and in the evening she just ¹⁴_____ at home.

C Correct the mistakes.
1 Dan likes dogs, but he no like cats.
2 Tariq drinks coffee, but he don't drink tea.
3 Sophia reads magazines, but she reads not books.
4 Lara works at the weekend, but she does work on Monday.
5 The hotel room has a television and a telephone, but it no have an internet connection.

D Complete the conversation.
A: ¹_____ you work?
B: No, I ²_____, but my wife ³_____.
A: Oh, what ⁴_____ she do?
B: She ⁵_____ English at a school.
A: Oh. And ⁶_____ she like it?
B: Yes, she ⁷_____. Well, she ⁸_____ like working in the evening, but she ⁹_____ her students.
A: And what ¹⁰_____ you do all day?
B: I ¹¹_____ TV and ¹²_____ with my friend Bob on the phone.
A: Oh, and what ¹³_____ Bob do?
B: He's a film reviewer. He ¹⁴_____ about films on TV.

2.3

A Look at the table. Use the information to write questions for answers 1–6.

train	leaves	8.30	$30
	arrives	10.15	
museum	opens	10.00	$15
	closes	6.00	

1 8.30   2 10.15   3 $30   4 10.00   5 6.00   6 $15
What time/When does the train leave?

B Read the text and correct the mistakes. Add *in*, *on* or *at* in ten places.

The weekend we do a lot Saturday, but Sunday we have a relaxing day. We get up 10 o'clock the morning and have a late breakfast. We have lunch about 2 o'clock and then the afternoon we relax at home. The evening we watch a DVD or something on TV and then we go to bed about 11.30 night.

3 LANGUAGE BANK

GRAMMAR

3.1 adverbs of frequency

never	hardly ever	sometimes	often	usually	always
0%	10%	40%	60%	80%	100%

Use adverbs of frequency to say how often you do something: *I **usually** have breakfast at home. She's **never** late.*

The adverbs go before most verbs: *He **never listens** to me* but after the verb *be*: *Sarah **is always** friendly.*

Usually and *sometimes* can also go at the beginning of a sentence: ***Sometimes** Ahmed phones me after midnight.*

modifiers

I'm		talkative.
Yuki's	very	good.
My friend's	really	happy.
He's/She's/It's	quite	boring.
We're	not very	interesting.
They're		

*I'm **quite** happy.* NOT ~~I'm happy quite~~.

3.2 have/has got

+	I/You/We/They	've (have)	got	three sisters.
	He/She/It	's (has)		
−	I/You/We/They	haven't		a phone.
	He/She/It	hasn't		

?	Have	I/you/we/they	got	an aunt?	Yes,	I/you/we/they	have.
				an iPod?	No,		haven't.
	Has	he/she/it			Yes,	he/she/it	has.
					No,		hasn't.

In questions, use *any* before plural nouns, and *a* before singular nouns: *Have you got **any** children? Have you got **a** car?*

Use *have/has got* to talk about family and possessions.
Use contractions when speaking, e.g. *I **'ve** got, she **'s** got.*
In the negative, use *any* before plural nouns: *I haven't got **any** brothers.*

3.3 making arrangements

What	do you want	to do?
What time		to go?
What	's	good for you?
Are		you free tonight?

making suggestions

| How about | going | to the cinema? |
| | meeting | at half past five? |

Use *How about* + infinitive + *-ing*.

responding to suggestions

| + | Sounds good.
That's a good idea.
OK. |
| − | Mmm. That's a problem.
Sorry, I'm busy. |

132

LB 3

PRACTICE

3.1

A Put the words in the correct order to make six sentences.
1 late / students / The / never / are
2 homework / their / always / They / do
3 hardly / ever / rains / here / It
4 TV / the morning / in / usually / We / watch / don't
5 quiet / I / am / very / sometimes
6 lesson / funny / is / The / often

B Add an adverb of frequency to each sentence. Use the information in brackets to help.
1 I get up early. (0%) *I never get up early.*
2 I have breakfast with my family. (100%)
3 My father reads the paper. (80%)
4 We're tired in the morning. (60%)
5 I get up before 7a.m. (10%)
6 I drink coffee. (0%)
7 He's late. (40%)

C Complete the sentences with *not very, quite, very* or *really* and an adjective from the box.

~~quiet~~ intelligent funny talkative good (x2) easy

1 Sue never talks. She's *very quiet*.
2 People like Juan because he's _____ and we laugh a lot.
3 This classroom is _____ – not too big, not too small.
4 The other students in this group are _____. They always get good marks in exams.
5 English is _____, but I like it.
6 I'm _____. I like to talk to people a lot to practise my English.
7 Mmm! This chocolate is _____!

3.2

A Complete the conversation with *have/has got*.
A: ¹_____ you ²_____ any brothers or sisters?
B: Yes, I ³_____ one sister, but I ⁴_____ any brothers.
A: ⁵_____ you ⁶_____ any children?
B: Yes, I ⁷_____. I ⁸_____ three sons and a daughter, Annie. She ⁹_____ a son and a daughter. And two of my sons ¹⁰_____ two children each. Charlie ¹¹_____ two sons, and Andy ¹²_____ two daughters.
A: And your sister? ¹³_____ she ¹⁴_____ any children?
B: Yes, Maggie ¹⁵_____ a son and a daughter, too.

B Complete the questions. Use the correct form of *be* or *have got*.
1 *Are* (you) married?
2 _____ (you) a mobile?
3 _____ (your classroom) a TV?
4 _____ (your best friend) very talkative?
5 _____ (you) usually early or late for class?
6 _____ (you) a diary with you?
7 _____ (you) cold?
8 _____ (your brother) twenty or twenty-one?

3.3

A Complete the conversation.
Paolo: Hi, Carl. ¹_____ _____ _____ on Thursday evening?
Carl: No, but ²_____ about Friday or Saturday?
Paolo: What's ³_____ _____ you?
Carl: Saturday's good. ⁴_____ _____ _____ _____ to do?
Paolo: ⁵_____ _____ _____ to the theatre?
Carl: Great. What's on?
Paolo: It's the Royal Shakespeare Company doing *Macbeth*.
Carl: Sounds good. What ⁶_____ _____ _____ _____ to meet?
Paolo: ⁷_____ _____ _____ at seven o'clock? At the theatre?
Carl: OK. See you there.

4 LANGUAGE BANK

GRAMMAR

4.1 there is/are

+	There	's		a balcony.
		are		three bedrooms.
–	There	isn't	a	garden.
		aren't	any	chairs.

Is	there	a TV in the bedroom?	Yes,	there	is.
			No,		isn't.
Are	there	two bedrooms?	Yes,	there	are.
		any shelves?	No,		aren't.

Use *there is* and *there are* to say that something exists.

Use *there is* and *there are* to talk about places and things and people in places: **There's** a health centre five minutes from here. **There's** a spider in the bathroom! **There are** only five students in class today.

In negatives and questions, with plurals, use *there aren't/are there + any + noun*: There aren't **any tables**. Are there **any chairs**?

4.2 can for possibility

+	I/You/ He/She/It/ We/They	can	come with me.
–		can't	

?	Can	I/you/ he/she/it/ we/they	buy English food?	Yes,	I/you/ he/she/it/ we/they	can.
				No,		can't

Use *can* to say something is possible and *can't (cannot)* to say something is impossible.

4.3 buying in shops

It's	too	big.
		small.
They're	very	expensive.
		long.

It's too big.

Use *very* + adjective with positive and negative ideas: It's **very** good. It's **very** expensive.

Use *too* + adjective with negative ideas: It's **too** small. = It's a problem for me.

Don't use *too* with positive ideas: It's **very** nice. NOT It's too nice.

It's	not	big	enough.
They're		small	
		long	

It's not big enough.

Use *not* + adjective + *enough* to explain what is wrong with an object: I'm sorry, it's **not** big **enough**. Have you got it in large?

Have you got it in	extra large/large/medium/small?
	green/blue?
How much	is it?
	are they?

LB 4

PRACTICE

4.1

A Write sentences with the prompts below. Use *there is/are* or *there isn't/aren't*.
1. 2 / table / kitchen   There are two tables in the kitchen.
2. 4 / chair / living room
3. 2 / bedroom / my flat
4. 0 / sofa / my living room
5. a bathroom / upstairs
6. 0 / any shelves / the bedroom

B Complete the questions with *is/are there*.
1. How many chairs _____ in the living room?
2. _____ a desk in your bedroom?
3. How many bedrooms _____ in your flat?
4. _____ a study?
5. _____ a separate dining room?
6. How many bathrooms _____ in your flat?

4.2

A Write questions about a hotel/apartment for pictures 1–5. Use *Can you … there?*

1. *Can you cook there?*
2. _____
3. _____
4. _____
5. _____

B Look at the table. Complete the sentences below with *can* or *can't*.

	seaside hotel	beach apartment
(pan)	no	yes
(racket)	yes	no
(cigarette)	no	no
(dog)	no	yes
(music)	no	yes

At the seaside hotel …
1. *you can't cook.*
2. _____
3. _____
4. _____
5. _____

At the beach apartment …
6. _____
7. _____
8. _____
9. _____
10. _____

4.3

A Complete the conversation.

Customer: Excuse me. ¹_____ _____ _____ this _____ large?
Assistant: Hold on. I'll check … Yes, here you are.
Customer: Oh, blue. ²_____ _____ _____ it _____ green?
Assistant: Large in green? No. Here's a medium. Is that OK?
Customer: Oh, no! That's ³_____ big _____.
Assistant: Ah, here's a large in purple!
Customer: Great. ⁴_____ _____ is it?
Assistant: £59.99.
Customer: Oh … that's too ⁵_____, sorry. Thanks anyway.

135

5 LANGUAGE BANK

GRAMMAR

5.1 Countable and uncountable nouns

There are two kinds of noun in English: countable nouns and uncountable nouns.

- Countable nouns are things you can count. They are singular or plural: *a banana, an apple, potatoes*
- Uncountable nouns are things you can't count in English: *water, rice, bread*. They are never plural. NOT *one water, two rices, three breads*
- Drinks are usually uncountable: *coffee, tea, juice* but you can say *a juice* (= a glass of juice) or *three coffees* (= three cups of coffee).
- It is also possible to use containers with the noun to show quantity: **a glass of** water, **two packets of** rice

Nouns with a/an, some, any

- Use *a/an* + singular countable noun: *I've got **an** apple.*
- Use *some* + plural countable noun or uncountable noun in positive sentences: *We've got **some** vegetables.*
- Use *any* + plural countable noun or uncountable noun in questions and negative sentences to ask about things: *Have you got **any** sweets? We haven't got **any** coffee.*
- Usually use *some* (NOT *any*) + plural countable noun or uncountable noun in questions to ask for things or to offer something to a person: *Can I have **some** coffee? Do you want **some** tea?*

Nouns with a/an, some, any

- Use *There* + *is/are* + *a/some* + singular/plural countable noun to say something exists: ***There's a** bottle of water. **There are some** carrots.*
- Use *There* + *is* + *some* + uncountable noun in the singular to say something exists: *There's **some** milk.* NOT *There are some milk.*
- Use *There isn't* + *a/an* + singular countable noun to say something doesn't exist: ***There isn't a** cucumber in the fridge.*
- Use *There aren't / isn't* + *any* + plural countable noun or uncountable noun to say something doesn't exist: ***There aren't any** tomatoes. **There isn't any** butter.*
- Use *Is* + *there* + *a/an* + singular countable noun to ask about something: ***Is there a** bottle of orange juice in the fridge?*
- Use *Are / is* + *there* + *any* + plural countable noun or uncountable noun to ask about something: ***Are there any** apples? **Is there any** salad?*

5.2 How much/many

Use *how much/many* to find out what amount of something someone has or there is.

- Ask questions with *how many* + plural countable nouns: ***How many** tomato**es are** there in that bag? **How many** vegetable**s** do you eat in a week?*
- Ask questions with *how much* + uncountable nouns: ***How much** sugar have we got? **How much** milk **is** there in the fridge?*

Quantifiers

Uncountable	
How much water do you drink every day?	A lot. / Lots. ▼ Quite a lot. Not much. None.

Countable	
How many apples do you eat?	A lot. / Lots. ▼ Quite a lot. Not many. None.

Use these quantifiers for short answers to *How much/many …?* *How much cheese have we got? **None**.*

Use *a lot/lots (of), quite a lot (of), not much/many* + noun: *I eat **lots of** fruit. I don't drink **much** water.*

We use *no* + noun. *There's **no** milk.* NOT *There's none milk.*

5.3 Ordering in a restaurant

Could I	have	a glass of water some vegetable soup	please?	+	Yes, of course. Yes, certainly.
Can I					
I'd	like		please.	−	I'm sorry, we haven't got any soup.

LB 5

PRACTICE

5.1

A Look at the sentences and correct the mistakes.
1 Do you often eat chickens?
2 Sylvie doesn't like fruits.
3 No, thanks. I don't eat sardine.
4 My parents hardly ever drink wines.
5 Does she eat meats?
6 I usually put butters on my bread, not margarines.
7 He doesn't like sugars in his tea.

B What does the customer buy? Write *a/an* or *some* and the types of food you see in the picture.
A = *some bread*

C Complete the conversation.
Man: What's for dinner?
Woman: Well, let's see. Oh no, we haven't got ¹_____ eggs.
Man: So I can't make an omelette. ²_____ there _____ spaghetti?
Woman: Yes, there's ³_____ packet of spaghetti.
Man: Have we got ⁴_____ tomatoes?
Woman: Yes, but there ⁵_____ only one.
Man: Oh. ⁶_____ there _____ butter?
Woman: Yeah, we've got ⁷_____ butter.
Man: Great. So dinner is … spaghetti with butter on it!?

5.2

A Complete the questions with *How much/many*.
1 _____ tea or coffee do you drink in the evening?
2 _____ people are there in this room?
3 _____ homework do you do every day?
4 _____ eggs are there in an omelette?
5 _____ hours do you sleep every night?
6 _____ children have you got?

B Complete the sentences about the picture. Use *a lot of*, *quite a lot of*, *not much/many*, *none* or *no*.
1 There <u>are a lot of</u> women.
2 There _____ men or children.
3 There _____ water.
4 There _____ empty glasses.
5 There _____ food.
6 There _____ fruit juice.

5.3

A Complete the conversation in a restaurant.
Waiter: Are you ready to order?
Customer: Yes, ¹_____ I have some tomato soup, _____?
Waiter: And for the main course?
Customer: I ²_____ like roast beef.
Waiter: What sort of vegetables ³_____ you _____?
Customer: ⁴_____ I have potatoes and green peas?
Waiter: ⁵_____ you _____ a salad with that?
Customer: No, thank you.
Waiter: And something to drink?
Customer: ⁶_____ like a mineral water, please.
Waiter: Yes, of course.

137

6 LANGUAGE BANK

GRAMMAR

6.1 past simple: was/were

+	I/He/She/It	was	happy.
	You/We/They	were	born in 2004.
–	I/He/She/It	wasn't	
	You/We/They	weren't	

?	Was	I/he/she/it	at home?	Yes,	I/he/she/it	was.
				No,		wasn't.
	Were	you/we/they		Yes,	you/we/they	were.
				No,		weren't.

The past simple of *be* is *was/were*. Use *was/were* to talk about the past.

When speaking, use contractions: *wasn't* = *was not*, *weren't* = *were not*.

6.2 past simple

regular verbs

+	I/You/He/She/It/We/They	started	a new school.	most verbs + -ed
		lived	in Spain.	verb ending in -e + -d
		studied	English.	verb ending in a consonant + -y, change to -ied
		travelled	a lot.	verb ending in a consonant–vowel–consonant, double the final consonant + -ed

Use the past simple to talk about things which started and finished in the past: *I **travelled** to Egypt last year.* (I'm not in Egypt now.)

irregular verbs

+	I/You/He/She/It We/They	went	home.
		had	a big meal.

Many common verbs have an irregular past simple form. Look at the list on page 127.

negatives with regular and irregular verbs

–	I/You/He/She/It We/They	didn't	like	the food.
			have	a DVD player.

The negative is the same for regular and irregular verbs.

Use *didn't* + verb: *I **didn't work** last week.* (regular) NOT *I didn't worked*. *They **didn't get** married.* (irregular) NOT *I didn't got married*.

Questions and short answers

Did	I/you/he/she/it/we/they	did	stop?	Yes,	I/you/he/she/it/we/they	did.
			come?	No,		didn't.
Where/When/Why			go?	We went to the park. We played tennis.
What/Who			see?	I saw Jane.
How			travel?	We took the bus to the park.

In questions, use (question word +) *did* + subject + infinitive: *Did you go?* NOT *Did you went?*

6.3 making conversation

Asking about the weekend	Answering	Showing interest
How was your weekend?	It was great/terrible!	
	Not bad/OK.	Really?
What did you do at the weekend?	Nothing special.	That sounds nice/great/lovely/good/interesting/terrible.
Where did you go?	I went to the park.	
What did you do?	I played tennis with my friends.	That's a shame.
Who did you go with?	John, Steve and Amy.	

In spoken English, when you show interest, it's possible to leave out *That*, e.g. *Sounds great/terrible!*

LB 6

PRACTICE

6.1

A Put the words in the correct order. Add capital letters.
1. child / were / a / you / happy?
2. was / holiday / your / how?
3. yesterday / concert / at / Jack / was / the?
4. were / last / night / the / open / windows?
5. people / the / many / at / there / how / were / party?

B Complete the answers to the questions in Exercise A.
1. Yes, I _____.
2. It _____ great, thanks.
3. No, he _____.
4. Yes, they _____.
5. There _____ about fifty.

6.2

A Complete the sentences with the verbs in the box. Use the past simple.

| dance   play (x2)   love   study (x2) |
| listen to   work |

1. Mick Jagger _____ economics in London in 1961.
2. Madonna _____ the drums in a band called *The Breakfast Club*.
3. When she was four, Shakira _____ on the table to some Arabic music.
4. Brad Pitt _____ as a driver before he was a film star.
5. Cate Blanchett _____ the piano every day when she was young.
6. Jean-Claude Van Damme _____ ballet for five years.
7. Shizuka Arakawa _____ swimming and ballet when she was young.
8. Ronaldinho _____ samba music when he was young.

B Read the text. Then complete the story about yesterday with the verbs in brackets in the correct form.

Tom usually gets up at six, does some exercise and walks to work. He eats lunch alone, leaves work at five, meets his girlfriend for dinner. Then he reads a book in the evening, drinks a cup of tea and goes to bed early.

But yesterday was different. he ¹*didn't get up* (not get up) at six, he ² _____ (get up) at eight. He ³ _____ (not do) any exercise and he ⁴ _____ (drive) to work. He ⁵ _____ (not have) lunch alone – he ⁶ _____ (meet) his friend Sally at a restaurant. She ⁷ _____ (tell) him about her problems, but he ⁸ _____ (not listen). He ⁹ _____ (not meet) his girlfriend for dinner – he ¹⁰ _____ (eat) alone, then ¹¹ _____ (watch) a DVD. Two things ¹² _____ (not change): he ¹³ _____ (drink) a cup of tea and ¹⁴ _____ (go) to bed early as usual.

C Complete the questions using the answers to help. Who is the famous person?

1. Born?
   When *was he born* ?
   In 1963. He was born in Kentucky, USA.
2. Lived when young?
   Where _____?
   In a lot of different places. His family moved twenty times.
3. Began film work?
   When _____?
   He began acting in films in 1984. His first film was *A Nightmare on Elm Street*.
4. What role had most fun playing?
   What _____?
   Captain Jack Sparrow in *Pirates of the Caribbean*.

6.3

A Complete the conversation.
A: Hi, Chris. How ¹_____ _____ weekend?
B: Not bad.
A: What ²_____ _____ do?
B: I stayed at home on Saturday and did my homework. On Sunday we went swimming.
A: ³_____ _____ good. Who did ⁴_____ _____ with?
B: With my sister and her family. They've got three kids.
A: Really? Where ⁵_____ _____ go?
B: Oh, just to the swimming pool. And you? What did you ⁶_____ _____ the weekend?
A: Liz and I went clubbing on Friday night. Then I stayed in bed all weekend.
B: ⁷_____ _____ great!
A: It wasn't great – I was ill.
B: Oh, ⁸_____ a shame!

7 LANGUAGE BANK

GRAMMAR

7.1 comparatives

adjective		comparative	rule
one-syllable adjectives some two-syllable adjectives	cold quiet	colder quieter	+ -er
adjectives: ending in -e	large	larger	+ -r
ending in -y	noisy	noisier	y + -ier
ending in a consonant + vowel + consonant	hot	hotter	double the final consonant
many two-syllable adjectives all longer adjectives	boring expensive	more boring more expensive	more + adjective
irregular adjectives	good bad	better worse	

Use comparatives (+ *than*) to compare things and people.
Use *than* not *that* with comparatives: *A restaurant is quieter **than** a disco.* NOT ~~A restaurant is quieter that a disco.~~

7.2 superlatives

adjective	comparative	superlative	rule
cold	colder	the coldest	*the* + *-est*
nice	nicer	the nicest	*the* + *-st*
friendly	friendlier	the friendliest	*the y* + *-iest*
big	bigger	the biggest	double the final consonant
boring interesting	more boring more interesting	the most boring the most interesting	*the most* + adjective
good bad	better worse	the best the worst	

Use superlatives to talk about the number one thing in a group: *Maria's spelling is **the best in the class**.*
Note: The spelling rules for superlatives are the same as for comparatives.

7.3 asking for/giving directions

Go	straight on. /ahead.	
	down/past	the High Street. /the bank.
Turn	left/right	into East Avenue.
Take	the first/second/third	left. /right.
It's	on the left/right.	

Use imperatives (e.g. *turn, take, go*) to give directions.
In speaking, it is also possible to add *You*: ***You** go past the cinema and turn left.*
To ask for directions, use *Can you tell me the way to* + place: ***Can you tell me the way to** the sports centre?*
When speaking, check information by repeating what you hear: *The **third** right? So, I take the **next left**?*
Correct information by stressing the correction: *No, the **first** right. No, the next **right**.*

140

LB 7

PRACTICE

7.1

A Write the comparative of the adjectives.

1. fast — _faster_
2. close — _____
3. big — _____
4. beautiful — _____
5. easy — _____
6. cheap — _____
7. important — _____
8. happy — _____

B Complete the sentences with comparatives. Use the adjectives in brackets to help.

1. A café is _quieter_ than a nightclub. (quiet)
2. Travelling by train is _____ _____ flying. (slow)
3. A nightclub is _____ _____ a café. (noisy)
4. It's _____ in India _____ in England. (hot)
5. Eating at a café is _____ _____ eating in a restaurant. (cheap)
6. The weather is _____ in autumn _____ in summer. (bad)

7.2

A Write the superlative of the adjectives.

1. great — _the greatest_
2. quiet — _____
3. comfortable — _____
4. close — _____
5. noisy — _____
6. cheap — _____
7. interesting — _____
8. hot — _____
9. fast — _____
10. crowded — _____

B Complete the sentences. Use the superlative of the adjectives in the box.

| ~~long~~ busy big high good old deep popular |

1. _The longest_ bridge in the world is the Pearl Bridge in Japan. It's 1,991 metres.
2. _____ tourist destination in Europe is Disneyland Paris. Over twelve million people visit it in a year.
3. _____ and _____ lake in the world is Lake Baikal, in southern Siberia, Russia. It's 1,600 metres deep and over twenty-five million years old.
4. _____ jungle (rainforest) in the world is the Amazon. It's four million square kilometres.
5. _____ mountain in the USA is Mount McKinley. It's 6,194 metres. _____ view is at the top.
6. _____ train station in the world is the Shinjuku Station in Tokyo. Over three million people use it every day and it has over 200 exits.

7.3

A Read the conversation. Add six more missing words.

A: Excuse ^me. Can you tell me way to the beach?

B: Yes, you right at the cinema. Then go straight for about five minutes.

A: Five minutes?

B: Yes, and then turn left Menier Avenue and then take second street on right. I think it's Grand Avenue. You can see the beach straight ahead.

A: Thank you very much.

141

8 LANGUAGE BANK

GRAMMAR

8.1 Present continuous

+	I	'm	having	a great time.
	He/She/It	's	sitting	on the balcony.
	You/We/They	're	waiting	for a train.

−	I	'm not	enjoying	this food.
	He/She/It	isn't	working	at the moment.
	You/We/They	aren't	doing	anything.

?	Am	I	leaving?
	Are	you/we/they	leaving?
	Is	he/she/it	working?

Yes,	I	am.
	you/we/they	are.
No,	I	'm not.
	you/we/they	aren't.
Yes,	he/she/it	is.
No,	he/she/it	isn't.

Use the present continuous to speak about something happening now / at this moment.

In speaking, usually use the contracted form: **I am not** = **I'm not**. NOT ~~I am not~~.

In the negative, also use: He's **not** working. They're **not** doing anything.

Spelling -ing

Most verbs + -ing	wait	waiting
	do	doing
Verbs ending in -e, e̶ + -ing	write	writing
	take	taking
Most verbs ending in a consonant–vowel–consonant, double the final consonant	swim	swimming
	run	running

8.2 Present simple and present continuous

Mario often	wears	a jacket and tie.
Now he	's wearing	jeans and a T-shirt.

What	do	you	do?	I'm a police officer.
	are		doing?	I'm writing down your number!

Use the present simple to talk about habits or routines: **We often watch** DVDs on Friday evenings.

Also use it to talk about things which are always true or true for a long time: **Elinor works** in the city centre.

Use the present continuous to speak about something happening at this moment: Sorry, I can't chat now. **I'm watching** a new DVD.

8.3 Asking for a recommendation

What do you recommend?	
Do you think I'd like	this DVD?
	it?

Giving a recommendation

What kind of	films	do you like?
I think	you'd like	Gold River.
I don't think		it.
There's a good	film	called Impact.

142

LB 8

PRACTICE

8.1

A Write the *-ing* form of the verbs.

1. live _____
2. go _____
3. come _____
4. put _____
5. feel _____
6. make _____
7. get _____
8. stand _____
9. drive _____
10. meet _____

B Write a phone conversation using the prompts below.

Bruno: Hi, Gerald. It's me. you / sleep? *Are you sleeping?*
Gerald: No, I'm at work. I / read.
Bruno: What / you / read?
Gerald: I / read some reports. What / you / do?
Bruno: Karl and I / play cards and listen / to music.
Gerald: Hey, why / you / not / work?
Bruno: I / take a break.
Gerald: Uh-oh. I / talk on the speaker phone. The boss / listen.
Bruno: you / joke?
Boss: No, he / not / joke!

8.2

A Complete the sentences with the verbs in the box in the correct form.

> ~~wear (x2)~~ listen to (x2) write have (x2)
> phone stay (x2) watch (x2)

1. I ____wear____ glasses but I ___'m not wearing___ them now.
2. I don't normally _____ TV, but I _____ it now.
3. We usually _____ salad for lunch, but today we _____ sandwiches.
4. I _____ my mother an email at the moment – usually I _____ her.
5. We often _____ classical music in the office, but today we _____ pop.
6. He usually _____ in a five-star hotel, but now he _____ in a self-catering apartment.

B Complete the questions with the verbs in brackets. Use the present simple or the present continuous.

1. ___Do___ you ___study___ English every day? (study)
2. _____ you _____ English now? (study)
3. _____ your best friend _____ every day? (work)
4. _____ your best friend _____ at the moment? (work)
5. _____ your teacher _____ blue today? (wear)
6. _____ your teacher often _____ blue? (wear)
7. _____ you usually _____ grammar exercises alone? (do)
8. _____ you _____ this exercise alone? (do)
9. _____ you _____ to English shows/music a lot? (listen to)
10. _____ you _____ to English shows/music at the moment? (listen to)

8.3

A Read the conversation and correct the mistakes.

Ines: I'd like to watch a good DVD. What recommend?
Pedro: What films you like?
Ines: Action films, mostly. Yes, and comedies.
Pedro: It's a good film called *Rush Hour*.
Ines: Who in it?
Pedro: Jackie Chan and Chris Tucker.
Ines: What's about?
Pedro: Jackie Chan is a detective and he comes to New York to help a friend.
Ines: You think I like?
Pedro: Yeah, I think so. I'll bring it tomorrow and you can borrow it.

9 LANGUAGE BANK

GRAMMAR

9.1 articles

no article		
usually use no article	before plural nouns when we speak in general	I like cats, but I don't like dogs. Sweets are bad for you.
	before cities and countries	Shanghai is in China. I went to Russia last year.
	in some phrases	go by car/train/bus/taxi go on foot go home, go to work/school be at home/work/school have breakfast/dinner/lunch

a/an		
usually use *a/an*	before singular nouns	It's a Ferrari. I've got a younger brother.
	before jobs	My sister's a teacher.

the		
usually use *the*	before nouns when there's only one	The president visited us last year. Can you close the door, please?
	in some phrases	in the morning/afternoon/evening at the weekend in the town/city centre on the right/left

With countries, use *the* with groups: **the** *United States,* **the** *United Arab Emirates.*

With times, use *in the morning/afternoon/evening* but use *at night* (no article).

9.2 can/can't, have to/don't have to

I/You/He/She/We/They	can	use	the bikes for free.
I/You/He/She/We/They	can't	park	in the city centre.
I/You/We/They	have to	pay	ten euros.
He/She/It	has to		
I/You/We/They	don't have to	pay	anything – it's free.
He/She/It	doesn't have to		

Use *can* when something is OK/permitted.
Use *can't* when something is not OK/not permitted.
Use *have to* when something is necessary/obligatory.
Use *don't have to* when something is not necessary/obligatory.
Compare:
You **can't** come to the party. (You didn't get an invitation.)
You **don't have to** come to the party. (You got an invitation, but it's OK to stay at home.)

9.3 apologising

Apologising		Responding
Sorry I'm late. I'm really/very sorry. I'm terribly/so sorry. I feel bad/terrible about this.		+ That's OK. No problem. Don't worry about it. No, really. It's fine.
I'm afraid Sorry, but	(+ reason) I missed the bus. I didn't hear my alarm clock. I lost my keys.	– I don't believe you. Don't let it happen again.

When speaking:
- to emphasise how sorry you are, use an adverb or *so* + *sorry*: *I'm terribly/so sorry.*
- to show how it makes you feel, use *feel* + adjective: *I feel terrible about the mess!*
- reply with *No, really. It's fine* when someone apologises again: **A:** *I'm so sorry.* **B:** *Don't worry about it.* **A:** *But I feel terrible …* **B:** *No, really. It's fine.*
- Use *Don't let it happen again* only when you're really angry.

144

PRACTICE

9.1

A Complete the text with *a/an*, *the* or no article (–).

Lucio is from [1] _Italy_ and he's [2] _____ doctor. He was born and grew up in [3] _____ Venice but now he lives just outside [4] _____ small town in the south. Every day, early in [5] _____ morning, he leaves [6] _____ home and drives to his clinic in [7] _____ town centre. He usually has [8] _____ lunch with [9] _____ colleagues and sometimes teaches in [10] _____ afternoon. At [11] _____ weekend, he often visits his brother's family. They live in the countryside, about two hours away by [12] _____ car.

B Complete the sentences with *a/an*, *the* or no article (–).

1 I think _–_ cars are safer than motorbikes.
2 I'd like ____ scooter for my birthday.
3 It's the best airline in ____ world.
4 I rode ____ bike to school when I was younger.
5 I hate ____ boats. I'm always sick!
6 I live in a small village and walk to ____ train station every day.

C Read the conversation. Find and correct six mistakes with *the*. (Two are correct.)

Pedro: Mrs Thorpe. Where can I buy **the** dictionary?
Mrs T: There's **the** bookshop in South Street. I think they sell **the** dictionaries. What kind do you want?
Pedro: I need **the** English–Spanish dictionary for my English class. **The** teacher said we have to get one. **The** only problem is that **the** books are very expensive here.
Mrs T: Maybe you can borrow one. Does your school have **the** library?
Pedro: Yes, it does. Good idea. I can ask there.

9.2

A Look at signs A–F. What do they mean? Underline the correct alternative.

1 Motorbikes *don't have to/can't* go here. They *have to/don't have to* go on another road.
2 You *can/have to* park here for free. You *can't/don't have to* pay for fifteen minutes parking.
3 Bikes *have to/can* keep left. People on foot *don't have to/can't* walk on the left.
4 You *can/can't* catch the bus here. You *have to/don't have to* wait more than ten minutes.
5 You *can't/don't have to* ride your bike. You *can/have to* get off and walk.
6 You *can/can't* take a taxi here. You *can/can't* park here.

B Complete the conversations. Use the correct form of *can/can't*, *have to/don't have to* and the verb in bold.

Conversation 1
A: You [1] _have to wear_ (wear) a jacket and tie to this dinner. It's a very formal party.
B: But it's so hot!
A: Well, you [2] _____ (wear) your light jacket.

Conversation 2
A: You [3] _____ (come) to the meeting. It's not very important.
B: That's good because I [4] _____ (come) – I'm too busy.

Conversation 3
A: I [5] _____ (get) a birthday present for Sandra. I completely forgot yesterday.
B: It's OK. You [6] _____ (get) anything. I bought her a present from both of us.
A: Thanks! What did you buy?

9.3

A Read the conversation and correct the six mistakes.

Teacher: Can I have your homework?
Student: Oh, I really sorry. I'm afraid of left it at home.
Teacher: Don't worry it. Did you do it?
Student: Yes, of course.
Teacher: Which part did you think was difficult?
Student: Sorry, both I don't remember.
Teacher: Did you *really* do it?
Student: Er … I afraid I forgot to do it.
Teacher: Don't left it happen again!

10 LANGUAGE BANK

GRAMMAR

10.1 be going to

+	I	'm	going to	be there	soon.
	He/She/It	's		eat	tonight.
	You/We/They	're		practise	tomorrow.
–	I	'm not			
	He/She/It	isn't			
	You/We/They	aren't			

Use *be going to* + verb to talk about plans and intentions: I**'m going to do** my homework **tonight**.

In the negative, also use *is/are not going to*: We **aren't going to go** to the concert.

With *be going to* + *go*, you don't need to repeat *go*: She**'s going** (to go) to the post office.

It is possible to use *be going to* with future time phrases, e.g. *tomorrow, soon, this weekend, next week, next month, next year, in two years*. **In two weeks** (time) I**'m going to be** on holiday!

?	Am	I	going to	speak to Eva today?
	Is	he/she		
	Are	you/we/they		

+	Yes,	I	am.
		he/she/it	is.
		we/you/they	are.
–	No,	I	'm not.
		he/she/it	isn't.
		we/you/they	aren't.

would like to

+	I/You/He/She/It/We/They	would / 'd	like to	go.
–		wouldn't		

?	Would	I/you/he/she/it/we/they	like to	drink some tea?

+	Yes,	I/you/he/she/it/we/they	would.
–	No,		wouldn't.

Use *I'd like to* + infinitive to talk about what you want to do: *It's hot.* I**'d like to go** for a swim.

You can also use *want to* + infinitive for the same idea: I **want to go** to the gym.

Note: *I'd like to* is more polite than *I want*.

10.2 will/might (not)/won't

+	I/You/He/She/It/We/They	'll (will)	go shopping.
		might	visit some friends.
–		might not	
		won't (will not)	

Use *might* + infinitive to predict the future if you are not certain: I **might see** Yuki tonight (= it's possible, but I'm not sure).

It is also possible to use *will*, *might*, *might not*, and *won't* with *there*: I think **there will be** a lot of people at the party.

?	Will	I/you/he/she/it/we/they	win?

+	Yes,	I/you/he/she/it/we/they	will.
–	No,		won't.

Use *will* + infinitive and *won't* + infinitive to predict the future when you are certain about it.

10.3 making suggestions

How about	going	to the zoo?
What about		
Why don't I/you/we	go	internet shopping?
Let's	cook	something.

Use *How/What about* + verb + *-ing* in questions: **What about** ha**ving** lunch now?
Use *Why don't* + subject + verb in questions: **Why don't we watch** a film?
Use *Let's* + verb in positive sentences: **Let's go** to the beach.

responding to suggestions

+	Great/Brilliant!
	(That's a) good idea.
	Sounds interesting.
	OK.
–	I don't really feel like going.
	That/It doesn't sound very good.
	That might be a problem.

146

PRACTICE

10.1

A Complete the sentences with the correct form of *be going to*. Use the verbs in brackets.
1 I _____ the cinema tonight. (go)
2 We _____ a flat next weekend. (look at)
3 _____ ready in time? (you / be)
4 We _____. (not wait)
5 They _____ a new car. (buy)
6 When _____ to Rome? (Steve / go)

B Underline the correct alternative.
1 I *'d like to go / 'm going* to the theatre, but there are no more tickets.
2 I *'d like to go / 'm going* to a concert tonight. I've got the tickets here.
3 We *'d like to / 're going to* buy a bigger flat, but we don't have enough money.
4 I *'d like to / 'm going to* take a trip to Zurich tomorrow. My train leaves at 7a.m.

C Complete the sentences with the words in the box.

like (x2)   don't   'd (x2)   would (x2)   want

A: Would you ¹_____ to go to the party?
B: Yes, I ²_____, but I've got too much work.
A: Would you ³_____ to dance?
B: No, thanks. I ⁴_____ like to sit down for a minute!
A: What ⁵_____ you like to do on your birthday tomorrow?
B: I don't know, I ⁶_____ want to think about it. I feel quite old!
A: Do you ⁷_____ to have dinner with me tonight?
B: I ⁸_____ love to!

10.2

A Complete the conversation with *'ll, will, won't* or *might*.
A: Oh, no. The dog ran away again!
B: Don't worry – he ¹_____ come back.
A: Are you sure he ²_____?
B: OK, he ³_____ not come back today – that's possible. But I'm sure he ⁴_____ come back tomorrow.
A: I don't believe you! He ⁵_____ come back. We ⁶_____ never see him again – I'm sure.
B: Oh, look … Here he is now!

B Circle the two correct alternatives.
1 He (will) / (won't) / might eat it – I'm sure!
2 It *might / 'll / won't* rain, so bring an umbrella.
3 There *might not / won't / might* be enough time to finish the whole film, so let's not start.
4 I *might not / 'll / won't* go by train. It's quicker by car.
5 She *might / won't / 'll* phone tomorrow so please take a message.
6 We *might / 'll / won't* be late, so don't wait for us.

10.3

A Put the words from the box in the correct places in the conversation.

~~about~~   problem   idea   don't   like   how   have

           about
Sam: I'm tired. How ∧ having a break now?
Jim: I don't feel stopping.
Sam: Oh, come on! Let's a coffee.
Jim: Why *you* make some coffee? I'll go on working.
Sam: That's a good. about a sandwich?
Jim: No thanks – I want to finish this.
Sam: Mmm. That might be a. You work, I'll have lunch.
Jim: It's not a problem for *me*!

11 LANGUAGE BANK

GRAMMAR

11.1 should/shouldn't

+	I/you/he/she/it/we/they	should	go to bed.
			drink lots of water.
–		shouldn't	take antibiotics.
			work.

?	Should	I/you/he/she/it/we/they	go	to the doctor?	Yes,	I/you/he/she/it/we/they	should.
					No,		shouldn't.

Use *should* + infinitive to give advice: You **should take** an aspirin
and to recommend: You **should see** that film.

Note: You **should try** this soup. NOT *You should to try this soup*.

11.2 adverbs

	adjective	adverb
Most adjectives, add *-ly*	bad	badly
	loud	loudly
	careful	carefully
Adjectives ending in *-y*, *-y* + *-ily*	easy	easily
	angry	angrily
Adjectives ending in *-le*, change to *-ly*	terrible	terribly
Irregular adverbs	good	well
	fast	fast NOT *fastly*
	hard (= difficult)	hard NOT *hardly*
	early	early
	late	late

Use adverbs of manner to say how you do something: I can swim **well**. She spoke **quietly**.

Use adverbs of time to say when you did something: I went to bed **early**. She had lunch **late**.

Use adverbs with verbs: He **drives** badly.

BUT with *be* and *feel*, use adjectives: The film **was** terrible. I **feel** terrible.

Use adjectives with nouns: He's a **bad driver**.

Adverbs often go after the verb: I **arrived early**. She **drove quickly** to the shops.

or after the verb phrase: I **started work early**. She **drove her car quickly**.

or at the end: I **arrived** at work **early**. She **drove** to the shops **quickly**.

11.3 offering to help

Problems	Offers		Thanking	Responses
I can't lift this case	I'll	do it.	Thanks a lot.	You're welcome.
It's hot in here	Let me	try.	That's kind of you.	No problem.
	Shall I	do it?	Thanks. I'm very grateful.	That's OK.
		try?		

Use *I'll* (NOT *I will*), *Let me* and *Shall I* + infinitive to offer help.

148

LB 11

PRACTICE

11.1

A Complete questions 1–6. Then match them with replies a)–f).

1 I don't have much time. _Should I_ send Kirsten an email? d)
2 Ben doesn't like the colour of his mobile. _____ get a new one?
3 Look at my hair – it's a mess! _____ get a haircut?
4 Some students never say anything in class. _____ speak more?
5 My daughter wants to travel in South America. _____ learn Spanish?
6 There are so many words we don't know. _____ buy an electronic dictionary?

a) Yes, you should. It's too long.
b) Yes, they should. It's important to practise.
c) No, he shouldn't. The old one is fine.
d) No, you shouldn't. Phone her – it's quicker.
e) Yes, she should if she has enough time.
f) Yes, you should get an English–English one.

B Complete the sentences with *should* or *shouldn't* and a verb from the box.

~~get~~ go have stay try wear change

1 My camera's very old. I _should get_ a new one.
2 You _____ this drink. It's delicious!
3 Do you think I _____ my money here or at the airport?
4 You _____ black. I think it doesn't look good on you – sorry!
5 They _____ by taxi. It's too expensive.
6 She looks tired. She _____ a holiday.
7 We _____ out in the sun too long. We'll get sunburnt.

11.2

A Complete the sentences. Use the adjective or adverb form of the word in brackets.

1 The teacher was very _____. She spoke to the students _____. (angry)
2 She dances _____. She's such a _____ dancer. (beautiful)
3 I passed the exam _____. It was _____. (easy)
4 Shhh – be _____. The baby's sleeping. We have to talk _____. (quiet)
5 She's a _____ teacher. She teaches _____. (good)
6 I sing _____. I'm a _____ singer. (terrible)

B Complete the story. Use the adverb forms of the adjectives in the box.

~~early~~ late easy quick angry slow

The other morning, I woke up ¹ _early_ because the neighbours were shouting ² _____. I didn't want to stay at home, so I made some breakfast ³ _____ and ran out of the door to work. I forgot to take an umbrella and it started raining so I got very wet. I got to the station at 7.50 and caught the eight o'clock train ⁴ _____. I was surprised when I looked round because the train was empty. Because of the rain, the train went very ⁵ _____ so I arrived at the office ⁶ _____. There was no one there. Then I realised that it was Sunday, and I didn't have to work!

11.3

A Complete the five conversations below. Use the verbs in brackets to help.

Conversation 1
A: I can't find the information anywhere.
B: I' _____ _____ on the computer. (check)

Conversation 2
A: I don't understand this homework.
B: _____ me _____ a look. (have)

Conversation 3
A: My hands are full. I can't carry all these things.
B: _____ I _____ something for you? (carry)

Conversation 4
A: The radio is too loud.
B: _____ I _____ it down? (turn)

Conversation 5
A: The top on this bottle is too tight.
B: _____ me try to _____ it. (open)

149

12 LANGUAGE BANK

GRAMMAR

12.1 present perfect

Use the present perfect to talk about past experiences in your life. Usually you don't know or say *when* exactly these things happened.

+	I/You/We/They	've	climbed	a volcano.
	He/She/It	's	travelled	around the world.
–	I/You/We/They	haven't	worked	in different countries.
	He/She/It	hasn't	studied	lots of languages.

Ever = 'in your life'. In the negative you can use *never*: I've **never** played golf.

?	Have	I/you/we/they	(ever) worked	in Australia?	Yes, No,	I/we/you/they	have. haven't.
	Has	he/she/it			Yes, No,	he/she/it	has. hasn't.

Make the present perfect with *have/has* + past participle.

For regular verbs, the past participles are the same as the past simple.

Many common verbs have an irregular past participle form. Look at the list on page 127.

I/You/We/They	've	been to	the Bahamas.
He/She/It	's	seen	Mount Fuji.

Go has two past participles: *been* and *gone*:

She's **gone** to India. = She went there and she's there now.

She's **been** to India. = She went there in the past and she came back.

12.2 present perfect or past simple

Use the present perfect to talk about past experiences in your life. You don't say exactly *when*: I**'ve travelled** in South America.

Use the past simple if you say *when* something happened: I **travelled** in Poland in May 2008.

When speaking, it is possible to start a conversation by asking a question in the present perfect and then asking about more details in the past simple:
A: **Have** you **ever been** to the USA?
B: Yes, I have. I **went** there two years ago.
A: **Did** you **like** it?
B: Yes, it **was** great!

I**'ve travelled** in South America.
   in South America
The past   NOW

I **travelled** in Poland in May 2008.
   went to Poland
The past   May 2008   NOW

12.3 telephoning

Calling a friend	Hi, Philippe. It's Debbie. Is Lise there?
Calling a business	Hello. This is Carla Rimini. Could I speak to Alan Jones, please?
Calling back	Could you ring back? Just ask him/her to call me. I'll call you back.
Leaving/taking a message	Could I leave a message for him/her? Could you give me the number? Let me check that.

Use *It's* + name (informal) or *This is* + name (formal) NOT ~~I am~~: Hello, **this is** Ali Hassan.

150

LB 12

PRACTICE

12.1
A Write sentences in the present perfect.
1. you / ever / eat / Japanese food?
2. I / eat / Japanese food two or three times
3. we / never / sleep / in a hotel before
4. they / drive / across Europe many times
5. he / ever / go / to England?
6. she / have / three husbands
7. I / spend / too much money
8. She / learn / Arabic, Spanish and Chinese
9. you / ever / climb / a mountain?
10. My parents / never / use / an iPod

B Correct ten mistakes in the conversation.
A: You have ever been to Australia?
B: No, I have. And you?
A: Yes, I've.
B: And have you gone to China, too?
A: No, but I been to Korea.
B: You've travel in many countries in your life …
A: Yes, I has. I've meeted a lot of people and I've try a lot of interesting food.
B: But you haven't learn to speak English perfectly!
A: Not yet …

12.2
A Read the email and underline the correct alternatives.

Hi Renata,

Thanks for the email. Lucky you … going to Italy next month! You asked me about Venice. Yes, ¹*I've been/ went* there. ²*I've been/went* there for a long weekend last year. ³*It has been/was* beautiful. ⁴*I've loved / loved* all the bridges and old squares. ⁵*I've also visited/also visited* Rome. ⁶*We have been/were* there in 2006. It's busier than Venice, but I know you like old buildings and churches, so maybe you'd like Rome better. ⁷*I've never travelled/never travelled* in the Italian countryside but my friend Emily ⁸*has driven/drove* around the south and she says it's lovely, but very hot at that time of year. Anyway, I'm sure you'll have a great time! Send me some photos.

Simone

B Complete the sentences using the prompts in brackets.
1. *Have you seen* Gangs of New York? (you / see)
   Yes, I ____saw____ it a few years ago.
2. _____ Sarah? (you / meet)
   Yes, we _____ last year.
3. _____ to Spain? (Lea / go)
   Yes, she _____ there last summer.
4. _____ an accident on his motorbike? (Paolo / ever have)
   Yes, he _____ a small accident a month ago.
5. _____ Anna Karenina? (you / read)
   Yes, I _____ it at university.
6. _____ school? (your children / finish)
   Yes, they _____ a long time ago.

12.3
A Complete Judy's sentences. Then write the correct response from Dan.

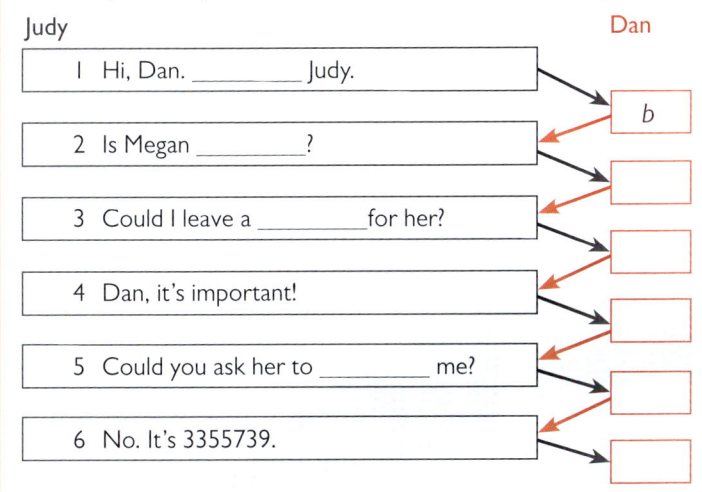

Judy
1. Hi, Dan. _____ Judy.
2. Is Megan _____?
3. Could I leave a _____ for her?
4. Dan, it's important!
5. Could you ask her to _____ me?
6. No. It's 3355739.

Dan
1. b
2. ___
3. ___
4. ___
5. ___
6. ___

a) 3355739. OK, got it. I'll tell her.
b) Oh, hi Judy.
c) No, she's gone out somewhere.
d) Has she got your number?
e) Let me just look … OK, I've got one.
f) A message … ? Oh, I can't find a pen. Could you ring me back?

151

PHOTO BANK

COUNTRIES AND NATIONALITIES

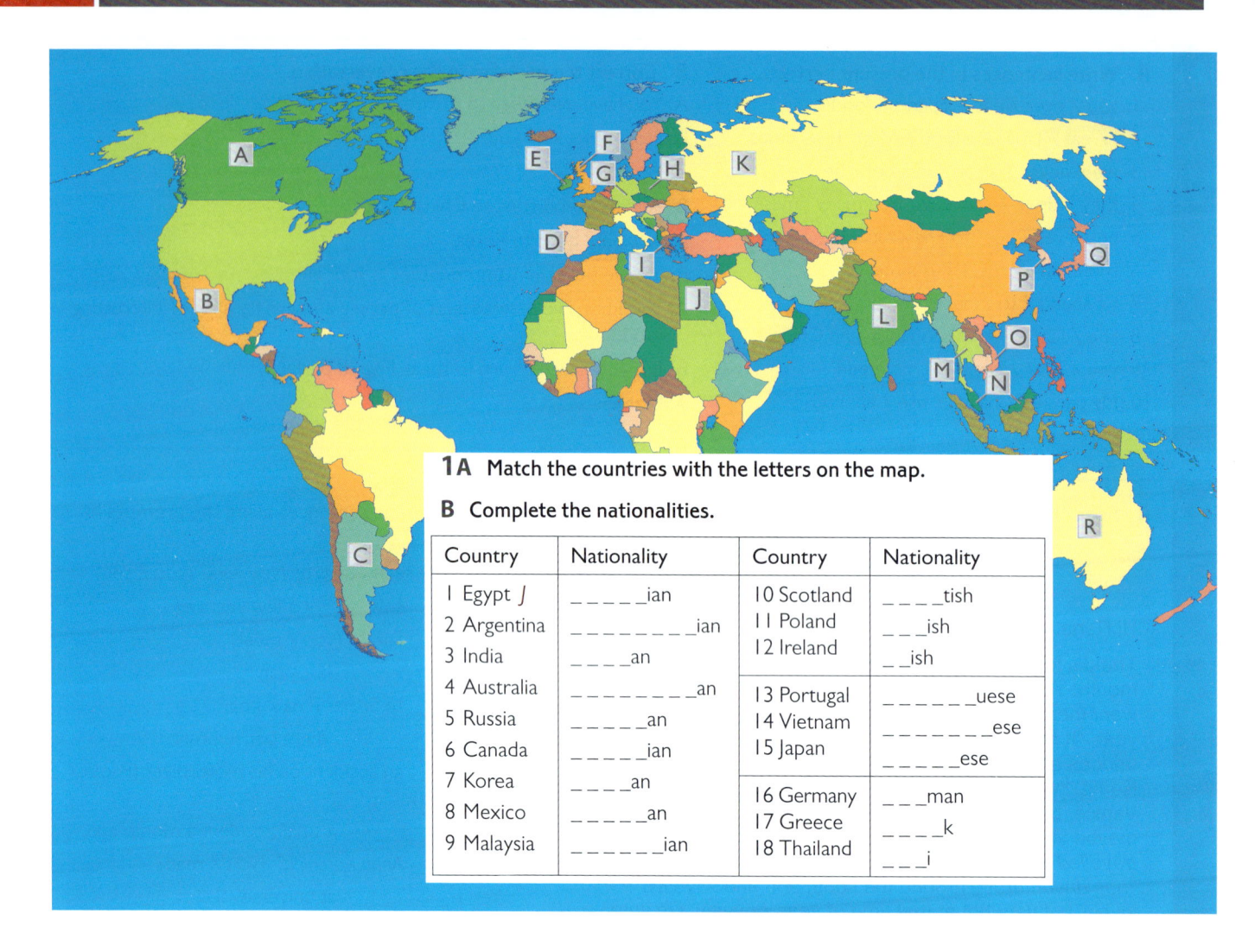

1A Match the countries with the letters on the map.

B Complete the nationalities.

Country	Nationality	Country	Nationality
1 Egypt J	_ _ _ _ ian	10 Scotland	_ _ _ tish
2 Argentina	_ _ _ _ _ _ ian	11 Poland	_ _ ish
3 India	_ _ _ an	12 Ireland	_ _ ish
4 Australia	_ _ _ _ _ _ an	13 Portugal	_ _ _ _ _ uese
5 Russia	_ _ _ _ an	14 Vietnam	_ _ _ _ _ _ ese
6 Canada	_ _ _ _ ian	15 Japan	_ _ _ _ _ ese
7 Korea	_ _ _ an	16 Germany	_ _ _ man
8 Mexico	_ _ _ _ an	17 Greece	_ _ _ _ k
9 Malaysia	_ _ _ _ _ ian	18 Thailand	_ _ _ i

EVERYDAY OBJECTS

1A Match the everyday objects with the photos.

B Complete the gaps with a, an or –.

1 *a* dictionary   A
2 _–_ stamps
3 ____ identity card
4 ____ sweets
5 ____ file
6 ____ tissues [pocket pack]
7 ____ umbrella
8 ____ glasses
9 ____ wallet
10 ____ comb
11 ____ driving licence
12 ____ coins
13 ____ chewing gum
14 ____ batteries
15 ____ credit card

PB

JOBS

1A Match the jobs with the pictures.

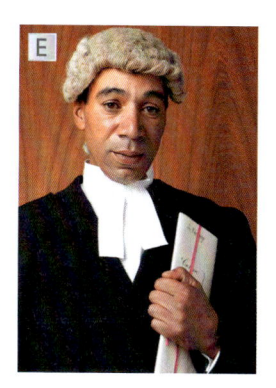

B Complete the gaps with *a* or *an*.

1 ____ lawyer
2 ____ teacher
3 ____ accountant
4 ____ police officer
5 ____ engineer
6 ____ politician
7 ____ hairdresser
8 ____ shop assistant
9 ____ chef
10 ____ doctor
11 ____ receptionist
12 ____ nurse
13 ____ personal assistant (PA)
14 ____ waiter/waitress
15 ____ sportsman/sportswoman
16 ____ actor/actress
17 ____ businessman/businesswoman

153

PHOTO BANK

FAMILY

A Frank Jackson
B Maggie Jackson
C Ann Barnes
D John Barnes
E Elizabeth Jackson
F Robert Jackson
G Katy Barnes
H Jake Barnes
I Mark Jackson
J Amy Jackson

1A Look at the family tree and write the people in the correct space below.

1 _____ are Jake's grandfather and grandmother.
2 _____ are Jake's father and mother (parents).
3 _____ is Elizabeth's husband.
4 _____ is John's wife.
5 _____ are Elizabeth and Robert's son and daughter.
6 _____ is Jake's sister.
7 _____ is Amy's brother.
8 _____ are Katy's aunt and uncle.
9 _____ are Mark's cousins.
10 _____ are Ann's nephew and niece.

B Choose one person from the family tree. Then use the words in the box to write how he/she is related to the other people.

father mother wife husband parents grandfather grandmother son daughter brother sister uncle aunt cousin niece nephew

Robert is Maggie's son. He's Elizabeth's …
_____
_____
_____

ROOMS AND FURNITURE

1A Match the names of the rooms and places with the photos.

1 garage
2 balcony
3 hall
4 kitchen
5 dining room
6 living room
7 stairs
8 home office
9 bedroom
10 bathroom
11 upstairs
12 downstairs

B Now label the items of the furniture using the words in the box below.

| armchair bath bed carpet cupboard |
| desk lamp plant rug shower sink |
| sofa table wardrobe washbasin |

2 Look at the pictures for thirty seconds. Then close your book and make a list of the furniture in each room.

155

PHOTO BANK

SHOPS

1 Match the names of the shops with the photos.

1 baker's
2 bookshop
3 butcher's
4 clothes shop
5 dry-cleaner's
6 electronics shop
7 greengrocer's
8 hairdresser's
9 internet café
10 pharmacy/chemist's
11 newsagent's
12 shoe shop
13 sports shop
14 supermarket

FOOD

1A Write countable (C) or uncountable (U) next to each word.

1 tomatoes
2 potatoes
3 onions
4 beans
5 peas
6 a cabbage
7 a lettuce
8 corn on the cob
9 a pepper
10 an orange
11 a pear
12 cake
13 crisps
14 biscuits
15 rolls
16 sugar
17 rice
18 pasta
19 cereal
20 herbs
21 spices
22 oil
23 yoghurt
24 beef
25 lamb
26 prawns

B Match the names of the food with the photos.

PHOTO BANK

APPEARANCE AND CLOTHES

1A Label the photos using the words in the box.

tall   short   slim*   overweight**
bald   straight hair   curly hair
long hair   short hair

* also use *thin*, but *slim* is more positive
** *fat* is also possible, but is very negative

B Match the names of the clothes with the photos.

1 socks
2 jeans
3 suit
4 jacket
5 trousers
6 shirt
7 tie
8 top
9 skirt
10 sweater
11 shorts
12 dress
13 T-shirt
14 coat

2 Write which words are adjectives (adj), uncountable nouns (U), countable singular nouns (C sing), countable plural nouns (C pl).

BODY PARTS

1 Match the names of the body parts with the photos.

1 arm
2 back
3 ear
4 eye
5 face
6 finger
7 foot
8 hand
9 head
10 knee
11 leg
12 elbow
13 neck
14 nose
15 shoulder
16 mouth
17 thumb
18 toe

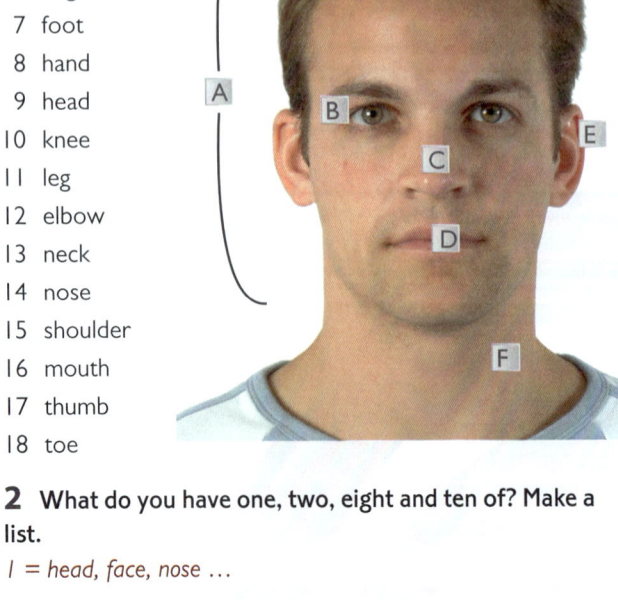

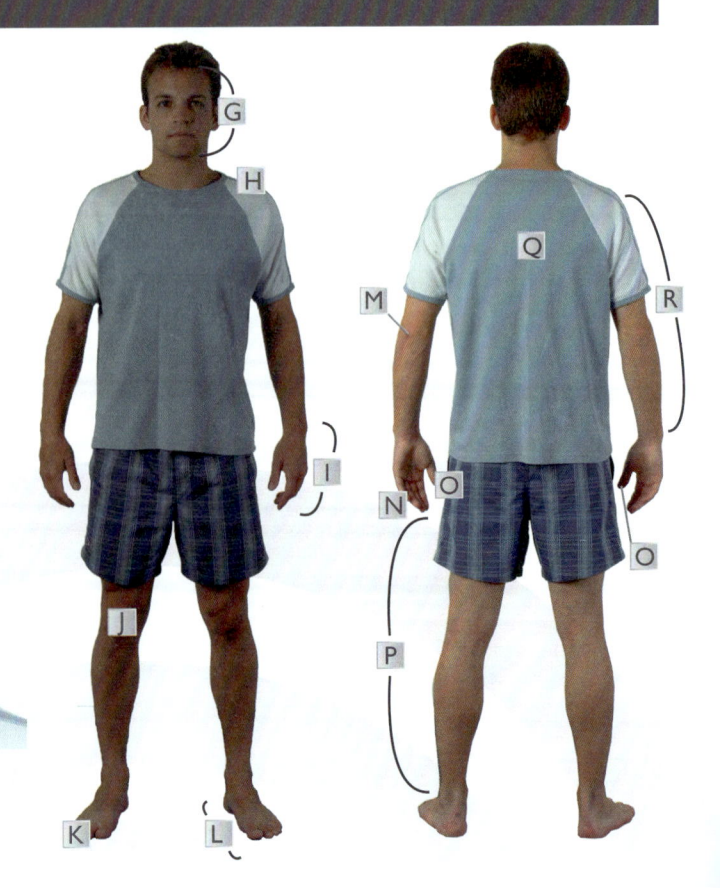

2 What do you have one, two, eight and ten of? Make a list.

1 = head, face, nose …

PB

TRANSPORT

1 Match the types of the transport with the photos.

1. a bike
2. a boat
3. a bus
4. a car
5. a ferry
6. a helicopter
7. a lorry/a truck
8. a motorbike
9. a plane
10. a scooter
11. a ship
12. a taxi
13. a train
14. a tram
15. an underground/ a subway train
16. a van

2 Put the words into the following transport groups:

a bike

- land
- sea
- air

159

COMMUNICATION BANK

6.1

8A Student B: write four important dates for you from last month and practise saying them.

B Work in pairs and take turns to ask and answer about your dates. Remember to sound interested and to give extra information.

A: *August the twelfth.*
B: *Why was that date important?*
A: *Because it was my birthday.*
B: *Really? What did you do? Did you have a good time?*

1.3

7 Student A: ask Student B the prices to complete your table. Then answer Student B's questions.

A: *How much is a sandwich and a tea?*
B: *Three twenty-five. How much is a sandwich and a coffee?*

Student A

	coffee	tea	juice
sandwich	3.50		3.75
burger			4.15
chips	2.20	1.95	
muffin		1.75	

9.2

7A Student B

Madrid
- 58 euros for 72 hours
- no public transport but free bus tour
- over 50 museums, and Madrid Fun Fair, Zoo, Aquarium

2.2

9A Student A: Read the texts. Write questions to ask your partner for the missing information.

1 Where … *does she work?*
2 When …
3 What time …
4 What …
5 What time …
6 What …
7 When …

Jeanette is a doctor – a flying doctor. She works in 1_____ for the Royal Flying Doctors of Australia and travels all over the country. She gets up at 5a.m., has a cup of coffee and goes to the airport at 2_____. She flies to a health centre and starts work. She usually visits two to three places every day and sees fifteen to twenty people. She has lunch at 3_____, but she has dinner late, at 8.30p.m., in one of the places she visits and sometimes she sleeps there! Then she comes back the next morning and 4_____ at 9a.m.

Henri is an acrobat and a father of three boys. He works in Switzerland at the National Circus. He gets up early and has breakfast at 5_____ with his boys. His wife drives the boys to school and Henri goes to the circus at 7a.m. In the morning he 6_____ and practises his high flying routine. On circus days, in the afternoon he sleeps and then has a sandwich at 5.30p.m. He doesn't eat dinner before a show. The evening show starts at 7.30p.m. Henri finishes work at about 7_____ and gets home at 11p.m.

B Ask Student B about the missing information. Complete your text.

4.2

6D Student A: write the buildings on the map on page 41.
The museum is on the left of the pharmacy.
The theatre is next to the museum.

E Ask Student B about the places below. Write them on your map. Then answer Student B's questions.
- the school
- the park

2.3

7A Student A: you work at the Tourist Information Centre. Look at the information below. Answer Student B's questions.

	Start time	Finish time	Leaves from	Price
Harbour tour	9.30a.m.	12.00p.m.	Pier 9, Central	HK$250
Island tour	9.00a.m	2.00p.m.	Outside the post office	HK$320

B Change roles. Student A: now you are a tourist in Hong Kong. Ask Student B questions. Complete the notes below.

	Start time	Finish time	Leaves from	Price
Night tour				
Rock concert				

Excuse me. Can you give me some information about the … ?
What time does it … ?

5.3

7C Student A

Today's specials

Spring special – Salad with cold chicken and fresh bread

Fisherman's platter – Fish, rice and salad

Roman holiday – Spaghetti with meatballs and a cucumber salad

9.1

6B Student B: look at the information about the Lightning Bug. Use a dictionary to check the meaning of any new words. Tell your partner about it. Why is it better than the Horseless Sulky?
- an American invented it in the 1930s
- it's completely safe – impossible to crash, it can't turn over
- there isn't any glass, only plastic windows
- it can stop faster than a car
- it can go up to 65 kilometres per hour

12.3

7B Student A: ask Student B for the telephone numbers. Answer Student B's questions.

A: What's Sam's phone number?
B: It's … What's Ahmed's phone number?
A: It's …

Sam	
Ahmed	5823031
Nina	
Chen	3662149
Simon	
Fatima	0870 1642513
Yuko	
Penny	00 281 5955427

5.2

5B Student A

(The underlined answers are correct.)
1 a) about 300 times   b) about 100 times
2 a) 750 litres   b) 7,500 litres
3 a) 200 bottles   b) 2,000 bottles
4 a) about 2,000   b) about 7,000

7.3

6C Student B: listen to Student A. Use the information below to correct any mistakes.
1 Kris lives in North Avenue.
2 His house is ten minutes from here.
3 It's on the right.

D Now check this information. Read it to Student A.
1 The bank's in West Street.
2 It's on the left.
3 Take the number 5 bus.

1.1

5B Check your answers to the quiz.

1
1 C   2 A   3 D   4 B

2
1 B   2 C   3 D   4 A

3
1 D   2 C   3 B   4 A

COMMUNICATION BANK

1.3

7 Student B: answer Student A's questions. Then ask Student A the prices to complete your table.

A: *How much is a sandwich and a tea?*
B: *Three twenty-five. How much is a sandwich and a coffee?*

	tea	juice	coffee
muffin		2.25	2.00
burger	3.65		3.90
chips		2.45	
sandwich	3.25		

4.3

7A Student A: you are a shop assistant in a sports shop. Look at the things in the list below. Write a different price for each. Then role-play the situation. Answer Student B's questions. Begin the conversation: *Good morning. Can I help you?*

- a football   €19.99
- trainers
- a swimming costume
- a football shirt

B Now you are a customer in an electronics shop. Role-play the situation. Ask Student B questions and try to buy the things below. When you buy something, write the price.

- camera battery
- blank CDs
- electronic dictionary
- headphones

5.3

7B Student B

Today's specials

Chef's Sunday special – Roast beef with potatoes and corn on the cob

Garden delight – Rice with three different vegetables (e.g. peas, green beans, carrots, peppers)

Summer mix – Salad and three kinds of meat: chicken, lamb and beef

4.2

6D Student B: write the buildings on the map on page 41.
1 The school is opposite the pharmacy.
2 The park is behind the sports centre.

E Answer Student A's questions. Then ask Student A about the places below. Write them on your map.
- the museum
- the theatre

10.2

2C Student B

SURVIVE IN THE DESERT!

In the desert, the temperature can change a lot. It can be very hot in the day, up to 55°C and then go down to 10°C at night. In the day, try to stay out of the sun and always put something between your body and the hot ground. Don't sleep on the ground – your body will get too warm from the hot sand. Wear a hat and a shirt to cover your head and arms. Remember to use sun cream and you won't get sunburnt.

You need to stay cool so drink water every hour. If you have food but no water, don't eat or your body will use too much water to digest your food. Try not to move or travel in the day when it's really hot – you might sweat too much.

There are many different types of small animals in the desert, so always wear shoes and gloves and look when you walk or before you put your hands down anywhere. When you get up after sleeping, always check your shoes and clothes. You don't want to step on a snake!

9.2

7A Student A

'I love Amsterdam'

* 53 euros for 72 hours
* all public transport
* free entry to over 25 museums
* 2 free boat tours
* 1 free cup of coffee

5.2

5B Student B

(The underlined answers are correct.)

5 a) about 50 times   b) <u>about 15 times</u>
6 a) <u>1,700</u>   b) 940
7 a) over 730 tubes   b) <u>over 270 tubes</u>
8 a) <u>about 2,000</u> b) about 7,000

8.1

5 Student A: Ask and answer questions to compare your picture with Student B's. Don't look at Student B's picture. Find eight differences in the pictures.

What's Mike doing? What's he wearing?

4.1

7B Look at the picture below for fifteen seconds. Then turn back to page 39 and correct the sentences.

COMMUNICATION BANK

11.3

6B Student B

Problem 1
I'm really tired.

Problem 2
I can't see the whiteboard. It's too dark in here.

Problem 3
I'm really thirsty, but I haven't got any money for a coffee.

2.3

2B Student B: ask and answer questions. Complete the times on the clocks.

A: *What's the time in number 1?*
B: *It's … What's the time in number 2?*
A: *It's …*

2.2

9A Student B: read the texts. Write questions to ask your partner for the missing information.

1 When … *does she get up?*   5 What time …
2 Where …   6 What …
3 What time …   7 When …
4 Where …

Jeanette is a doctor – a flying doctor. She works in Queensland for the Royal Flying Doctors of Australia and travels all over the country. She gets up at ¹_____, has a cup of coffee and goes to the airport at 7a.m. She flies to ²_____ and starts work. She usually visits two to three places every day and sees fifteen to twenty people. She has lunch at 12, but she has dinner late, at ³_____, in one of the places she visits and sometimes she sleeps there! Then she comes back the next morning and gets home at 9a.m.

Henri is an acrobat and a father of three boys. He works in ⁴_____ at the National Circus. He gets up early and has breakfast at 6a.m. with his boys. His wife drives the boys to school and Henri goes to the circus at ⁵_____. In the morning he does exercises and practises his high flying routine. On circus days, in the afternoon he ⁶_____ and then has a sandwich at 5.30p.m. He doesn't eat dinner before a show. The evening show starts at 7.30p.m. Henri finishes work at about 10p.m. and gets home at ⁷_____ p.m.

B Ask Student A about the missing information. Complete your text.

9.1

6B Student A: look at the information about the Horseless Sulky. Use a dictionary to check the meaning of any new words. Tell your partner about it. Why is it better than the Lightning Bug?

- an Italian invented it in the 1930s
- it's easy to get into and out of
- it's easy to see things on the left and right
- it's easy to turn
- it can go up to 190 kilometres per hour

9.2

7A Student C

Prague

- 790 crowns (32 euros) for 4 days
- free entry to over 50 museums and sights
- unlimited travel on Prague transport system (for an extra 330 crowns or 13 euros)

7.3

6C Student A: check this information. Read it to Student B.

1 Kris lives in North Road.
2 His house is five minutes from here.
3 It's on the left.

D Now listen to Student B. Use the information below to correct any mistakes.

1 The bank's in East Street.
2 It's on the right.
3 Take the number 9 bus.

6.1

8A Student A: write four important dates for you from last year and practise saying them.

B Work in pairs and take turns to ask and answer about your dates. Remember to sound interested and to give extra information.

A: August the twelfth.
B: Why was that date important?
A: Because I was in France, in Paris.
B: Really? Why did you go? Did you like it?

3.2

2B Student A: read the text. Circle the numbers in the box which are in the text. What do they refer to?

(12)　17　11　8　1　7　9　6　15

12 children in the Lewis family

For Tracy and Pete Lewis 'Big is beautiful' when you talk about families. They've got 12 children – 11 girls and a boy. Ages range from daughter Shaznay (2) to Carly (19).

Life in the Lewis house starts at 6.30 in the morning. Tracy serves the kids breakfast in 2 sittings – 6 children have breakfast from 6.30 until 7, then the other 6 have breakfast from 7 to 7.30. For breakfast every day they usually eat 2 boxes of cereal and drink 7 litres of milk. Then Tracy makes packed lunches for the children and drives them all to school. At 9.30 she's back home and she starts making dinner.

Tracy and Pete's son, Charles (15), is the only boy in the house. 'I'm lucky because I've got my own bedroom. My sisters all share bedrooms.'

How do Charles's parents feel about their big family? Pete says, 'It's never boring in our house. It's great doing everything together and I really enjoy being in such a large, happy family.'

And the biggest problem? 'Waiting for the bathroom!' The house has got only 1 bathroom!

10.2

2C Student A

SURVIVE AT SEA!

Surviving at sea is difficult. The biggest problems are the weather, food and drink. In cold weather, try to stay dry and never sit on the bottom of the raft – there's usually water there and you'll get wet. In hot weather, wear a hat and a shirt to cover your head and arms. Remember to use sun cream and you won't get sunburnt.

Drinking water is the most important thing. With water only and no food, you can live for ten days or longer. Your body loses a lot of water when you sweat, so relax and try to sleep a lot, too. If you don't have water, don't eat because your body will use too much water to digest your food. Never drink seawater. It is too salty and you'll get thirsty.

In the open sea, fish is your most important food and it's also easy to catch. Most fish are safe to eat and you can drink water from fish eyes as well. But never put rubbish into the water – sharks might come! Try not to move around too much because you don't want to fall off the raft with sharks near.

COMMUNICATION BANK

8.1

5 Student B: ask and answer questions to compare your picture with Student A's. Don't look at Student A's picture. Find eight differences in the pictures.

What's Mike doing? What's he wearing?

2.3

2B Student A: ask and answer questions. Complete the times on the clocks.

A: What's the time in number 1?
B: It's … What's the time in number 2?
A: It's …

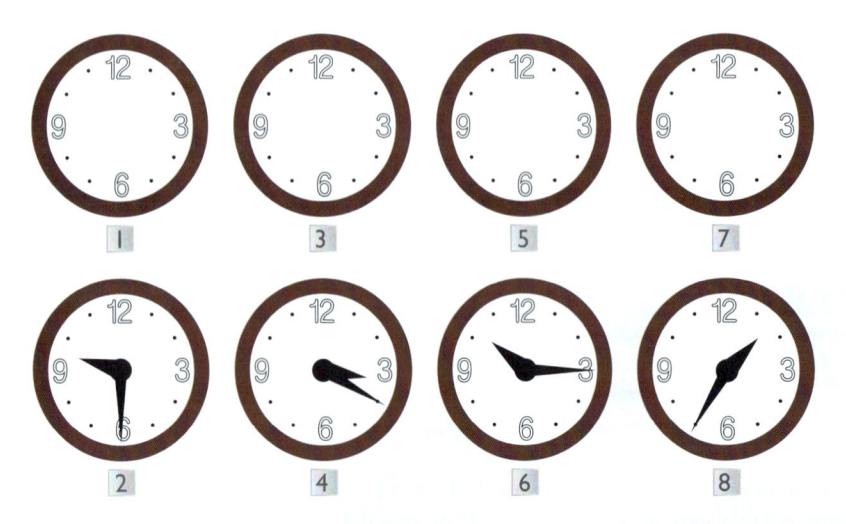

11.3

6B Student A
Problem 1
It's cold in here.

Problem 2
This computer doesn't work.

Problem 3
It's too noisy. The music's too loud and I can't concentrate.

12.3

7B Student B: answer Student A's questions. Ask Student A for the telephone numbers.

A: What's Sam's phone number?
B: It's … What's Ahmed's phone number?
A: It's …

Sam	9240473
Ahmed	
Nina	7886301
Chen	
Simon	0463 3739912
Fatima	
Yuko	00 44 2816933
Penny	

166

AUDIO SCRIPTS

LEAD-IN Recording 2
1 What does 'capital' mean?
2 I don't understand.
3 Could you repeat that?
4 Could you spell that?
5 Could you write it?
6 Which page is it?

UNIT 1 Recording 1
Conversation 1
T=Tour guide M=Man W=Woman
T: Hello. Are you Mr and Mrs Burns?
M: Yes, we are.
T: Hello. I'm Elena Garcia from YouTourist.
W: Hello. Nice to meet you.
T: And you.
Conversation 2
M=Mia L=Lily
M: Hi, Lily. How are you?
L: Great, thanks. And you?
M: Not so bad.
Conversation 3
J=John A=Ana Ju=Juan
J: Juan, this is Ana.
A: Hi, Juan.
Ju: Hi. Nice to meet you.
A: Are you in the same class?
Ju: No, I'm not a student. We're friends.
Conversation 4
S=Sophie Raworth
S: Good evening and welcome to the BBC News at One.
Conversation 5
R=Receptionist C=Chris
R: Good afternoon. Can I help you?
C: Yes. I'm here to see Mr Miller.
R: Is your name Simpson?
C: No, it isn't. My name's Jackson.
R: Oh, sorry. Please take a seat, Mr Jackson.

UNIT 1 Recording 5
M=Marco R=Rob K=Kate
M: Oh, that's my flight! Bye, Rob, Kate. I have to go!
R: OK. Bye, Marco. Have a good trip!
K: Yeah. Have a good trip, Marco!
M: Thanks. You, too. Bye!
R: He's a nice guy, Marco.
K: Yeah, he is. Wait a minute – is this my bag?
R: No, that's mine. This is your bag.
K: Wait, look. What are these?
R: Those? They're DVDs. But they aren't mine.
K: And they aren't mine.
R: What's that?
K: It's a book about Rome, but it isn't mine. Is it yours?
R: Oh no. That's Marco's …
K: And that bag?

R: Just a minute.
K: Oh good. Those are my sunglasses.
R: Oh, no …
K: And that's my laptop and my MP3 player.
R: So Marco's got my bag. Total disaster. Marco! Marco!!

UNIT 1 Recording 9
Conversation 1
T=Tourist S=Shop assistant
T: Excuse me. Do you speak English?
S: Yes. Can I help you?
T: Can I have one of those, please?
S: One of these batteries? For your camera?
T: Yes, that's right.
S: OK. That's eleven euros, please.
Conversation 2
T=Tourist C=Clerk
T: Excuse me. Do you speak English?
C: Yes. Can I help you?
T: Could I change this money, please?
C: Fine. That's four hundred and fifty pounds. Here you are – one hundred, two, three, four hundred. And ten, twenty, thirty, forty, fifty. Four hundred and fifty.
T: Thank you.
C: You're welcome.
Conversation 3
T=Tourist W=Waiter
T: Can I have a sandwich and a cola, please?
W: That's six euros.
T: Ah, I only have five euros. How much is the sandwich?
W: Four euros fifty. And the cola is one fifty.
T: OK. Could I have the sandwich, but no cola?
W: That's four fifty.
T: Thank you.
Conversation 4
TS=Ticket seller T=Tourist
TS: Can I help you?
T: Could I have a single to Sydney, please?
TS: Today?
T: Yes.
TS: That's twenty-five dollars.
T: Here you are. Which platform is it?
TS: Platform three.
T: Thanks.

UNIT 1 Recording 10
1 Can I have a sandwich, please?
2 Can I have one of those batteries, please?
3 Could I have a single to Sydney, please?
4 Could I change this money, please?

UNIT 1 Recording 12
T=Tourist W=Waiter
T: Can I have a sandwich and a cola, please?
W: That's six euros.

T: Ah, I only have five euros. How much is the sandwich?
W: Four euros fifty. And the cola is one fifty.
T: OK. Could I have the sandwich, but no cola?
W: That's four fifty.

UNIT 1 Recording 13
M1=1st man M2=2nd man
W1=1st woman W2=2nd woman
Conversation 1
M1: How much is an orange juice?
W1: It's two euros twenty.
Conversation 2
W2: A single ticket is four euros eighty and a taxi is thirteen euros.
Conversation 3
M2: That's two euros fifty for the coffee, and another three seventy-five for the sandwich and a bottle of water – that's one thirty. That's seven euros and fifty-five cents altogether.

UNIT 1 Recording 14
R=Receptionist G=Guest
R: Good evening. Can I help you?
G: Good evening. Yes, I have a reservation. My name's Baumann.
R: Ah, yes. Mr Baumann. For two nights?
G: That's right.
R: Could I ask you to complete this form?
G: Oh, I haven't got my glasses. Can you help?
R: Certainly. What's your family name?
G: Baumann.
R: Could you spell that?
G: B-a-u-m-a-n-n.
R: Is that double 'n'?
G: Yes, that's right.
R: Your first name?
G: Jeff.
R: And what's your phone number?
G: 212 4742 285.
R: OK. You're in room 407. That's on the fourth floor. The lift's over there.
G: Room 407?
R: Yes, and this is your keycard.
G: Thank you. What time's breakfast?
R: From seven to ten.
G: And where is it?
R: In the restaurant, over there.
G: Thank you.
R: Have a good stay.
G: Thanks.

UNIT 2 Recording 1
M=Man W=Woman
W: Come on! You just sit around all day. Why don't you *do* something?
M: What?
W: I don't know – get an interest, go out, meet people …

167

AUDIO SCRIPTS

M: Why?
W: It's good for you! Join a group … or something. Look, here are some interesting ones. The Film group, The Travel group, the Sport group and the Laid-back group.
M: The Laid-back group?!
W: Yes, well. So which is the right group for you?
M: Oh, I don't know …
W: OK. Let's see. Do you do a lot of sport?
M: No, I don't. Not really. Well, not at all. I don't like it.
W: OK. Do you like films?
M: Yes, I do. Everyone likes films …
W: OK!
M: But I don't watch them very much.
W: Oh. Well, do you like meeting people then?
M: Ah, yes, I do.
W: OK!! And do you travel a lot?
M: Me – travel? No, I don't, but I like … the idea.
W: Well, do you take a lot of photos when you travel?
M: No, I don't. Hmm. Sorry.
W: Right. That's it!
M: That's it?
W: OK. One more question: Do you relax a lot?
M: That's a strange question! Of course I do. I *really* like relaxing.
W: Yes, that's true …
M: So, which group do you think is right for me?
W: Well, *this* one … of course!

UNIT 2 Recording 3
I=Interviewer P=Pilot W=Window washer

I: And today on Radio 99 we talk to some high flyers – men and women who work in very high places around the world: high buildings or mountains or planes. Our first guest has breakfast with his family in London, lunch on a plane, and dinner in Singapore. He leaves home on Monday morning and only gets home on Thursday. Of course he's a pilot, and he flies the long-distance London to Singapore route for British Airways. Good morning, Daniel.
P: Good morning.
I: Well, you travel a lot … but do you actually like it?
P: Yes, yes I do.
I: And what does your family think about your job?
P: Well, they're OK about it. I mean, they think it's a good job. It's true that I'm not at home for three or four days a week. But I phone my family from the plane and from the airport in Singapore. Yes. They like my job and my routine, for them it's normal.
I: You have a boy and a girl, is that right?
P: Yes, that's right – six and eight years old. William and Sonia.
I: And William … does he want to be a pilot?
P: No, he doesn't! He doesn't want to fly.

He wants to be a teacher. But Sonia wants to be a pilot like me.
I: OK. Thanks, Dan. Let's move on. Our next guest is also a high flyer – but of a very different kind. He's a window washer from New York. He washes windows on high-rise buildings in the city. He leaves home at six every day and starts work at seven. He has breakfast on the thirtieth floor – actually *outside* the thirtieth floor – he has lunch on the fortieth floor, and works all day in sun or rain. He finishes work at five and gets home for dinner. So why does someone become a window washer, Ted?
W: Well, my father washes windows; my older brother washes windows … so I wash windows. I love it up high above the cars and the people. The only problem is the rain … and the cold.
I: What does your family think about your job?
W: My wife doesn't like it. She thinks it's crazy. But she loves the money, it's very good money. And my son wants to be a window washer. It's normal in my family – it's a tradition.
I: So, you work all day outside the building.
W: Yeah, that's right.
I: You eat there, you phone your wife from there …
W: Yeah. Oh, and I even read my emails from there. It's my office.
I: Well then, I have a question … Where *does* a window washer … you know, urm … go to the bathroom?
W: Oh, well … that's a window washer's secret!

UNIT 2 Recording 9
A and B=Tourists C=Tour operator

A: Oh look, Tourist information. We can ask there.
B: OK. You ask.
A: No, you ask. My English isn't very good.
B: You speak English very well. You ask.
A: No, you ask.
B: No, *you* ask.
A: OK … Excuse me. Do you speak English?
C: Yes, can I help you?
A: Yes, thank you, my friend has a question.
B: Nooo … ohhh … uh … OK … We want to take a tour.
C: OK. Which tour is that? The Hong Kong Island tour, the Harbour tour, the Hong Kong by night tour?
B: Uhhh … I don't understand anything.
A: She asked which tour.
B: Oh, the Hong Kong Island tour.
C: Ah, the Island tour, good choice, and I think we have a couple of places left on the tour tomorrow morning if you're interested in that one …
B: Thank you, goodbye.
C: Oh. Goodbye.
A: What's the problem?
B: I don't understand her. She speaks too fast!

A: Oh, come on! Let's go back.
B: No, I don't want to. I feel sooo stupid!
A: Oh, come on.

UNIT 2 Recording 11
A and B=Tourists C=Tour operator

A: Hello. We're back.
C: Hello again! So, do you want the Hong Kong Island tour?
A: Yes. Er. Could you speak more slowly, please?
C: Of course. Would you like to take the tour tomorrow morning or afternoon?
A: Tomorrow morning. What time does it start?
C: At eight o'clock exactly.
A: Excuse me, eight o'clock …?
C: Yes, at eight.
A: And where does it leave from?
C: The bus leaves from the front gate here.
A: Sorry, could you repeat that?
C: The bus leaves from the front gate.
A: The front gate? Here? Outside?
C: Yes, just over there. Do you see the sign?
B: Yes, I can see the sign. I can see it!
A: And when does the tour finish?
C: The bus arrives back here at 1p.m.
A: 1p.m. OK. How much does it cost?
C: 320 dollars per person.
A: 320 dollars. So, 640 dollars for two.
C: That's right.
A: OK, that's good. So could we have two tickets for tomorrow morning, please?
B: Er, do you take credit cards?
C: Yes, of course …

UNIT 2 Recording 14
M=Man W=Woman

M: Oh no! Look at this mess. Where's the hoover?
W: Urm … Oh, here it is. I am surprised, Mark. Do you like cleaning?
M: Yes, I love it!
W: Uh, really?! Why?
M: Well, I study all week and by Friday my apartment looks terrible!
W: Right …
M: So on Saturdays I clean all morning. It makes me feel good. What about you? Do you like cleaning?
W: No, I don't! I hate it. I don't like cleaning or washing.
M: So … what do you like doing?
W: At home, I like doing nothing! Well, I like playing video games and watching TV, you know … just relaxing.
M: Me, too. But *after* the cleaning!

UNIT 3 Recording 1
intelligent, kind, talkative, friendly, funny, stupid, unkind, quiet, unfriendly, serious

AS

UNIT 3 Recording 2

A: I don't like talkative people, and my friend José is usually very quiet. People think he's not very friendly because he's quiet and often serious, but in fact he's really friendly and he's sometimes very funny – not all the time, but sometimes. We don't like doing the same things, so we hardly ever do things together, maybe two or three times a year. For example, he likes computer games and staying at home and I go out a lot … but it's not a problem. When we meet, he always asks me how I am, and he really listens to me. And when he phones me with a problem, I always listen to him. He's a good friend and we usually understand each other well.

B: My friend Rosa is usually very funny – she makes jokes and we laugh a lot. We like the same things, we're always together. We often go out to clubs – two or three times a week – and to parties … She talks a lot, and she's a friendly person, but are we really close friends? I don't know … I think I'm a good friend to her, but she … when I have a problem, she hardly ever listens to me. So sometimes she's not very kind. She's an intelligent person, and I sometimes feel stupid around her. We don't always understand each other, but you know, she's a good friend … I think.

UNIT 3 Recording 5

J=Jack R=Ron

J: Hello?
R: Hi, Jack. It's Ron.
J: Oh, hi. How are you?
R: Fine, thanks. And you?
J: OK.
R: Uh, well, I'm at my new office, you know I've got a new job … Uh, the work's quite interesting and the people are very friendly … Hello, are you there?
J: Yes. Yes, I'm still here.
R: … and the work isn't too difficult … Hello, are you there?
J: Yes.
R: Oh … and, well, I haven't got my own office and one of the people in my office is really unfriendly … Are you there?
J: Yes, I'm here.
R: Anyway, are you free tonight?
J: Yeah, I think I am. What do you want to do?
R: How about going to the cinema? I'd like to see the new Will Smith film.
J: Will Smith … ah, wait, I'm busy. Sorry …
R: Oh … OK, well, maybe next time.
J: Yeah, see you.
R: Bye.

UNIT 3 Recording 6

D=Denise R=Ron

D: Hello?
R: Hi, Denise. It's Ron.
D: Oh, hi. How are you?
R: Fine, thanks. And you?
D: I'm OK. How's your new job?
R: Good. The work's quite interesting and the people are quite friendly …
D: Uh-huh.
R: … and the work isn't too difficult.
D: That's great.
R: It's not perfect. I haven't got my own office and one of the people in my room is really unfriendly …
D: Oh, that's a shame!
R: Yeah. Anyway, are you free tonight?
D: Yeah, I think so. What do you want to do?
R: How about going to the cinema? I'd like to see the new Will Smith film.
D: Sounds good. Where's it on?
R: At the ABC in town.
D: OK. What time do you want to go?
R: It's on at six o'clock and at half past eight. What's good for you?
D: I finish work at five. So six is good.
R: Right. How about meeting at … er … half past five at the cinema?
D: Yes, that's fine.
R: Great! See you there.
D: Yeah. Oh, how about inviting Jack?
R: Hmm. *You* call him!
D: OK. Bye.
R: Bye.

UNIT 3 Recording 8

1 I've got a new job!
  That's fantastic!
2 I haven't got any money.
3 I've got a new boyfriend …
4 … but he's not a very nice person.
5 Oh, look – rain!
6 My English teacher is great!

UNIT 3 Recording 10

W=Woman M=Man

W: What's a special occasion in your country?
M: Hogmanay.
W: Hog … er … man …?
M: Hog-man-ay. Let me tell you about it. OK … Hogmanay happens in Scotland on New Year's Day. In our families, on the day before Hogmanay, we always clean the house – all day – because it's important to start the New Year in a clean house.
Then, in the evening, we usually have a big party with friends and family. At midnight we stand in a circle, join hands, sing '*Auld Lang Syne*' … you know. '*Should auld acquaintance be forgot* …'. I think people sing this in a lot of countries now.
We also have a special custom. After midnight, the first person who visits the house gives presents to the family, usually shortbread or coal. This brings good luck. Then we eat and drink. The party often goes on all night. I like it because all our friends and family come together and it's a great start to the New Year!

UNIT 4 Recording 2

W=Woman M=Man

W: Hi! It's me.
M: Hi, Mum! Come on in.
W: Here, I brought you a plant. A small plant for your microflat!
M: Thanks, it's great! I'll put it here on the dining room table.
W: Oh, so this is the dining room.
M: Yes, well, this is where I eat.
W: There are only two chairs? It's good your father isn't here.
M: Mum, it's a microflat. There isn't a lot of furniture.
W: It's very … sweet. Now, is there a living room?
M: Well, there isn't a separate living room. This *is* the living room. Just here.
W: Oh, I see. Yes, there's a sofa and a TV … yes, it *is* a living room.
M: And here's the kitchen.
W: Oh, I see, three rooms in one – the dining room, the living room and the kitchen.
M: Mum, it's a microflat.
W: Is there a bedroom? Or do you sleep on the sofa?
M: Of course there's a bedroom. Come through here …
W: Yes …
M: Here it is.
W: This is nice … but there aren't any shelves. Where do you put your things?
M: There's a wardrobe here.
W: Oh, but look, there *is* a bathroom!
M: Mum …
W: … and a toilet!
M: Mum … Listen, do you want a drink? Let's go out to the balcony …
W: The balcony! Is there really a balcony?
M: Of course there's a balcony. It's a microflat.

UNIT 4 Recording 7

1 You can post a letter with UK stamps.
2 You can't play American football.
3 Can you buy medicine?
4 Can you change money?
5 You can't go to a French class.
6 You can speak English all day!

UNIT 4 Recording 8

1 The supermarket is opposite the bank.
2 The cinema is on the right of the bank.
3 The post office is on the left of the supermarket and opposite the cinema.
4 The sports centre is near the post office.

UNIT 4 Recording 10

Conversation 1
A=Assistant C=Customer

A: Can I help you?
C: No, thanks. I'm just looking.

169

AUDIO SCRIPTS

Conversation 2
A=Assistant C=Customer
A: Can I help you?
C: Yes, how much is that?
A: 19.99.
C: OK. Where are the changing rooms?
A: Over there, next to the mirrors.
C: Thanks.
A: How is it?
C: Hmm. It's too small. Have you got it in large?
A: Sorry, no.
C: Mmm. It's not big enough … No, it isn't right. Thanks anyway.
A: No problem.

Conversation 3
A=Assistant C=Customer
C: Uhhh … Excuse me.
A: Yes, can I help you?
C: I need one of these for my camera. This one's dead.
A: Let's see. What type is that?
C: Uhh … let's see, the number is DLK-760.
A: Here you are. That's 8.99.
C: That's fine. I'll take it.

Conversation 4
A=Assistant C=Customer
C: Excuse me?
A: Yes, can I help you?
C: Yes, how much is this?
A: Uh, let's see … it's 22.95.
C: Have you got it in paperback?
A: Er, yes, I think so. Here. It's 6.99.
C: Oh good … but this is English–English. Have you got an English–Arabic one?
A: No, I'm sorry, we haven't.
C: All right. I'll have this one. The paperback.

Conversation 5
A=Assistant C=Customer
A: Can I help you?
C: Yes, can I try these trainers?
A: What size are you?
C: Thirty-eight.
A: These are size thirty-eight. How are they?
C: Yes … urm … good, thanks. How much are they?
A: One hundred and twenty euros. Would you like to buy them?
C: One hundred and twenty? Er … I'm not sure. I need to think about it. Thanks.
A: Fine. No problem.

UNIT 4 Recording 12

One of my favourite places in the world is Lake Titicaca. It's between Bolivia and Peru and is, urm, about 4,000 metres above sea level. The water is always very, very cold. I go there every year with my family and we stay in a small town near the lake. When I'm there I usually go out on the lake in a boat, and sometimes I visit one of the small islands. Sometimes there are big waves on the lake, but it's usually very quiet. So why do I like the lake? Well, I love its deep blue colour and it's a great place to relax.

UNIT 5 Recording 2

1 Hi. My name's Luis, from Spain. Welcome to my fridge! What have we got here? Well, there's some chicken and some fish – some sardines. They're for the barbecue tonight. It's my wife Carmen's birthday. And we've got some fruit: grapes and an apple. And of course, the baby's milk. And we've got some wine and some fruit juice for the barbecue. And at the back there's a … oh no! Where is it? Carmen! Where's your birthday cake?
2 Hi, I'm Amy. I'm from Canada and I'm a vegetarian. And this is my fridge! On the top shelf I have some cheese, yeah, lots of cheese and a cucumber. And I've got some carrots. I love carrots! And on the next shelf, I've got some eggs and some yoghurt. Of course, I haven't got any meat. Hey, what's this? Look, a hot dog! Why is this here? And here I've got a bottle of water and lots of milk.
3 Hi, everyone. I'm Mike and I'm Australian. So, this is my fridge. Er … I've got some leftovers from … er from last week. And I've got lots of cola and … oh look, a banana – why's that in the fridge? I don't eat fruit. And there's some bread, it's quite old, and some butter, yup, that's very old. Well, that's me! I don't go shopping a lot. I usually eat at the university.

UNIT 5 Recording 5

How much food does an average person eat in a lifetime? And how much drink? The answer is *a lot*!!!
Do you eat meat? Well, an average meat-eater eats 21 sheep in their lifetime and 1,200 chickens. Does that sound quite a lot? The good news is that he or she only eats 4½ cows. If you're a vegetarian, maybe you like beans? Well, on average British and American people eat 845 cans of baked beans in their life.
And why is weight a problem for so many people? How many cookies does the average American eat? The answer is an amazing 35,000. And chocolate? Over 10,000 bars!
And how much water or tea do people drink in their lifetime? Well, it's interesting that a person drinks about 60,000 litres of water and people in the UK drink about 75,000 cups of tea. Maybe it isn't surprising that people use 61 rolls of toilet paper a year. That's about 4,300 in their lifetime!

UNIT 5 Recording 6

Wa=Waiter M=Man W=Woman
Wa: Good evening. A table for two?
M: Yes, please.
Wa: By the window?
M: That's fine.
Wa: Can I take your coats?
M/W: Thank you.
Wa: Would you like something to drink?
W: Er … yes, please. Could I have an orange juice?
M: And I'd like a cola, please. And can we have a bottle of mineral water?
Wa: Certainly. The menu …
M: Thank you.
Wa: Tonight's special is Chicken à la Chef de Saint Germaine de Paris Rive Gauche.
W: What's that?
Wa: It's grilled chicken with potatoes and green beans.
W: Is it French?
Wa: Not really …
W: But it has a French name.
Wa: Well, that's true … it's very good …
Wa: Are you ready to order?
M: Yes, I'd like some soup and the special.
W: The same for me, please.
Wa: Thank you.

UNIT 5 Recording 9

A: Afternoon, what can I get you?
B: Uhhh … the Jackpot special, please.
A: Is that eat in or takeaway?
B: Take away.
A: Large fries with that?
B: No, medium …
A: Something to drink?
B: A cola.
A: Small, medium or large?
B: Small.
A: Anything else?
B: No thanks.
A: That'll be 9.95.
B: OK.

UNIT 5 Recording 10

1 A<u>f</u>ternoon. What can I <u>get</u> you?
2 <u>Small</u>, <u>medium</u> or <u>large</u>?
3 Is that <u>eat in</u> or <u>takeaway</u>?
4 <u>Any</u>thing else?
5 Thanks. Have a <u>nice day</u>!

UNIT 5 Recording 11

M=Man W=Woman
W: The name of our dish is the Italian special. It's very easy to make. You need some prawns, a can of Italian tomatoes, a large onion, a red pepper and two celery sticks – the vegetables need to be cut into small pieces. You also need some pasta, olive oil, black pepper and lots of herbs.
M: You heat the oil in a frying pan and then put all the vegetables in together for about two minutes. Then you throw in the prawns, some black pepper and the tomatoes. Then add the herbs. You cook everything for a minute or two …
W: … and leave to cook slowly. Heat some water in a pan and add the pasta. Cook for three minutes then take the pasta out of the water. Mix with the sauce and then eat our dish with some salad.
M: It's delicious. You'll love it!

UNIT 6 Recording 1

1 Cars were important to Lewis Hamilton from an early age. He was a quiet boy, and one of his favourite activities was to play with radio-controlled cars. His other hobby was karate and he was a black belt at the age of twelve.

2 Shizuka Arakawa from Japan was the Olympic ice-skating champion in 2006, but skating wasn't her favourite sport when she was younger. She loved swimming and her other hobby was ballet.

3 Tennis player Rafael Nadal, or 'Rafa', is Spanish and was born in Manacor, Majorca. He was always a very good tennis player, but when he was young, his favourite sport was football. His favourite food was pasta and his favourite film was *Gladiator*.

4 When she was younger, Cate Blanchett's favourite film star was Harrison Ford. Her hobby was playing the piano and she was really good.

5 When she was very young, Colombian singer Shakira's favourite activities were writing poems and dancing. At the age of four, when she was at a restaurant with her father, she danced on the table to some Arabic music.

6 Rowan Atkinson is famous as Mr Bean. When he was young his favourite TV show was *Monty Python's Flying Circus* and his favourite actors were John Cleese and Charlie Chaplin.

UNIT 6 Recording 2

1 She's very kind.
2 She was very kind.
3 They were my favourite band.
4 They're my favourite band.
5 It isn't very funny.
6 It wasn't very funny.
7 We were very happy.
8 We're very happy.

UNIT 6 Recording 3

1 She was very kind.
2 They were my favourite band.
3 It wasn't very funny.
4 We were very happy.

UNIT 6 Recording 5

A: Do you know all the dates?
B: Let's check. OK. Christmas Day is the twenty-fifth of December. Everyone knows that.
A: And New Year's Day is January the first.
B: Valentine's Day – well, you always forget – that's February the fourteenth. Halloween is the thirty-first of October …
A: And World Health Day?
B: I don't know. Let me check the internet. Guess.
A: Uh, March the second?
B: No, it's April the seventh.
A: OK, but I know the last one. Independence Day in the USA is the fourth of July.
B: Bingo. Well done!

UNIT 6 Recording 6

Lia was born in Yugoslavia on the 14th July 1931. She lived in a small village and went to school when she was seven. In 1944, her family moved from Yugoslavia to Hungary because of the war. She wanted to go to university, but there was no money, so she started working in a sugar factory at seventeen. She had sugar for lunch and dinner every day for three years. She got married at twenty-five. She didn't have any children, but children always liked her. In 1969, she moved to Lake Balaton in Hungary and made a lot of money selling ice cream with her sister. She bought a house with the money, and now she rents rooms there.

Carol was born in the USA on the 14th July 1931. She went to a school for child actors in New York and at eight years old she had her own radio programme. For a few years, she stopped going to school and studied at home with her mother. She became a well-known radio actress. Later, she worked in a bookshop in New York. She met her husband there in 1951. They got married and had five children. In the 1990s, she didn't see her children very much because they lived abroad. She and her husband visited them sometimes. In 2002, they bought a house by the sea and now their children come and visit them.

UNIT 6 Recording 8

I=Isabel M=Marek

I: Hi, Marek. How was your weekend?
M: OK. And yours? What did you do?
I: I went for a walk. It was great!
M: Who did you go with?
I: With my boyfriend, Diego. He's a football player.
M: Oh. Where did you go?
I: By the river. It was really beautiful.
M: That sounds good.
I: And you? What did you do?
M: Oh, I played football, cleaned the flat.
I: Who did you play football with?
M: With some guys from work. We play every weekend.
I: Really? Where did you play?
M: In the park. There's a football pitch there.
I: Did you win?
M: Of course. I scored five goals!
I: Ha! I don't believe you!

UNIT 6 Recording 9

I=Interviewer B=Baruti Kaleb

I: Thank you for coming on the show, Baruti. We are all very interested to know more about your work. But, first of all, let's start from the beginning … urm, where were you born?
B: I was born in Johannesburg in 1962.
I: Can I ask you about your childhood?
B: Yes, of course. I was the fourth child in a very big family – there were eleven of us. My father was a teacher and my mother cleaned houses for rich people.
I: Did you go to school?
B: Yes, I did. Education was very important to my parents.
I: When did you decide to work with poor children?
B: When I was in school, one of my friends lost his parents. He had no family … urm … no living grandparents, so he moved to a house for orphans. I visited him and when I saw his life there I decided to work with orphans.
I: When did you open your orphanage?
B: We opened it in 1996.
I: We?
B: Yes, my wife and I. We got married in 1990.
I: And who's your hero?
B: I'm glad you asked that – it's Mother Teresa. I often think about her words: 'I can do no great things, only small things with great love.'
I: That's very interesting. I have one more question: What's your favourite book?
B: Let me think about that. I like many books, but *Long Walk to Freedom* is one of my favourites. It's the story of Nelson Mandela's life in his own words.
I: That sounds interesting, thank you. OK … now, it's time to ask the audience for questions. Are there any questions for Baruti? … Yes, you at the back …

UNIT 7 Recording 2

M=Man W=Woman

M: So, how do you usually travel? By plane or train?
W: Train. I think travelling by train's more comfortable than flying. And I don't like flying.
M: I put 'plane' because flying is faster than going by train.
W: Not always! OK, next question. Where do you like to stay: in a hotel or a self-catering apartment?
M: In an apartment. And you?
W: In a hotel.
M: Oh. But a hotel is more expensive than an apartment!
W: Yeah, but it's more comfortable. Hmm …. next question. What do you prefer to do: go sightseeing or relax on a beach?
M: Oh, that's easy! I hate beach holidays! Boring!
W: OK – there's one we answered the same. So we agree about that.
M: Yeah, sightseeing's definitely more interesting!
W: Right. When do you like to go: in spring or summer?
M: In spring – I don't really like hot weather. Tourist places are more crowded in summer.
W: True. But the weather's better. Summer

AUDIO SCRIPTS

is hotter than spring. I love hot weather.
M: Well, we don't agree there. Anyway, next question. What do you like to eat: local dishes or the food you usually eat?
W: Local dishes, I think. You?
M: Definitely! That's two answers the same!
W: Hmm, interesting. Next … what do you like to do in the evening? Go to a club or go to a restaurant?
M: Well, go to a restaurant.
W: Oh, good. Me, too. It's much quieter than a club.
M: Yes, I agree. Restaurants are quieter … more relaxing.
W: And the last question … how long is your perfect holiday?
M: Three months.
W: You can't have *three* months! The answer is either a week or a month.
M: OK, a month then.
W: Me, too!
W: So we've got four answers the same!
M: Maybe we *can* travel together …

UNIT 7 Recording 5
I=Interviewer P=Passenger

I: So, Jeff. A few questions about the trip. What was the coldest place you visited?
P: The coldest place was Mount Everest. We stayed at Everest base camp and the temperature was minus thirty.
I: Really? And what was the hottest place?
P: Well, it was hot in Pakistan, but the Red Desert in Australia was hotter.
I: Ah, was it? And what was the friendliest place?
P: That's an impossible question. I can't say. We met so many fantastic people. Everyone was wonderful.
I: OK. What was the longest you travelled in one day?
P: One day we travelled about 400 kilometres in Pakistan. That was a long day!
I: Very! So, what was the most beautiful building you saw?
P: There were some great ones in Nepal and Bali, but my favourite building was the Taj Mahal in India. I think it's the most beautiful building in the world.
I: Yes, it is. So, what was the most amazing experience of the journey?
P: Seeing a tiger in the tiger reserve in the Himalayas. A-ma-a-a-zing!

UNIT 7 Recording 6
A: Excuse me. Can you tell me the way to the Pier, please?
B: Yeah, you go down West Street until the end.
A: Straight on?
B: Yeah. And then turn left and you'll see the Pier.
A: Thanks very much.

UNIT 7 Recording 8
A: You go out of this car park and turn right. So that's right into Church Street. Then take the third right, I think it's called New Road.
B: The first right.
A: No, the third right. And you go straight on until the end of the road and then turn left. After about one minute you'll see it on the left. You can't miss it!
B: So third right, erm, left at the end of the road and then … ?
A: It's on the left.
B: On the left.
A: Yeah.
B: Fine. Thanks a lot.
A: You're welcome.

UNIT 7 Recording 10
M=Man W=Woman

M: We want to talk about Rimini, an old city on the Adriatic coast in Italy. It's got a beautiful beach and you can swim in the sea in the summer. One of the most important places in Rimini is the cathedral, and also the Arch of Augustus.
W: Ah, but for me the most important place is the beach.
M: Yes, for me, too. And at night, the bars on the beach. You can go dancing – it's really good fun …
W: And what about the food? Well, a typical food from Rimini is *puntarelle* or pasta with fresh vegetables, but the fish is really amazing. The city is by the sea so the fish is very fresh.
M: So, we think Rimini is a beautiful, relaxing place. You can sit on the beach all day, eat great food and dance all night.

UNIT 8 Recording 3
Conversation 1
A: Is it a man or a woman?
B: A woman.
A: What does she look like?
B: I think she's in her thirties. She's got long, dark hair and dark eyes. She's wearing make-up.
A: Hmm. Is it Michelle Yeoh?
B: Yes.

Conversation 2
A: Is it a man or a woman?
B: A man.
A: What does he look like?
B: He's got short, dark, curly hair. He's got a beard and a moustache. He's black.
A: Oh, I know … it's Will Smith.
B: Sure is!

UNIT 8 Recording 4
I=Interviewer

I: Hello and welcome to *Fashion Now*, with me, Dan Taylor. In today's programme, we ask the question, 'What is Beauty?' Do men today *really* like women with blonde hair and blue eyes? And do women like the James Bond look – tall, dark and very masculine, or do they like something different now? Are ideas about beauty changing? We went out to see what you *really* think …

UNIT 8 Recording 5
I=Interviewer W1=1st woman
W2=2nd woman W3=3rd woman
M1=1st man M2=2nd man

I: Excuse me, ladies. Do you have a moment?
W1: Yes?
I: Just a quick question. Research says that these days women prefer men with feminine faces …
W1: Really?
I: Yes. It's true … honestly!
W1: I don't agree at all. I like masculine faces …
I: Can I show you some photos?
W1: Sure.
I: So which of these guys do you like best?
W1: Sean Connery. He's definitely the best looking man here. And he's tall, isn't he? Yeah … I like tall men. And I like a man with a beard.
I: Uh-huh. What about you?
W2: Mmm. I'm not sure. I like this one, what's his name?
I: It's Gael García Bernal. He's a Mexican film star.
W2: Yeah? Well, he's got quite a feminine face and he's very good-looking. I like his eyes – he's got dark brown eyes and I like men with dark eyes and black hair. But I think it's more in the personality … in the smile … so I like this one best. Will Smith. He's got a really nice smile.
I: Thank you. And here's another lady. Excuse me. Have you got a moment?
W3: Well …
I: I'm doing a survey about the changing face of beauty. Can I ask you some questions?
W3: Yes, OK. Yes.
I: I've got some photos here. Can you tell me which of these people you like? Do you think any of them are good-looking?
W3: Well, I don't really like any of them …
I: No? So what sort of man *do* you like?
W3: What sort of man do I like? Well, my husband's over there. I think he's good-looking. I like his hair. I love guys with red hair.
I: Which one? The one looking in the shop window?
W3: No, he's over there. He's wearing a white T-shirt and he's talking to … that blonde woman … Excuse me …
I: And then I talked to some men to find out if they really prefer blondes – just like they did fifty years ago. Do you think it's true that men prefer blondes, sir?
M1: What? No, not at all! Beauty comes in all shapes and sizes and ages. Look at this photo of Judi Dench. She's lovely. She isn't young, but she's got beautiful grey eyes and she always wears beautiful clothes. She looks kind and intelligent.

M2: Yeah, she does. But I still prefer blondes, you know … like Scarlett Johansson. She's lovely … slim, blonde hair, blue eyes – that's the sort of woman I like.
M1: Scarlett Johansson, *slim*?
M2: Well, OK … but she's not *fat*.
M1: No, that's true…
I: OK, guys. Thanks for talking to us …

UNIT 8 Recording 6
Conversation 1
M=Man W=Woman

W: OK … what do you feel like watching?
M: Hmm. I don't know really. What do you recommend?
W: Erm, … Well, how about *French Kiss*? Do you know it?
M: No, I don't think so. What's it about?
W: Well, it's a romantic comedy. It's about an American woman. She goes to France and meets a French guy and … they fall in love. It's quite old, but it's really funny.
M: Sounds OK, I suppose. Who's in it?
W: Meg Ryan and Kevin Kline.
M: Oh, I like Meg Ryan. Mmm. Do you think I'd like it?
W: Yeah, I think so. You like comedies, don't you? And it's very funny.
M: Yeah, OK. Why don't we get it then?
W: Great. Excuse me. Can we have this one, please?

Conversation 2
W=Woman M=Man

W: What was the last DVD you saw?
M: Erm, Let me think. Oh – I know, it was *Speed*.
W: *Speed*? Is it new? What's it about?
M: No, a bit old actually. It's an action film. It's about a bus and it can't stop. It has to go at top speed or … or it explodes. It's great!
W: Right. Who's in it?
M: Sandra Bullock and … the guy is, the actor is, er … Keanu Reeves.
W: Mmm. Do you think *I'd* like it?
M: Well, do you like action films?
W: Not really. I prefer romantic films and dramas.
M: Oh, then I *don't* think you'd like it …. Er, well. Oh, I know. I think you'd like that French film, you know, with the actress Juliette Binoche. What's it called? Oh, yeah: *Chocolat*.
W: *Chocolat*? Do I know it?… Oh …with Johnny Depp? Mmm! Now that *is* a good recommendation. Have you got the DVD?

UNIT 8 Recording 7
1 What do you recommend?
2 How about *French Kiss*?
3 Do you think I'd like it?
4 I don't think you'd like it.
5 I think you'd like that French film.

UNIT 8 Recording 9
Recently I went to a concert in the park with my boyfriend and some other friends … It was in City Park … We went because we all like the band, Double-X, and we listen to their music all the time.

The concert only lasted two hours, but we took a picnic with us and went out early in the afternoon – it was a free concert, you see, so there were already a lot of people sitting out in the park in front of the stage. We got a really good place, close to the stage. We chatted and lay in the sun all afternoon … and then in the evening more and more people came and it got quite crowded. Then the concert started and well, it was … fantastic! Double-X is an amazing band … and better *live*! I really liked the concert because everyone was dancing and singing – we had a great time.

UNIT 9 Recording 1
G=Guide V1=1st visitor
V2=2nd visitor V3=3rd visitor

G: So, ladies and gentlemen … Let's move into the transport section now. Could you all come over this way? Let's look at these photos. As you can see, these early methods of transport have two things in common … they're all great ideas, great ways to travel through the air rather than on the ground … but they weren't successful! There was a big problem with each one.
V1: But the monorail – that was successful …
G: Well, yes and no…. Look at this photo on the left. It's from the World Fair in Seattle. That was in 1962. Monorails were a very popular idea in America at that time. People wanted to leave their cars at home and go to work by public transport. But they weren't successful – monorails are difficult to build and expensive to keep in good condition. So you're right. There are some monorails in the world … but not very many!
V2: Hey … Look at this photo. Is that a car under a plane?
G: Oh, yes. This was a very interesting idea. People wanted to fly from Los Angeles to New York … and then drive straight into the city centre from the airport.
V2: No way! How?
G: Well, the idea was that the car came off the bottom of the plane and then … you got in and drove away. This was in the 1940s. Ah, yes. Look … here's the date: 1948. It was a nice idea – no airports or waiting around – but it wasn't successful.
V2: Why not?
G: There was an engineering problem … the car was too heavy and small planes weren't strong enough to carry them.
V3: What's this? A helicopter in the garage?
G: Yes, indeed. We laugh at this now, but people were very serious about it at the time. People wanted to leave home in the morning, say goodbye to the family and go to work by private helicopter. The idea was very popular … but of course, it was impossible. Helicopters are very difficult to fly … and can you imagine the traffic problems in the sky … So noisy!
V2: Yes. Very noisy … There's far too much traffic these days in my opinion.
G: I agree. People should go to work by bike … or on foot. By far the best way to travel …

UNIT 9 Recording 3
1 There was a problem.
2 It was a good idea.
3 The photo on the left.
4 In the city centre.

UNIT 9 Recording 5
1 Tourists can use the bikes.
2 Children can't use the bikes.
3 Users have to give their credit card details.
4 You don't have to pay for the first half hour.

UNIT 9 Recording 7
L=Liam K=Kamal

K: Hey, Liam. Did you stay in bed too long this morning?
L: Ha-ha! It's these trains – they're terrible!
K: Why? What happened *this* time?
L: Well, first of all, the train was late leaving the station, but only about a quarter of an hour or so. After that, it just went at walking speed – all the way to London. Really! There was a guy on a bike on the road next to us … I think he got to London before we did!
K: Well, you're two hours late … and the boss wants to see you.

K: Hey, Liam. The boss wants to see you. Whoa! What happened to you? You're all wet!
L: Believe me, it's a *long* story. First of all, I got up late because I didn't hear my alarm, so I only woke up at 8.30. I ran to the train station – usually I walk – but I missed the train by two minutes! Then I waited for the next train, the 9.15, and everything was fine until we just stopped – just *stopped* – in the middle of nowhere. The guard said that there was a signal problem. After that, the air-conditioning stopped working, so it was like an oven – at least a thousand degrees! Finally, after forty minutes, we started moving … very, very slowly. What could I do? Uh-oh, there's the boss.
K: Yeah. She's not happy. Two and a half hours late, Liam … Good luck!

UNIT 9 Recording 9
A=Attendant P=Passenger

A: Your meal, sir.
P: Thank you. Erm, excuse me.
A: Yes, can I help you?
P: Hope so! I'm sorry, but there's a small problem here … I ordered a vegetarian meal – but this is meat.
A: Oh, just a moment … I checked and we don't have a record of your order.
P: What?! But I *always* order vegetarian. I'm a frequent flyer.

AUDIO SCRIPTS

A: I understand, sir, but we don't have any more vegetarian meals.
P: I don't believe it! You always have extra meals in business class.
A: Yes, but this is economy class.
P: You don't understand. Let me explain one more time. I don't eat meat. I ordered vegetarian. I can't fly to Tokyo without dinner. It's your job to bring me a meal. A business class vegetarian meal is fine.
A: Just a moment. Here you are, sir. A vegetarian meal.
P: Thank you … but this is already open. And it's cold. Urm, can I speak to the person in charge, please?

UNIT 10 Recording 1
I=Interviewer E=Elaine A=Aled
I: Elaine and Aled, the luckiest couple in Britain today … welcome to the programme!
E/A: Thank you.
I: So Elaine, tell us about that moment when you found out.
E: I saw the winning numbers on television and I phoned Aled straight away!
A: I didn't believe her at first. I thought 'You're lying!'
E: I didn't believe myself! I was in shock!
I: And is it true that you're *not* going to stop working?
A: That's right. We enjoy our jobs and we've got lots of friends here. I don't like doing nothing. I think hard work's good for you.
E: Definitely. People think working in a fast food restaurant is boring … but it's not. We have a lot of fun. It's an important part of our life.
I: So what are you going to do with the money?
E: Well, first of all, we're going to get married this summer. We already had plans to get married before we won the lottery, maybe in two years, but now we can do it this summer.
I: Congratulations!
A: Or next summer.
I: Ah …
E: *This* summer.
A: And we'd like to move. At the moment I'm living with my parents and Elaine's living with hers. So we're going to look for a house to buy.
E: By the sea.
A: Yes, maybe by the sea, or …
I: Are you going to take a break? Travel around the world maybe?
A: No, I don't think so, but we're going to have a holiday. We're going to the Canary Islands.
I: Fabulous. And have you got any other plans? Maybe a new car … or clothes?
E: Yeah, I'm going to buy some new clothes. I'm going shopping with my mum and sister this weekend. Cars …? Well, Aled doesn't drive so no, he isn't going to buy a car.

A: Right … not now … but I'd like to learn to drive and then maybe in the future …
I: What would you like to drive?
A: I'd like a Mercedes … or maybe, or maybe a Ferrari.
E: But we haven't got plans to buy a car now.
I: OK – great! Thanks very much for talking to us today. Oh, just one last question … How did you celebrate when you first heard the news?
E: Well … we went out and had a burger!

UNIT 10 Recording 6
Conversation 1
M=Man W=Woman
W: Hi, Sergio. Let's do something different tomorrow. It's Saturday.
M: OK … How about going to an art gallery? There's a new exhibition on at the Tate.
W: Ur, I don't really feel like doing that. I'd like to stay in. What about having a 'movie marathon'? You know, we could just sit at home all day and watch films, eat junk food …
M: Mmm … Do we have to? I saw a film last night. I don't want to sit around all day anyway. I know! Let's cook something. Or I can.
W: Sounds lovely. Why don't we invite Augusto and Carla for lunch?
M: Brilliant! I'll try a new recipe and we can have a food tasting.

Conversation 2
M=Man W=Woman
W: Hey, Tom. Are you busy this weekend?
M: Er … No, I don't think so.
W: Great. Let's do something!
M: OK. What do you want to do?
W: Well … How about going for a bike ride and having a picnic?
M: A bike ride? That sounds a bit tiring … Why don't we play computer games?
W: You're joking!
M: No, really. Why not?
W: Well … because, I sit in front of my computer all week – I'm not going to turn it on tomorrow! Look, let's go to the theatre. Actually, there's a Shakespeare play on in the park: *Romeo and Juliet*.
M: Hmm. I can never understand Shakespeare plays …
W: OK, well, why don't we read it together first?
M: Oh, but can we get tickets?
W: Yes. It's free.
M: Ah, fantastic! Come on then …

UNIT 10 Recording 7
1 How about going to the zoo?
2 What about doing something more relaxing?
3 Why don't we do some internet shopping?
4 Let's go to the theatre.

UNIT 10 Recording 9
In Dublin today, it'll be hot and sunny with

temperatures up to twenty-five degrees Celsius. Tomorrow will be cloudy, but quite warm, with a high of twenty. Things will change on Friday night: it'll be a wet night with rain from midnight to early next morning. The temperature will fall to ten so it'll feel quite cool, but the rain will stop, so we'll have a dry day all Saturday. Sunday will be windy and cloudy … and very cold, so make sure you wear your winter coat!

UNIT 10 Recording 10
1 Oh, I think spring is the best. I love it when the flowers come out and the birds start singing … that's when everything is so fresh. It's the perfect time to take a walk along the Danube.
2 It rained every day, but we had a great time. We went to museums, sat in cafés and played cards.
3 In winter I love skiing … getting up early to spend the whole day on the mountain skiing – fantastic! I love having a hot chocolate in a local café at the end of the afternoon – it's the perfect time to do that.
4 I really don't like it when it's very hot, especially in the city. There are so many tourists about – I get so hot and tired … it's awful!
5 Oh, I really like it when it's hot and then there's a big summer storm, with lots and lots of rain … I love the way the air cools down and it feels fresher.
6 Well, definitely not in the rainy season! I think the best time to visit Malaysia is May to September because after that it gets really wet – it feels like it never stops raining!

UNIT 11 Recording 2
P=Presenter D=Doctor
P: And this week in *Health Matters*, we're talking about colds and flu. What's the difference, and more importantly, how to cure them? With me in the studio is Dr Elizabeth Harper. Dr Harper … How is flu different from a common cold?
D: Well, flu starts very suddenly. One minute you're fine, the next minute you feel terrible. You've got a headache – often a very bad headache – and a cough. You've got a sore throat and your arms and legs hurt. You're very hot. Usually you've got a temperature of over thirty-eight degrees centigrade and you're too ill to do anything. You can't work. You just want to go home and go to bed. Sometimes you have to stay in bed for a week or more.
P: Awful. I see, yes. And what about a typical cold?
D: A cold starts slowly. Maybe it takes two or three days to start. It's a cold when you've got a sore throat … or a cough and a runny nose and you don't feel very well. But – and here's the big difference – if you can get up and go to work, then you've probably got a cold, *not* flu. After a week you feel better. After flu, you often feel very tired for a very long time, maybe two or three weeks!
P: Mmm. OK, so the next question …

174

UNIT 11 Recording 4

W1=1st woman W2=2nd woman
W3=3rd woman M1=1st man
M2=2nd man M3=3rd man

Situation 1
W1: Oh, no. My papers!
M1: Here, let me help. What a mess!
W1: Thank you very much.
M1: No problem.

Situation 2
W2: Er … Excuse me … sir?
M2: Uhhh …
W2: Are you all right? Shall I call an ambulance?
M2: No … Yes … Uh… Thanks so much …
W2: That's OK.

Situation 3
W3: Hmm … Uh … Mmm …
M3: Oh, look. I'll do that for you. Where do you want it?
W3: Just over here, in front of the window … Thanks a lot. That's kind of you.
M3: You're welcome.

UNIT 11 Recording 7

P=Pharmacist C=Customer

P: Hello, can I help you?
C: Yes, have you got anything for an earache?
P: An earache? Hmm … When did it start?
C: Yesterday afternoon. I took some paracetamol, but it didn't help.
P: And do you have any other pain?
C: No, just my ear.
P: Do you often have earaches?
C: No, it's the first time, but it hurts a lot.
P: OK. I'm going to give you some ear drops. They're very mild.
C: Sorry, I don't understand. Mild?
P: They're not very strong. Put these drops in your ear, three times daily.
C: Three times a day?
P: That's right. When you get up, at lunch and just before you go to bed. If it doesn't get better, you should see a doctor.
C: Thank you. How much is that?

UNIT 12 Recording 1

I=Interviewer S1=1st speaker
S2=2nd speaker S3=3rd speaker

Interview 1
I: Excuse me. Do you have a second? We're asking people about experiences of a lifetime … for a survey.
S1: Oh … Er, yes, if it's quick.
I: Great! Could you look at this list? Have you done any of these things?
S1: Hmm … Yes, yes, I have actually. Well, one of them! I've been to Guatemala and I've climbed that volcano, I think.
I: Anything else?
S1: No, no, I don't think so. Sorry, I have to run …

Interview 2
I: Excuse me …
S2: What?
I: Have you ever ridden an elephant?
S2: What? Why? Uh, no. No, I haven't …
I: We're doing a survey on experiences of a lifetime. Can I show you this list? Have you done any of these activities?
S2: Oh, OK. OK. Let's see … Er … No, no, no, no. Oh, I've sailed down the Nile … so that's one thing. In fact I went to Egypt last year, with the wife … our wedding anniversary …

Interview 3
I: Excuse me. We're doing a survey … about experiences of a lifetime.
S3: Right …
I: Two minutes. Could you just look at this list? Have you done any of these things?
S3: OK. Well … I don't travel that much, so … I haven't been to Iceland … but it looks nice – swimming in a thermal spa looks fun.
I: And the other things?
S3: Hmm … no … well, I've seen some of them on TV. Is that OK? Does that count?

UNIT 12 Recording 4

Conversation 1
A: Hello.
B: Hi, Sean. It's Debbie.
A: Hi, Debbie. What's up?
B: Is Kevin there?
A: No, he's not. He went out about ten minutes ago.
B: Oh …
A: What's up?
B: Well, I locked the keys in the car. Kevin has the spare key.
A: Oh, what a drag!
B: Could I leave a message for him?
A: Of course.
B: Just ask him to call me.
A: On your mobile?
B: No, that's in the car … I'll give you a number.
A: Hold on … OK, go ahead.
B: OK, let's see … It's 3-double 2, 6-3, 2-8.
A: Got it. I'll tell him.
B: Thanks, bye.
A: Bye.

Conversation 2
A: Berkley Bank.
B: Hello. Could I speak to customer services, please?
A: Just a moment.
C: Customer services.
B: Hello, I've got a problem. I think I've lost my credit card.
C: I see. I'm sorry, this line is very bad. Where are you calling from?
B: I'm in Madrid, actually. In fact I'm calling from a public phone and I've only got one minute on this card. Could you ring me back?
C: Of course. Could you give me the number there?
B: Just a moment … It's 34 for Spain, 91 for Madrid, then 308 5238.
C: Let me check that. 34 91 308 5238.
B: That's right.
C: Fine. Put the phone down – I'll call you back straight away.
B: Thank you.

Conversation 3
A: Hello?
B: Oh, thank goodness. Hello, uh … Who's this?
A: My name's Marianne.
B: Thanks for picking up.
A: Well, the phone rang so I picked it up.
B: Yes, well, that's my cell phone. And you found it.
A: Oh, OK … It's yours. Do you want to get it back?
B: Yes, thanks. Where are you?
A: Central Park, by the fountain. It was here in the grass.
B: Ah, yes … I thought it might be.
A: So where are you?
B: Not far away. I can be there in ten minutes.
A: OK, I'll wait here.
B: Great. Thanks a lot!

UNIT 12 Recording 8

This happened in Australia … when I was about twenty-five. I spent a few days at a hotel in Alice Springs and went to Ayers Rock and … well, anyway, one day, I went out for a walk … in the outback.

It was a lovely day so I walked and walked … and then I realised I didn't really know where I was. I was a bit stupid, really… because I decided to go further … I guess I thought I'd find the way back. Urm … anyway, after that I heard some dogs.

First I heard them barking, and then I saw them … there was a group – maybe five or six dogs, wild dogs, coming towards me. I felt really frightened, but I remembered some advice I, er … urm, I read in my guidebook: Don't move, and don't look at the dogs. So I froze, like a statue …. I didn't move … and I looked at a tree, not at the dogs, and didn't move my eyes. The dogs were all around me, jumping and barking … I thought they were going to bite me. Then one dog *did* bite my arm, just a little, but still I didn't move.

In the end, after about twenty minutes, the dogs went away. I stayed there for a few more minutes and then luckily found my way back to the hotel. It was the most frightening experience I've ever had!

Pearson Education Limited
Edinburgh Gate
Harlow
Essex CM20 2JE
England

and Associated Companies throughout the world.

www.pearsonelt.com

© Pearson Education Limited 2011

The right of Frances Eales and Steve Oakes to be identified as authors of this Work has been asserted by them in accordance with the Copyright, Designs and Patents Act 1988.

All rights reserved; no part of this publication may be reproduced, stored in a retrieval system, or transmitted in any form or by any means, electronic, mechanical, photocopying, recording, or otherwise without the prior written permission of the Publishers.

First published 2011

Sixth impression 2014

ISBN: 978-1-4082-7606-8

Set in Gill Sans Book 9.75/11.5

Printed in Slovakia by Neografia

Acknowledgements

The publishers and authors would like to thank the following people and their institutions for their feedback and comments during the development of the material:

Reporters: Australia: Jane Comyns-Carr; **Germany:** Irene Ofteringer; **Ireland:** Fiona Gallagher; **Italy:** David Barnes, Elizabeth Gregson, Elizabeth Kalton, Thomas Malvica, Claire Maxwell; **Poland:** Dorota Adaszewska, Sylwia Sroda; **Spain:** Robert Armitage, Anabel Fernandez, Will Moreton; **United Kingdom:** Filiz Aydinlioglu, Andrew Briston, Olivia Date, Gareth Eldridge, Helen Elmerstig, Eileen Flannigan, Paula Kler, Alastair Lane, Andrea Merckel, Sheila Parrott, David Penny, Rich Quarterman, Emma Stobart, Alison Tomura

We are grateful to the following for permission to reproduce copyright material:

Text: Interview 3.2 adapted from Interview with Vladimir Chernenko "Family of 19 is never bored", *The Sacramento Bee*, 5 January 2006 (Erika Chavez), copyright © The Sacramento Bee 2006; Extract 3.2 from "Birds of a feather meet the southside's broodiest mom" published on www.bbc.co.uk 15 January 2003 copyright © The BBC; Extract 7.2 adapted from www.oz-bus.com copyright © OzBus; Extract 11.3 from "Good Samaritan?" by Michael Coombes published on www.bbc.co.uk 26 July 2006 copyright © The BBC.

Fawlty Towers written by John Cleese and Connie Booth

Illustration acknowledgements: Lyndon Hayes pgs9, 163t, 166; Mister Paul pgs10, 11, 48, 137; Harry Malt pgs28, 81, 92, 101, 106, 109, 129, 132, 134, 135, 141, 142, 143, 147, 150, 164, 166; Jurgen Ziewe p38; Infomen pgs40, 41, 72, 73, 163b; Peter Grundy pgs53, 121; Joel Holland p54; Vince McIndoe pgs88, 89; Otto Steininger p109; Dermot Flynn p111; Matt Herring p112.

Photo acknowledgements: The publisher would like to thank the following for their kind permission to reproduce their photographs:

(Key: b-bottom; c-centre; l-left; r-right; t-top)

7 Andrew Hackett, www.viewphotographic.co.uk: Andrew Hackett / photographersdirect.com (p12). **BBC Photo Library:** (p14). **Corbis:** Heide Benser (p8). **Photolibrary.com:** Lester Lefkowitz (p10). **8 BBC Photo Library:** (A). **Getty Images:** Andersen Ross (D); David Lees (C). **Photolibrary.com:** Photo Alto (B). **Rex Features:** Image Source (E). **12 Alamy Images:** Ken Welsh (B). **Axiom Photographic Agency Ltd:** Andrew Watson (b). **13 Alamy Images:** Vanda Woolsey (D). **Art Directors and TRIP photo Library:** (C). **Getty Images:** Andrew Hetherington (b). **14 BBC Photo Library:** (tl) (tr). **14-15 BBC Photo Library:** (b). **15 BBC Photo Library:** (br). **17 Alamy Images:** Chris Howes/Wild Places Photography (p22); funkytravel London - Paul Williams (p24). **Buzz Pictures:** Dean O'Flaherty (p20). **Corbis:** Roy Morsch (p18). **18 Photolibrary.com:** Corbis (t); Digital Vision (tc); Moodboard (bc). **PunchStock:** moodboard (b). **19 Alamy Images:** David Stares (b). **20 www.dreamstime.com:** (E) (F). **iStockphoto:** (D) (I). **Jupiter Unlimited:** (A) (H) (B) (C). **Photolibrary.com:** Fancy (G). **21 BBC Photo Library:** Jeff Overs (cl). **Corbis:** Barry Lewis (t). **Rex Features:** Nils Jorgensen (b). **22 www.dreamstime.com:** (A). **Adrian Japp:** Adrian Japp / Photographersdirect.com (D). **alveyandtowers.com:** (E). **PunchStock:** Digital Vision (tourists). **Rosina Redwood :** Rosina Redwood / Photographersdirect.com (F). **Ureche Marius Liviu Photography:** Ureche Marius Liviu Photography / Photographersdirect.com (B); Ureche Marius Liviu / Photographersdirect.com (C). **22-23 Photoshot Holdings Limited:** World Pictures (t/background). **23 DK Images:** Nigel Hicks (r). **iStockphoto:** (l) (c). **24 Photolibrary.com:** Comstock (bl). **Rex Features:** Nils Jorgensen (tl). **24-25 Alamy Images:** funkytravel London - Paul Williams (main). **27 Alamy Images:** Ian Walter (p30). **Getty Images:** Louis Laurent Grandadam (p28); Neo Vision (p32). **Spectrum Photofile:** Spectrum Photofile / Photographersdirect.com (p34). **29 Getty Images:** Eileen Bach. **30 Getty Images:** Monica Davey / AFP. **31 Photolibrary.com:** Purestock. **32 Alamy Images:** Directphoto.org (l). **Corbis:** Jon Hicks (r). **33 Alamy Images:** John Elk III (bc/montage); Sergio Pitamitz (br/montage). **Gareth Boden:** (br). **Rex Features:** Ilpo Musto (t/montage). **34 Rex Features:** Geoffrey Swaine (bl). **34-35 Photolibrary.com:** Walter Bibikow (main). **35 Alamy Images:** Mary Evans Picture Library (sheet music). **iStockphoto:** (biscuits) (coal) (cleaning items). **37 Photolibrary.com:** Blend Images (p42); Shubroto Chattopadhyay (p44). **Rex Features:** Ken Straiton (p40). **View Pictures Ltd:** Edmund Sumner (p38). **38 Smoothe / Piercy Conner Architects :** (tl). **40 Alamy Images:** amama images inc. (b). **42 Alamy Images:** Rubberball (b). **Photolibrary.com:** Image Source (t). **42-43 Photolibrary.com:** Digital Vision (background). **43 Getty Images:** Andersen Ross (b). **Photolibrary.com:** Digital Vision (t). **44 Alamy Images:** Images of Africa Photobank (B). **Corbis:** Arnaud Chicurel (C). **FLPA Images of Nature:** Suzi Eszterhas/Minden Pictures (D). **International Photobank Ltd:** (A). **Photolibrary.com:** Image Source (E). **44-45 Corbis:** Ron Watts (background). **47 Alamy Images:** Agripicture Images (p50); foodfolio (p48). **BBC Photo Library:** (p54). **iStockphoto:** (p52). **49 iStockphoto:** (c) (r). **Photolibrary.com:** Creatas (l). **50 www.dreamstime.com:** (K). **Alamy Images:** Alistair Heap (beans can). **Alamy Images:** Alistair Heap (beans can); The Daniel Heighton Food Collection (B). **DK Images:** Susanna Price (J). **iStockphoto:** (H) (I). **Jupiter Unlimited:** (A) (D) (E) (F) (G) (C) (tr). **POD - Pearson Online Database:** (K). **51 Alamy Images:** David Muscroft (b). **Getty Images:** Bay Hippisley (b). **52 Photolibrary.com:** Digital Vision (b); John Howard (t). **52-53 Getty Images:** Mike Blank (t). **54-55 Corbis:** Jon Hicks (background). **55 BBC Photo Library:** (b). **56 Copyright (c) Brand X Pictures.** **57 Corbis:** John Turner (p58). **Getty Images:** Rick Gershon (p60). **Rex Features:** Steve Bell (p64). **SuperStock:** Corbis (p62). **58 Alamy Images:** United Archives GmbH (A). **Getty Images:** Vladimir Rys/Bongarts (B). **Press Association Images:** (E). **Rex Features:** Lehtikuva OY (C); © Universal/Everett (F) (D). **60 Steven Oakes:** (l) (c) (r). **61 Steven Oakes:** (l) (c) (r). **62 Photolibrary.com:** Goodshoot (b). **SuperStock:** Comstock (t). **63 Alamy Images:** Colin Underhill (c). **Press Association Images:** Paul Faith (tr). **64 FAMOUS:** (tl). **iStockphoto:** (football). **Lebrecht Music and Arts Photo Library:** Laurie Lewis (br). **Photolibrary.com:** Chad Ehlers (bl); Roy Rainford (building). **Pictures Colour Library Ltd:** (cars). **65 Lebrecht Music and Arts Photo Library:** (b). **67 Photolibrary.com:** Chad Ehlers (p74); Digital Vision (p72); Image Source (p68). **Rex Features:** The Travel Library (p70). **68 Alamy Images:** Caro (D). **Photolibrary.com:** Digital Vision (B). **Rex Features:** The Travel Library (A). **Photolibrary.com:** Spectrum Colour Library / HIP (C). **69 Hesvan Huizen Fotografie B.V. :** Hesvan Huizen Fotografie B.V. / Photographersdirect.com (tent). **Photolibrary.com:** Cultura (beach); Image Source (boat); Noel Hendrickson (horse riding). **Rex Features:** Stuart Black/The Travel Library (sign post). **70 Axiom Photographic Agency Ltd:** J. Sparshatt (A). **Rex Features:** David Pearson (D); Image Source (E). **STILL Pictures The Whole Earth Photo Library:** Biosphoto / Klein J.-L. & Hubert M.-L (C). **Travel Library Ltd, The:** John Carr (B). **71 Alamy Images:** D A Barnes (tl). **Corbis:** David Samuel Robbins (r). **Rex Features:** Image Source (bl). **Spectrum Photofile:** (bus). **72 Alamy Images:** M J Perris (C). **Rex Features:** KPA/Zuma (B); The Travel Library (A). **73 Photolibrary.com:** Corbis. **Aflo Co. Ltd.** (bl). **Getty Images:** altrendo images (cr); Nicolas Russell (tl). **Photolibrary.com:** Brand X Pictures (br); Oswald Jan (cl). **TopFoto:** (tr). **74-75 Getty Images:** Chad Ehlers (main). **75 Getty Images:** altrendo images (br). **76 Photolibrary.com:** Jack Hobhouse (p84). **Getty Images:** John D McHugh/AFP (p80). **Press Association Images:** Fiona Hanson (p78). **Vickie Burt:** Vickie Burt / Photographersdirect.com (p82). **78 Corbis:** Daniel Attia (t); Moons (l). **Getty Images:** Jochen Tack (br). **79 Getty Images:** Zac Macaulay (b). **Photolibrary.com:** Corbis (t). **80 Corbis:** Kurt Krieger (tr); Peter Andrews (br); Rafael Roa (bl). **Getty Images:** Frederick M. Brown (tl). **81 Corbis:** Kurt Krieger (t). **Getty Images:** Avik Gilboa (b). **82 Ronald Grant Archive:** 20th Century Fox (B); 20th Century Fox (B); New Line Cinema (A); Paramount Pictures (H). **Rex Features:** Magnolia/Everett (F). **83 Getty Images:** Workbook Stock/Kristin Burns (b). **Ronald Grant Archive:** Columbia Pictures (D); © Walt Disney (G). **Kobal Collection Ltd:** Universal / Playtone (c). **84 Alamy Images:** David Pearson (br); Mai Chen (br). **84-85 Alamy Images:** Edward Westmacott (background). **85 Press Association Images:** Jon Crwys-Williams (br). **87 Getty Images:** Elis Years (p92). **Photolibrary.com:** Xavier Subias (p90). **Science Faction:** Peter Ginter (p94). **SuperStock:** Etienne (p88). **90 Alamy Images:** Pablo Valentini (b). **91 POD - Pearson Online Database:** Image Source (bl); Photodisc (t). **93 Alamy Images:** Jack Sullivan (br). **Getty Images:** Christopher Furlong (tr); Tim Graham (bl). **Press Association Images:** Matt Dunham (tl). **94-95 Corbis:** Ashley Cooper (aeroplane); Ralf-Finn Hestoft (background). **95 Alamy Images:** CoverSpot (tr/montage); vario images GmbH & Co.KG (cl/montage). **Corbis:** Marc Asnin (bl/montage). **Getty Images:** Photo and Co (tl/montage). **Photolibrary.com:** Image Source (br/montage); Will Datene (cr/montage). **97 Alamy Images:** E.J. Baumeister Jr. (p104). **Corbis:** Simon Marcus (p102). **Getty Images:** Gregor Schuster (p98). **Photolibrary.com:** Geoff Renner (p100). **98 Photolibrary.com:** Blend Images (couple). **TopFoto:** (shop). **99 Alamy Images:** Ace Stock Ltd (jogger); Bubbles Photolibrary (bags); Ian Thraves (barbecue); igroover (at desk). **Getty Images:** Paul Viant (wedding couple); Stuart O'Sullivan (shaking hands). **Photolibrary.com:** Corbis (with plant). **100 Alamy Images:** Chris Cooper-Smith (tl); Daniel H. Bailey (tr); Travelscape Images (br). **Corbis:** Alfred Saerchinger (bl). **102 Alamy Images:** Lars Johansson (c); PYMCA (tr). **Corbis:** Anthony West (cl). **Getty Images:** Jim Cummins (tl). **Photolibrary.com:** Brand X Pictures (bl); Creatas (b). **SuperStock:** Corbis/Tim Pannell (cr). **104 Alamy Images:** Ian Dobbs (A); Steve Bloom Images (D). **Corbis:** Onne van der Wal (B). **iStockphoto:** (E) (C). **Photolibrary.com:** (F). **104-105 iStockphoto:** (background). **105 Alamy Images:** Alex Segre (tl); David Noble Photography (tr) (bl). **Photolibrary.com:** (B). **107 Alamy Images:** D. Hurst (p108). **Aurora Photos Inc:** Daniel Lai (p114). **Getty Images:** Felbert + Eickenberg (p112); Tao Associates (p110). **108 Alamy Images:** Charles Mistral (B); Chris Rout (C). **Corbis:** Steve Prezant (D); Turbo (A). **Getty Images:** Oliver Lang (E). **110 PhotoDisc.** **112 Alamy Images:** Alvey and Towers (r). **Photofusion Picture Library:** Bob Watkins (l). **113 Alamy Images:** Sally and Richard Greenhill (b). **alveyandtowers.com:** Peter Alvey (t). **114 iStockphoto:** (A) (D). **Jupiter Unlimited:** (F) (C). **Photolibrary.com:** Corbis (E); Corbis (B). **Rex Features:** Richard Young (b). **117 Ronald Grant Archive:** New Line Cinema (p120). **Image Quest Marine:** (p124). **Masterfile UK Ltd:** (p122). **Rex Features:** The Travel Library (p118). **118 Alamy Images:** David Noble Photography (E). **Ardea:** Chuck McDougal (A). **Corbis:** Jose Fuste Raga (B); Peter Adams (D). **Eye Ubiquitous / Hutchison:** Elliot Walker (C). **120 Ronald Grant Archive:** (tl); LucasFilm/Paramount Pictures (br). **Kobal Collection Ltd:** LucasFilm Ltd/Paramount (bl); MGM / EON / Jay Maidment (tr). **121 Alamy Images:** Martin Florin Emmanuel. **122-123 Getty Images:** Don Spiro. **123 Alamy Images:** Chris Howes/Wild Places Photography (inset). **124 Rex Features:** Buzz Pictures (r). **iStockphoto:** (shark) (rat) (tiger) (spider) (bear) (snake). **124-125 Image Quest Marine:** (main). **152 iStockphoto:** (D) (E) (H) (I) (M) (N) (t) (B) (C) (L). **Jupiter Unlimited:** (J) (G) (O). **Pearson Education Ltd:** (A). **Rex Features:** 24/7 Media (F). **shutterstock:** (K). **153 Alamy Images:** Danny Clifford (J). **Blend:** (G). **iStockphoto:** (D) (A) (F) (M) (O) (Q) (L) (B). **Jupiter Unlimited:** (H) (I) (K) (N). **Photolibrary.com:** Corbis (P); White (E). **Rex Features:** Ron Sachs (C). **154 Bananastock:** (E) (F) (H) (J) (C). **iStockphoto:** (A) (D) (B). **Jupiter Unlimited:** (G). **155 www.dreamstime.com:** (D) (E) (G). **iStockphoto:** (A). **Jupiter Unlimited:** (F) (H) (inset H) (B) (C). **156 www.dreamstime.com:** (A) (N) (B) (L). **Alamy Images:** Adrian Sherratt (J); Gary Roebuck (G); LondonPhotos - Homer Sykes (M); Peter Titmuss (K); uk retail Alan King (C). **iStockphoto:** (E) (H). **Jupiter Unlimited:** (D) (F). **Photolibrary.com:** Polka Dot (I). **157 www.dreamstime.com:** (P) (S) (Q). **Trevor Clifford:** (I) (J) (G) (K) (C) (L). **Copyright (c) Brand X Pictures:** (A) (V) (X). **iStockphoto:** (E) (D) (H) (M) (U) (Z) (R) (T). **Jupiter Unlimited:** (F) (N) (O) (W) (Y) (B). **158 Alamy Images:** Johnny Greig people (cr/top row). **Corbis:** Kate Mitchell (r/top row). **Getty Images:** Jose Luis Pelaez (cl/top row). **iStockphoto:** (r/centre row). **Pearson Education Ltd:** (bl) (bc) (br). **Photolibrary.com:** Corbis (cl/centre row); Creatas (l/centre row); Digital Vision (cr/centre row); Tim Garcha (l/top row). **159 www.dreamstime.com:** (N) (O). **iStockphoto:** (D) (E) (G) (H) (I) (J) (K) (M) (P) (B) (L). **Jupiter Unlimited:** (C) (A) (F). **160 Corbis:** VALLON FABRICE (br). **Getty Images:** PNC (bl). **iStockphoto:** (tc). **Newspix:** Cifra Manuela (tr). **Photolibrary.com:** Digital Vision (bc). **162 Alamy Images:** Ian Dagnall (b). **Jupiter Unlimited:** Stockexpert (t). **164 Corbis:** VALLON FABRICE (br). **iStockphoto:** (tr). **Newspix:** Cifra Manuela. **Photolibrary.com:** Digital Vision (bl). **165 Alamy Images:** Jon Arnold Images Ltd

All other images © Pearson Education

Every effort has been made to trace the copyright holders and we apologise in advance for any unintentional omissions. We would be pleased to insert the appropriate acknowledgement in any subsequent edition of this publication.